INTEGRAL PUBLISHING HOUSE

Streams of Wisdom

Streams of Wisdom

An Advanced Guide to Spiritual Develoment

By Dustin DiPerna
Foreword by Ken Wilber

Integral Publishing House

Published by Integral Publishing House

First Edition

Cover Design by James Redenbaugh

Author photo taken by David Vergne

IntegralPublishingHouse.com

ISBN 978-0-9892289-3-0

Printed and Bound in the United States

In honor of my Teachers

Table of Contents

Figures and Illustrations

Foreword
By Ken Wilber

It is truly a pleasure—and honor—to write the foreword to Dustin DiPerna's *Streams of Wisdom*. I'm also, if I may be allowed some self-serving noise, very proud of this book, the reason being that— as Dustin openly allows—the book is essentially based on my work and my thought (but with, I hasten to add, a substantial amount of original additions and an enormous amount of supporting detail, most of which I did not include in my original outlines). But this is exactly the way that I would like to see my work in Integral Theory used, because generally when writing in any "pioneering" area (if I may be allowed a little more self-serving noise), I generally write what are essentially outlines for the new area—general maps of the new integral world—knowing, or least hoping, that I have provided enough guidelines for others to follow and fill in the details with more rigor and sophistication. (This has happened, for example, with the brilliant Integral Ecology, Integral Economics, Integral Psychotherapy, Integral Criminology, and so on.) And now Dustin has done so with his series in Integral Religion and Spirituality, and the results are truly wonderful.

Integral Theory, as it shows up in Integral Spirituality and Religion is based on a few fundamental ideas, some of them quite novel. One, every event has at least four perspectives (called quadrants— namely, the interior and exterior of the individual and the collective, or "I," "We," "It," and "Its"—or, again, art, morals, and science, or first-person, second-person, and third-person modes, counting the two exterior modes as one). These quadrants show development—namely, through developmental lines or streams that grow and evolve through developmental levels or waves (e.g., multiple intelligences, such as cognitive intelligence, moral intelligence, self intelligence, spiritual intelligence, kinesthetic intelligence, emotional intelligence—with all of these streams growing through essentially similar waves or levels of complexity). The "deep structures or patterns of these levels are

15

basically similar wherever they appear, although their "surface features" or patterns vary considerably from culture to culture. In addition to these lines and levels or structures of consciousness, there are states of consciousness (e.g., waking, dreaming, deep sleep, meditative). Finally, rounding out this Integral outline, there are types, which are patterns that continue to appear at each level of development (such as masculine/feminine, or Enneagram types, etc.). All in all, that gives us five major elements that every human being in the world possesses (indeed, every sentient being), and the point about an integral approach is that if you want to have a truly comprehensive and inclusive picture of any event, you need to include all five elements.

This is as true for religion and spirituality as for anything else. (Although the word "spirituality" is usually used to refer to the more interior aspects of religion, and "religion" to the more exterior, institutional aspects, I will use them synonymously unless otherwise indicated.) Religion has all five dimensions or elements: quadrants, levels, lines, states, and types. Virtually all five of those assertions are novel, they—and especially their connectivity—is what makes the Integral Theory approach to religion so new and creative, capable of handling some very difficult questions that have eluded humankind virtually from the start (see Integral Spirituality for a further discussion of this). This book, *Streams of Wisdom*, includes all five of these elements with particular focus on the distinctions between states of consciousness and structures of consciousness.

When we examine these two elements in more detail, Integral Theory suggests – and Dustin's work confirms – that every individual has a dual center of gravity. Every human being has both a structure center of gravity (or structure-stage) and a state center of gravity (or state-stage). We usually determine the structure center of gravity by using the stage of self-development or ego development (but any line or group of lines can be used). These stages move from archaic, to magic, to mythic, to rational, to pluralistic, to integral. For one's state center of gravity we usually use the basic path of gross, subtle, causal, witness, and nondual. Everyone is born with a dual center of gravity: archaic and gross. This basic notion of a dual center of gravity is part of an overall understanding of a kosmic address.

States and Structures are particularly important when we look at world religions. One of the things each tradition tends to do – generally speaking –is to give emphasis to one or the other of those types of self. Most fundamental religions, for example, focus only on a particular narrative – whether that is the beginning of the universe, the natural state, no sin, illusion, maya, suffering. From that position they offer a way out of that problem. Salvation, then, becomes accepting the truth of that narrative; believing in one major adept personal savior, whether that be Mohhamed or Jesus, - etc. If you "believe" then when you die you'll go to a particular heaven. When the focus is on the narrative, and all beliefs center around it, the tradition is oriented toward a particular level of expression (often mythic/amber) and gives emphasis to the needs of the relative self at that stage. In this way, the tradition focuses on the individual's center of gravity as it shows up in structures.

The other type of emphasis gives preference to the psycho-technology of consciousness change of a particular tradition. This element focuses on changing one's center of gravity in states. Relatively speaking, technologies of consciousness change are rarer than the other type of engagement that give more emphasis to the structures of religion.

When we look to Western developmental models for support in state cultivation, we notice that there is little information about meditative stages. According to current conventional models, states like waking, dreaming, and deep sleep are temporary. Modern researchers don't believe its possible that one can establish a permanent vantage point that brings full wakefulness into each on an ongoing basis. Most Western researchers are only vaguely aware of the truly infinite dimensions of the observing self. They are often aware of it but not to the extent that self can be realized. And most are even more unaware of the degree of extraordinary liberation or freedom that can be realized, and virtually nothing is known of nondual suchness as vantage point. All of this is because as natural states – waking, dreaming, and deep sleep, don't turn into vantage points or center of gravity except through training... shifting from gross, to subtle to causal to turyia to turiyatita. And so if we want solid evidence in this domain of state development we have to turn to our world's great wisdom traditions. Wisdom traditions have maintained lineages overtime that preserve knowledge about consciousness transformation.

We are left with this very important distinction between structures and states. These are the two different dimensions that we tend to work through as human beings. Naturally we want to make sure that all religions are doing both. It's fine to work with structures as they show up in various levels of spiritual intelligence. This means that we want to work with higher stages not just mythic narrative based levels. There is an amber Jesus, an orange Jesus, a green Jesus, a turquoise Jesus. We can also make sure that our great wisdom traditions are drawing on some aspect of their own lineage transmission for state-stages. This means that they all include some effective form of contemplative practice. Father Thomas Keating, for instance, stated that, "Christianity only really starting ignoring contemplative development at the counter reformation. Prior to that, it was common." And it was certainly common in the early centuries of Christianity.

And so with an integral approach, we want to make sure that we are introducing both of those. We want to make sure that the religious traditions have as full and complete development in spiritual intelligence and a robust path to introduce states of consciousness as they progress through vantage points. With any integral orientation to spirituality or religion, neither of those can be left out and both need to be pursued.

As we move toward a trans-lineage, universal spirituality, it becomes clearer and clearer that many paths have traditions of their own that can draw on to introduce true spiritual awakening. Those paths that don't, we'll have to introduce some sort of meditative practice as part of their dharma. Re-coding both structures and states is possible for the very first time.

Dustin puts true substance behind the basic outlines I've offered in my work on Integral Spirituality. With examples from the world's great traditions, Dustin articulates the key elements of spiritual development. Using an advanced integral outline he expands the basic distinction between structures and states, described above, to include four major vectors of human growth: (1) states; (2) state-stages; (3) structures; and (4) structure-stages. For the purposes of this volume, Dustin treats structures and structure-stages as a single category allowing him to give emphasis to the distinction between states and state-stages. In volume 2 of his series, *Evolution's Ally*, Dustin provides a more refined differentiation between structures and structure-stages. Altogether, his first two volumes give a full exposition of the four most important vectors of spiritual growth.

Dustin's offering here in *Streams of Wisdom*, and in his larger corpus of books on Integral Religion and Spirituality, provides a series of brilliant first steps toward a vibrant trans-lineage spiritually. This work gives me true hope that the kosmic grooves we are laying will help ensure that the world that our children inherit will be more whole, more loving, and more integral than ever before.

Ken Wilber
author of Integral Spirituality

Acknowledgments

This book was made possible by a generous gift of financial support from Cindy Wigglesworth. Cindy's contribution has served at least two philanthropic ends that I'd like to acknowledge. First, and close to my own heart, Cindy's support has allowed my own dreams to flourish. As a result of her generosity, I was able to spend the past year and a half researching and writing this book full time. Second, in as much as the content of this book helps to clarify several key aspects of spiritual development from an Integral perspective, Cindy's support also helps to facilitate a gift to spiritual practitioners interested in Integral studies all over the globe. I overflow with gratitude for the incredible opportunity Cindy has made possible and can only hope that the content provided in the following pages is worthy of her confidence and faith in me. If this book does indeed contribute to our shared understanding of spiritual development, may it be for the benefit of all beings.

I am also deeply indebted to my two spiritual and intellectual mentors, Ken Wilber and Daniel P. Brown. Both Wilber and Brown are quite familiar with the other's genius but have not collaborated on a written project since the publication of the book *Transformations of Consciousness* in 1986. As a student of both Wilber and Brown, it is a true privilege to have received their teachings. The two systems that Brown and Wilber have developed complement each other's in such a way that I believe their up-to-date integration provides one of the very best models of spiritual development available today.

I would like to note as well that the distinctions Dan has made between what he calls the "event perspective" and "mind perspective" serve as foundational elements of this book. To this end, I must also give additional credit where credit is due. Although I first learned the distinctions between "event perspective" and "mind perspective" from Dan, he learned the distinctions from Denma Locho Rinpoche, former abbot of the Tibetan Namgyal Monastery. It is with great honor that I give thanks to Dan, Denma Locho, and the lineage of wisdom that they each represent. Without the insights of their wisdom-stream flowing through me, this book would not be possible.

This book is also the product of several interdependent relative minds and hearts. In addition to the generous financial support offered by Cindy Wiggelsworth and the extraordinary mentorship of Wilber and Brown, this book is a direct result of my community of spiritual brothers and sisters.

For the beautiful graphics and figures, I thank Mathias Weitbrecht and James Redenbaugh. Mathias, from Visual Facilitators, was responsible for the majority of the graphics and for coming up with the general style and aesthetic. Mathias supports change and facilitates the unfolding of potential through visualization. Both by hand work (being one of the top graphic recorders) as well as in digital format (process visualization, info graphics, etc.) his work contributes to the evolution of consciousness in a rapidly changing world -- IntegralInformationArchitecture.com and visualfacilitators.com. James helped with a few final touches needed to design and create the spiritual development cubes (figures 15, 16, 17, 18, and E). A huge thank you to both of you.

During my time in graduate school while living in Cambridge, Massachusetts, I was blessed to have close friends who shared my passion for spiritual growth and awakening. I'd like to thank several individuals in particular from my Cambridge community. First, a warm thank you to my two roommates during that time, Mark Schmanko and Ben Williams. Our intense 4:30am daily practice schedule helped to build a foundation of mutual trust and commitment like nothing I had ever experienced. I'd like to thank John Churchill and Robert Wolsky. John for your support in the Mahamudra stream and for introducing me to Dr. Brown and Robert for your willingness to explore the potential of inter-subjective dynamics and practices. I'd also like to extend gratitude to Kenzo An, Rodrigo Tarraza, Morgan Dix, Vedren Peric, Dan Capone, Ted Saad, Mike Sullivan, Scott Arbeit, and all the others from the local Boston community not mentioned. You are all a part of this book in collaborative consciousness. The penetrating "we spaces" that we cultivated together continue to teach me what it means to be together in true spiritual brotherhood. Thank you.

I also give heartfelt thanks to Bruce and Sharon Lyon. Our time together in San Francisco and in the deserts of Egypt has taught me what it means to love "for no reason at all." Your love flows through these pages. I am grateful.

I'd to thank Olivia Hansen and Julie Flaherty for your incredible love and ongoing financial support during the last legs of the editing process. Each of you supported me in such a monumental way.

I also extend gratitude to my Integral family in Denver. Thanks to Clint Fuhs, Brian Berger, Ali Akalin, Colin Bigelow, Andrea Engle, Rollie Stanich, Nicole Fegley, Kelly Bearer, Michael LaGattuta, and the rest of Ken's close students. Our interaction, dialogue and friendship have helped to make this book what it is.

I'd like to thank Andrew Cohen and other senior students in his community (e.g., Elizabeth Debold, Jeff Carreira, and Mike Wombacher) through whom I've gained deeper insight into the dynamics of what they call a "Higher We." My understanding of what it means to be in community will forever be molded by my experiences with all of you.

I offer gratitude to Sally Kempton (Swami Durgananda) for the stories and affirmation she shared about the early emergence of inter-subjective non-duality that took place among some of Muktananda's senior students, and to Terry Patten for relaying experiences of inter-subjective non-duality that also took place among some of the students of Adi Da Samraj. Along this line, I also thank Adi Da Samraj himself. Although I never met him in person, I heard him speak once referring to all of humanity as one "Great Tradition." Although using the phrase —The Great Human Tradition— as I do throughout the book, was not a conscious attempt to follow Adi Da's transmission, it seems appropriate to honor his work and influence.

Finally, and most fundamentally, I would like to thank my wife Amanda for her unending support. Sharing Daniel P. Brown as meditation teacher has opened up worlds of dialogue and practice between us that I benefit from endlessly. This book would truly have not been possible without her support and her particular perspective on Dan's teachings. She is a true mentor for me when it comes to framing these sorts of complex spiritual conceptualizations to a more general audience. Without her, I might easily find myself lost in a level of specificity that loses a broader audience. Amanda, darling, I love you. Thank you.

As a final statement in this section, I'd like to make the point directly that the insights offered in the book are, unavoidably, limited to my own level of spiritual development. I do not offer these teachings from the position of authority or as representative of any particular tradition or lineage stream. Rather, I offer this book from my own direct experience as advice that has helped to shape my path. As such the insights are necessarily biased in certain ways by the experiences I've had and the practice communities and traditions of which I am a part. My hope is that the perspective offered here might help others as they navigate similar territory. Ultimately, as the ideas outlined in this book are compared, challenged, and supported by practitioners inside of other lineage streams, I hope that we can, together, more deeply reveal the universal human lineage of which we are all a part.

In humble recognition of the great beings who have evolved beyond the view presented here, I yield to your wisdom. Corrections and improvements that bring greater benefit to our human family are always welcome.

Introduction

We stand *in streams of wisdom*. Today, the insights of nearly all of the great wisdom traditions of Earth are available to us. With this level of access to Earth's wisdom, we are presented an opportunity. We have the opportunity to lay out the spiritual insights from all traditions in front of us and to examine them side by side, all at once. We have the opportunity to take in the whole of what is available to us as human beings rather than restricting ourselves to a single tradition, culture, or historical time period. We have the opportunity to synthesize humanity's knowledge of spiritual development from a truly global perspective and in a way that is dedicated to serving the benefit of all. When we look at the spiritual lineages of Earth through this lens of opportunity, we see that all of humanity is a single tradition. I call this single lineage of humanity *The Great Human Tradition*.

My work here, in this book, begins to point to several of the underlying elements of a Great Human Tradition. In order to do so, I draw together the profound and sacred insights garnered in our world's great religious traditions and integrate them with the conventional streams of wisdom uncovered by modern Western psychology. This bridge between the contemplative and the conventional creates a link that allows a massive swath of the human population to access the wisdom of our traditions who might otherwise be closed off to it.

The integrative approach I bring is based on the work first pioneered by my own teachers Ken Wilber and Daniel P. Brown. Both Brown and Wilber demonstrate a clear competency for the integration of contemplative and conventional approaches to psychology and spirituality. Their efforts were first highlighted together in their co-edited volume *Transformations of Consciousness*. Since then, both Brown and Wilber have continued to show how universal *deep structures* appear across traditions and in varying cultural contexts. When these deep structures are articulated and made obvious they set a foundation for a more holistic, more integral approach to spiritual development. This book builds upon and further supports their original research. The details I offer here would not be possible were I not able to stand on their shoulders.

This book is divided into three parts. In Part 1, I introduce several key elements of the meta-theoretical framework that Wilber calls Integral Theory. Integral Theory serves as the main orientation for my work. I begin with an introduction to the Four Quadrants/Quadrivia and demonstrate how the various methodological approaches used today in the academic study of spiritual development often preference one particular perspective while ignoring others. Next, I provide a general overview of what Wilber calls states and structures. In doing so, I show how each of these elements relates to specific aspects of Integral Theory (e.g., The Wilber-Combs Matrix, Wilber's notion of "dual center of gravity"). In order to offer more granularity to the discussion and to set the context for the rest of the series, I briefly point out here how the original categories of states and structures can be expanded to account for the four core vectors of spiritual development: states, state-stages, structures, and structure-stages.

In Part 2, I draw on our world's religious traditions to explore various examples of three of these four core vectors: state-stages, structure-stages, and states in full detail. Chapter 2 focuses on the stabilization of identity through state-stages. My work follows the lead of Daniel P. Brown and refers to state-stages as shifts in *vantage points*. I do my best to articulate each vantage point clearly so as to give the reader a true sense of the territory. In chapter 3, I introduce a concept that Wilber calls structure-stages. Structure-stages provide the fuel to operationalize the second core vector of growth. Depending on the context, I sometimes refer to structure-stages using the term *spiritual intelligence*. In chapter 4, I introduce the concept of states and show how spiritual practitioners can enter into different experiences with regard to gross, subtle, and causal realms. At the end of Part 2, in chapter 5, I introduce a three-dimensional model I call the Spiritual Development Cube. The Spiritual Development Cube is a visual way to show how these three aspects of spiritual development (state-stages, structure-stages, and states) relate to each other in an ongoing and dynamic way. The Spiritual Development Cube, along with the other insights brought forward in this book, help to expand upon the ideas outlined by other researchers and elaborate some points that have thus far only been explained implicitly. For instance, although the insights garnered through use of the Spiritual Development Cube are implicit in a concept that Wilber calls "dual-center of gravity," the implications of this new model have not yet been unpacked.

In a similar way, the distinctions between state-stages, structure-stages, and states are implicit in Brown's work as well. Given Brown's background in Western Psychology he is aware of the difference between structure-stages of the relative mind (i.e., stages of spiritual intelligence that enact various *views* of reality) and what he calls vantage points (state-stages). He is also aware of the difference between vantage points (state-stages) and the capacity for experiences in various states and realms. However, many of these distinctions are not brought to full and explicit expression in his work. The model presented here makes all of these distinctions clear in hopes of easing the path for practitioners. These are distinctions that I struggled to understand in my own spiritual development and I offer them here with the hope of eradicating similar confusion in others.

In Part 3, I offer three closing chapters that speak to the implications of a deeper understanding of spiritual development and the fuller recognition of our Great Human Tradition. In chapter 6, I explore how a better understanding of spiritual development might lead to benefits on both individual and collective scales. Here, I make the case for why honoring both conventional and contemplative aspects of development would be a positive move for us all. In chapter 7, I bring a hopeful view of how, together, we might enter into a new phase of conscious evolution. I leave the reader with a vision of our kosmic future and the various ways that an Integral model of spiritual development might offer guidance for something I call a Bright Alliance. In chapter 8, I shift the focus to the reader. There I express several areas of direct responsibility that each of us must lean into if we are to manifest this next, promising phase of human evolution.

I hope that in some small way, this book can help to show others where they are on the path and what areas of spiritual growth still lie ahead of them.

The Series in Integral Religion and Spirituality

This book, *Streams of Wisdom*, serves as volume 1 in a series dedicated to Integral Religion and Spirituality. In addition to the core elements of Integral Theory (quadrants, levels, lines, states, and types), the series outlines four major vectors of human growth as it moves through (1) states; (2) state-stages; (3) structures; and (4) structure-stages. As an introductory volume in the series, I focus the attention and scope on three of these four vectors. As I've outlined above, my general attempt is to articulate the distinctions between state-stages, structure-stages, and states in a bit more explicit detail, while simultaneously drawing on the world's great religious traditions for support. In describing these three dimensions of growth, my aim is to demonstrate that any description of a universal human spirituality ought to include each of them, lest it run the risk of missing a major dimension of spiritual growth.

In the second volume of the series, *Evolution's Ally*, I shift the focus to study the vectors of structures and structure-stages in greater detail. With an emphasis on our world's religious traditions (Islam, Christianity, Hinduism, and Buddhism), the entire analysis in volume 2 attempts to pinpoint why religion tends to serve as a blockade to human evolution and how, instead, it might be transformed into an ally for human progress. In doing so, I introduce a new dimension of academic study I call Developmental Religious Pluralism. The core chapters of volume 2 provide evidence to support Wilber's notion of the *conveyor belt*.[1] The conveyor belt explains that religious traditions are not composed of homogeneous practitioners but rather a complex pool of individuals each of whom rests at a particular structure-stage of development. Each structure-stage enacts a different version of the tradition. As a result, we find that there is not just one version of each tradition, but rather a version of every tradition appropriate for each stage of development. This means that there is a magic version of Christianity, a mythic version, a rational version, a pluralistic version, and an integral version. Just as there is a magic version of Buddhism, a mythic version, a rational version, a pluralistic version and an integral version. If clearer maps of the progressive unfolding of each of these stages can be successfully outlined within each tradition, then there is a chance to transform our world's religious traditions into vehicles of evolution. In short, Volume 2 attempts to do just that. By tracing each level of interpretation across the world's most popular traditions, it shows how religion can play a positive role in the future of humanity.

Although both books can certainly stand-alone as contributions in their own right, each book's strength grows exponentially when read together and all four vectors of spiritual growth are understood.

Preliminary Definitions and Distinctions

Before proceeding, four distinctions need to be made by way of clear definitions:

1) *The term spiritual development.* Although this whole book is in essence a sophisticated definition of the term, a brief statement is useful here to provide a foundation. Spiritual development, as I use the term, refers broadly to the spiritual unfolding of an individual over time. It includes: (a) deepening one's sense of identity through state-stages, (b) increasing complexity of thought through structure-stages of spiritual intelligence, (c) as well as the capacity to cultivate access to specific states, realms, and planes of reality.

2) *A differentiation between the terms spiritual development (defined above) and another commonly used term, spiritual intelligence.* I use the word spiritual intelligence to refer to a specific line of development. That means that within the frame of multiple intelligences, one specific area of growth is the development through structure-stages with regard to ultimate concern. I base much (but not all) of my understanding of spiritual intelligence on the work of James Fowler. Fowler's approach and methodology is commonly referred to as faith development theory.[2] Fowler's research serves as one of the primary indicators of one's structure-stage of spiritual intelligence. (Volume 2 of this series explores spiritual intelligence in detail.)

In short, the over-arching and more general term of spiritual development includes the more specific term spiritual intelligence. Conversely, the term spiritual intelligence, as I will be using it, does not necessarily account for the whole gamut of spiritual development (i.e., spiritual intelligence does not necessarily include vantage point development or state/realm access).[3]

3) *The two terms religious experience and spiritual experience.* Unless

27

otherwise noted in context, I use both terms as synonyms to refer to the same category of human experience. Rather than the more ordinary experience of religion that might simply result from being a religious adherent (e.g., What is the experience of being a Christian or a Muslim?), I use both terms to refer specifically to peak mystical experiences that result in temporary and permanent shifts in one's perception of ultimate reality.[4]

The Primacy of Practice

In 1931, Alfred Korzybski coined the phrase "the map is not the territory."[5] Korzybski first used the phrase as a metaphor to help explain his theory of general semantics. Wilber, too, is famous for adopting the idiom. In Wilber's context, the phrase usually refers to the fact that the Integral map is not the same as the experiential territory. In other words, just having a conceptual understanding of the various quadrants, levels, lines, states, types, and potential shadows, does not indicate that one has fully come to know each dimension in their own experience firsthand. The map, whether it refers to Wilber's model of reality or Korzybski's representational use of language, always represents a limited third-person account of a given topic. In a similar way, although understanding spiritual development is important, a conceptual grasp of the process and goal is certainly not enough if we seek individual and collective transformation.

Understanding the difference between the map and the territory is particularly important when discussing spiritual development. A conceptual understanding of the process of spiritual development (the map) is not the same as undergoing the process of spiritual development and transformation itself (the territory). While it is true that the two ideas are deeply related, it is also important that the two are not conflated.

Once we have disaggregated first-person territories from third-person maps, it becomes obvious that individuals often possess varying combinations of conceptual and experiential realization. For instance, a person may have a sound conceptual understanding of spiritual awakening but little actualization in first-person experience. Conversely, a person may have a significant degree of spiritual actualization but lack the proper third-person conceptual framework to make sense of his or her experience. In the ideal situation, individuals and societies ought to balance the conceptual with the experiential.

Following this injunctive distinction, one of the first caveats to impart to the reader is that understanding the maps outlined in this book should not be confused with the actual experience of spiritual development itself. Although some of the ideas proposed here may indeed be psychoactive, creating shifts in state, context, or, perhaps, certain realizations, the model is not a replacement for finding a teacher and practicing in earnest on one's own. All of these ideas can become a reality in your own experience and, to the degree to which these maps make sense to you, there is a moral obligation that you make them manifest and stable in your own life and personal experience.

PART 1: An Integral Context

Chapter 1
An Integral Approach

Integral theorist Ken Wilber spent the last four decades analyzing and organizing human knowledge. The fruits of his efforts resulted in a type of cross-paradigmatic map-making that enables vast amounts of information to be organized into a single integrative framework. The majority of this first chapter introduces several of Wilber's key insights and shows how each helps to set the foundation for a more comprehensive understanding of spiritual development.

Organizing the Field of Spiritual Development

Wilber's Integral Theory encourages us to begin our analysis with the working assumption that *everyone holds a piece of the puzzle that is both true and simultaneously partial.* One of the best ways to put this working assumption into action is through an application of what Wilber calls the Four Quadrants.

Anytime we take into account a greater number of perspectives, we create more space to take in the whole of any occurrence.[6] The Four Quadrants are one of the easiest ways we can actively view reality in a multi-perspectival way. The Four Quadrants represent an individual perspective, a collective perspective, and an interior and exterior of each. Figure 1 below provides a graphic representation of the Four Quadrant Model.[7]

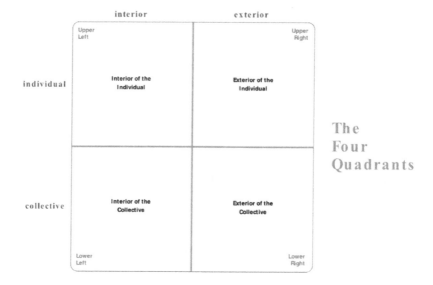

Figure 1: The Four Quadrants

Integral Theory suggests that any given occurrence can be viewed using the four basic orientations shown in figure 1.[8] The two upper quadrants represent individual perspectives. The two lower quadrants represent collective perspectives. The left-hand quadrants represent the interior perspectives and the right-hand quadrants represent exterior perspectives. Throughout this book, I'll refer to each of these as upper right (UR), upper left (UL), lower right (LR), and lower left (LL) for short.

Let's look at an example. Your experience right now is composed of all Four Quadrants. When you turn your attention to your UR Quadrant you notice your own exterior. This includes your physical body and all of your behaviors. When you turn your attention to your UL Quadrant you notice the interior of your experience. This includes all of your thoughts, emotions, and intentions. Your LL Quadrant relates to the interior aspects of your reality that you share with others. This may include shared beliefs, shared intentions, and areas of mutual understanding. The LL Quadrant represents the aspect of you that is embedded in and moving in the world as culture. Your LR Quadrant relates to the exterior aspects of the reality you share with others. This includes the shared political, economic, social and environmental systems that arise as part of your reality. All Four Quadrants are a direct part of your experience right now. They don't arise one at a time, but rather all at once. Your Four Quadrants are always present. They co-arise and tetra-mesh to form every occurrence your've ever experienced.

Now, we can look from the Four Quadrants, as we just did in the paragraph above, and we can also look at the Four Quadrants. Looking at the Four Quadrants allows us to use these four fundamental perspectives as an organizing tool for knowledge. When viewed in this way, the Four Quadrants help us to appropriately separate and distinguish one methodological approach from another.[9] Given the vast amount of research conducted over the past hundred years into the nature of spiritual development, it is useful to have a tool like the Four Quadrants that can make sense of everything and understand it in the context of a more comprehensive whole. When working with academic knowledge, as we do below, the Four Quadrants help us to see which perspective(s) a particular scholar preferences and which perspective(s) he or she leaves out.

Let's take a deeper look at the scholarship available today on spiritual development. The average scholar does his or her best to coordinate vast amounts of information haphazardly, usually without any sort of meta-framework. Often he or she gives preference to one particular methodology (or one particular quadrant) over another. With the Four Quadrants in place, however, instead of weighing one specific approach over another, all methodologies are given equal value and integrated into a single comprehensive frame.[10] Figure 2 below shows this type of organization in graphic form. (All of the researchers listed in figure 2 are described in full in Appendix 1. Readers interested in more details and supporting evidence are pointed there.)

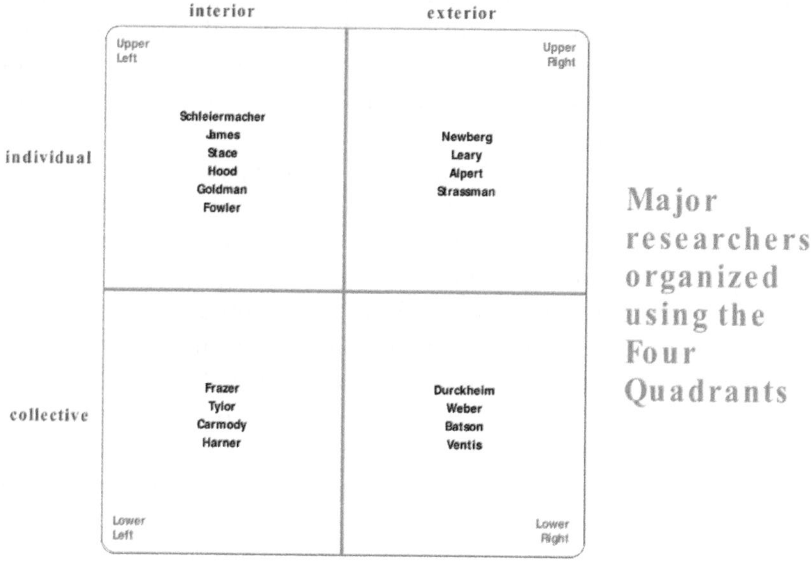

interior   exterior

	interior	exterior	
individual	Upper Left Schleiermacher James Stace Hood Goldman Fowler	Newberg Leary Alpert Strassman	Upper Right
collective	Frazer Tylor Carmody Harner	Durckheim Weber Batson Ventis	
	Lower Left	Lower Right	

Major researchers organized using the Four Quadrants

Figure 2: Major researchers organized using the Four Quadrants

Today's most influential researchers into the nature of religious experience and spiritual development can be categorized according to the specific methodology they use. Figure 2 lists several scholars and the methodological approach with which they can be most closely associated.[11]

In figure 2, Hood, Stace, and Fowler are all associated with UL Quadrant methodologies. This means that each of them focus their work on the interior of the individual. Scholars like Hood and Stace focus on states of consciousness. Fowler focuses on structures of consciousness. Neuroscientists like Newberg and psychopharmacologists like Strassman focus the majority of their attention on the UR Quadrant. This means they give emphasis to physiological correlates of spiritual experience that show up in the exterior of individual experience. Newberg focuses on the brain itself through neuroimaging and mapping. Strassman focuses on the active neurotransmitter dimethyltryptamine (DMT) and its role in inducing spiritual experience. The same is true for the two lower, collective quadrants. Anthropologists like Harner and Frazer focus on the LL Quadrant. This involves research into the interior of the collective in order to examine the shared values of particular groups. In Harner's case he conducted a massive amount of research through actual participation in shamanic experience with indigenous populations. Harner's focus on the interior of the collective can be directly contrasted to the socioeconomic and systemic dynamics of spiritual experience that scholars like Ventis and Batson examine. Ventis and Batson give emphasis to the exterior of the collective or what Integral Theory calls the LR Quadrant. (See Appendix 1 for supporting material.)

It is important to note that an Integral analysis is not meant to pigeonhole any particular scholar into a specific quadrant. Many scholars, especially more recent theorists, who are careful to account for postmodern sensitivities, are aware of areas of influence outside of their primary methodology. However, these other perspectives are often only examined superficially, and rarely are they ever included into any sort of meta-framework or synthesis. The Four Quadrants prove invaluable to sort through and organize what might otherwise seem like an overwhelming amount of information.

A More Balanced Approach

In articulating the Great Human Tradition, a single and unbroken lineage of humanity, I attempt to provide as balanced an analysis as possible, considering all relevant factors. Because all quadrants arise simultaneously and because all quadrants are valuable and irreducible perspectives on reality, each plays a role in co-creating any given event or occurrence. Spiritual experience in the Upper Left and its correlating brain changes in the Upper Right are concurrently molded and shaped by the social dynamics of the Lower Right and the shared cultural values and expectations in the Lower Left. As Wilber aptly puts it, all quadrants "tetra-arise and tetra-mesh as mutual dimensions of every occasion, all the way up, all the way down."[12]

I agree with Wilber that this model seems to be one of the most comprehensive explanations we have thus far to do justice to all the research available. All researchers hold views that are true but partial. All provide something of significant value but most usually leave out a piece of the puzzle.[13] The Great Human Tradition is based, both explicitly and implicitly, on the fact that reality tetra-arises. (For a detailed explanation of how the Four Quadrants lay the foundation for the Eight Zones, and for some of the most relevant research in the field of spiritual development associated with each zone, see the endnotes.)[14] [15]

Four Core Elements of Spiritual Development

In addition to giving us the Four Quadrants, Wilber began laying the foundation for the Great Human Tradition with the articulation of the difference between what he calls "states and structures" in his book *Integral Spirituality*. The Wilber-Combs matrix is one of the primary models used to describe the difference between these two types of experiences within the Integral framework.[16] The Wilber-Combs matrix is usually labeled as follows:

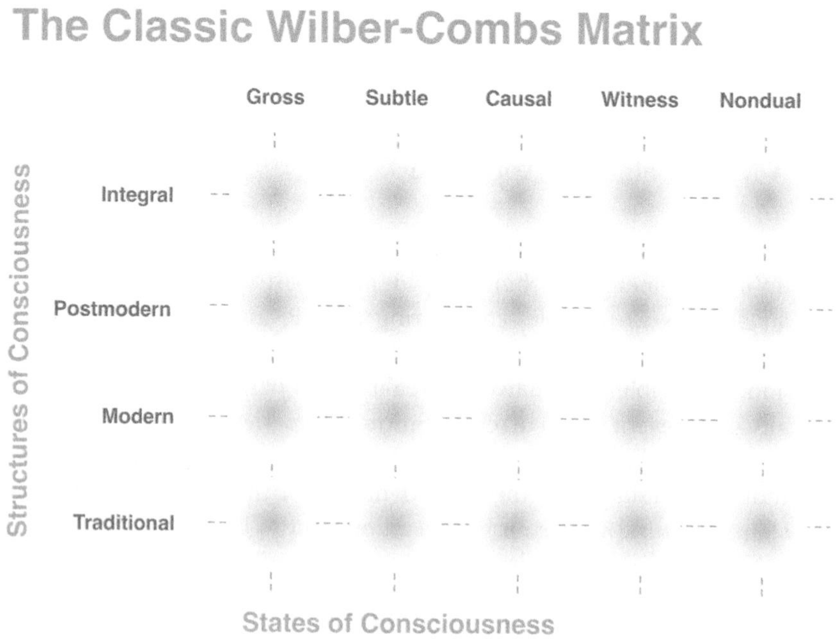

The Classic Wilber-Combs Matrix

	Gross	Subtle	Causal	Witness	Nondual
Integral					
Postmodern					
Modern					
Traditional					

(Vertical axis label: Structures of Consciousness)

(Horizontal axis label: States of Consciousness)

Figure 3: The Classic Wilber-Combs Matrix

The vertical dimension of the Wilber-Combs Matrix represents *structural* development. Structural development as it shows up in structure-stages indicates the increasing lenses of complexity through which the relative self views, interprets, and engages with the world. In the Integral model in general, and the Wilber-Combs Matrix in particular, structures-stages of development (e.g., levels, waves) range from traditional, to modern, to postmodern, to Integral and beyond. These same stages are sometimes called mythic, rational, pluralistic, and Integral, respectively.[17] The number of levels or names of demarcation that we employ to denote vertical growth are less important than the fact that we include some indicator of increasing levels of structural complexity. In the case of this book, when I refer to structure-stage development, I will most often be referring to one's stage of religious orientation or what we will call spiritual intelligence. The main point here is that every wave of structural development enacts a different view of reality. (Note: In volume 2, I draw the important distinction between structures and structure-stages.)

The horizontal dimension across the top of the matrix is used to signify states of consciousness. The five major states pointed out on the Wilber-Combs matrix range from gross to subtle to causal to witness to nondual. I discuss various types of states in chapters 2 and 4.

The development of the Wilber-Combs Matrix helped to point out three important breakthroughs. First, the two-vector matrix clearly disaggregates states of consciousness from structures of consciousness. This important distinction was not always obvious. Four decades ago, members of the humanistic and transpersonal psychology movements assumed that states of consciousness were simply examples of higher stages of human development.[18] In these early models, scholars assumed that after the major stages of *conventional* Western psychological development, a human being would then enter into psychic, subtle, causal, and nondual stages of *contemplative* development, as shown in figure 4 below:

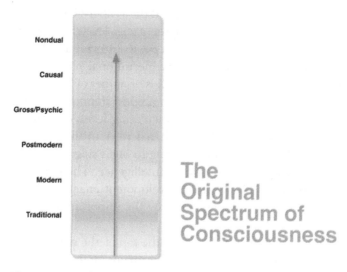

Figure 4: The spectrum of consciousness as originally perceived by early transpersonal researchers

This model shows states (gross, subtle, causal, nondual) stacked on top of structure-stages (traditional, modern, postmodern), which is now thought to be a partial understanding.

Empirical studies[19] now show that the stages of conventional Western developmental psychology (structure-stages) and the contemplative stages to which the spiritual mystics point (state-stages) represent two different types of spiritual development.[20] Stages of Western psychological growth, as represented in the vertical dimension of the Wilber-Combs Matrix, tend to focus on Wilber's Upper Left quadrant using a third-person approach, whereas states of consciousness offered in detail by mystics of both East and West and shown across the top of the matrix horizontally represent a first-person perspective of the Upper Left quadrant.[21]

Second, the parsing apart of states from structure-stages revealed that various states of consciousness are available at every stage of development.[22] Instead of assuming, like early transpersonal researchers, that contemplative states of consciousness were simply the domain of the most highly evolved human beings, the Wilber-Combs Matrix elucidates the fact that states are universally available.[23] Just as all beings wake, dream, and experience deep sleep, passing each day through gross, subtle, and causal realms, all beings also have access to states of consciousness gross, subtle, or causal. That means, as the graph in figure 3 shows, that even if an individual has traditional or modern structure-stage of development, he or she can still access a gross, subtle, or causal state of consciousness.[24] States are available at every structure-stage.

Third, the Wilber-Combs Matrix points to the fact that every state will naturally be interpreted through (or more precisely "enacted by") the structure-stage of the development that he or she has stabilized.[25] This means that an individual at a traditional level of development who has a subtle state experience will necessarily interpret that experience through a traditional lens. A modern person will interpret it through a modern lens, a post-modern person through a postmodern lens, and so on; all the way up the spectrum of structural development. When we add in all the information available at our disposal given the Four Quadrants of Integral theory, we see that the individual interpretation will not only be a result of the structure-stage of development but will also be conditioned by the shared values of the culture as well as the social and systemic elements of the surrounding environment (in other words it will be interpreted according to the Four Quadrants).[26]

Let's unpack the example a little further to elucidate how much nuance and sophistication the Integral model can bring to an analysis of spiritual experience. Imagine a Christian practitioner holding a traditional structure-stage of development has a subtle state experience of luminosity full of love. Due to the cultural influences and biasing perspectives of his or her tradition, he or she might automatically determine that the subtle contact with luminous love represented contact with Jesus.

In a different cultural and social context, a Hindu at a traditional stage of development might have the same subtle experience of light and love but might interpret the experience as communion with Krishna. In both cases, the brain activity in the Upper Right would show the same exterior correlates to the same interior subtle state experience. However, the experience itself shows up in vastly different ways due to the factors in the other quadrants.

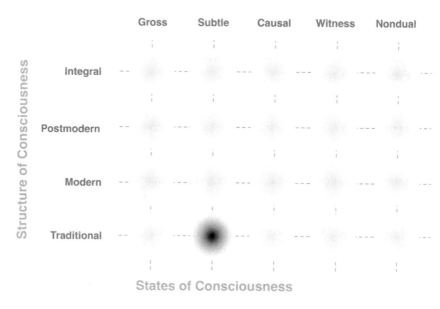

Figure 5: Wilber-Combs Matrix highlighting a traditional level of development and a subtle state experience

Notice the darkened circle in figure 5. The Wilber-Combs Matrix above does an adequate job marking a subtle state experience in relation to a traditional level of development. If, however, we want an even more detailed analysis that includes additional factors (i.e., religious tradition or socio-cultural influences), it is helpful to write out a full equation that includes the quadrants as well:

Christian (Shared LL+LR) + Traditional (Structure-Stage) + Subtle Luminosity (State) = an experience of Jesus interpreted to reinforce religious superiority

or

Hindu (Shared LL+LR) + Traditional (Structure-Stage) + Subtle Luminosity (State) = An experience of Krishna interpreted to reinforce religious superiority

In both of the examples provided, due to the traditional (ethno-centric)

structure-stage of consciousness through which the experience is interpreted, the person undergoing the experience might be even more certain that their particular cultural or religious worldview is correct. That means that now that a traditional Christian adherent thinks that she has seen Jesus, she may be even more certain that Christianity is the one true religion. Similarly, if a Hindu adherent with a traditional structure-stage of development thinks that he has contacted Krishna, he is likely to be even more certain that Hinduism holds the exclusive truth. Due to the adherent's stage of structural development, this type of experience is likely to reinforce ethnocentric views about their own religious superiority.

In contrast, a Christian or Hindu with a postmodern structure-stage of psychological development might have the same subtle experience but interpret it in a completely different fashion (this is shown in figure 6 below):

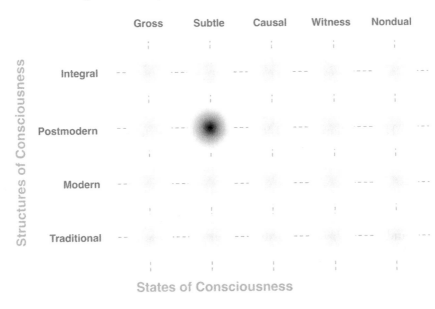

Figure 6: Wilber-Combs Matrix highlighting a postmodern level of development and a subtle state experience

Figure 6 shows a subtle state experience enacted at a postmodern structure-stage of development. In the case of both a traditional structure-stage and the postmodern structure-stage the experience is still co-created by the shared religious values and social expectations in the LL and LR quadrants. This means that the Christian would still see Jesus and the Hindu would still see Krishna. Similarly, brain activity in the UR would also match. However, despite these similarities, the interpretation of the event would be uniquely influenced by the structure-stage of spiritual intelligence. Whereas the adherent at a traditional level is now even more ethnocentric and certain that his or her specific worldview is exclusively correct, the individual at a postmodern level of development might be fully aware of the conditioned nature of his or her experience and thus even more convinced that such experiences are universal, across traditions and available to all.

Written out, full equations of a subtle experience enacted by postmodern structure would read as follows:

Christian (Shared LL+LR) + Postmodern (Structure-Stage) + Subtle Luminosity (State) = An experience of Jesus interpreted to support a universal potential for all human beings.

or

Hindu (Shared LL+LR) + Postmodern (Structure-Stage) + Subtle Luminosity (State) = An experience of Krishna interpreted to support a universal potential for all human beings.

These types of insights are just the beginning of the depth and clarity brought forth with an Integral lens. The Wilber-Combs Matrix and the use of the Four Quadrants provide a fantastic model to examine spiritual experience and spiritual development. It is my hope that scholars of Integral Religious Studies in the future will use these types of distinctions as a starting point.

Unpacking the Wilber-Combs Matrix
States + State-Stages + Structures + Structure-Stages

This book (along with other books in the series) builds upon ideas implicit in the classic Wilber-Combs Matrix outlined above to further elucidate its usefulness. The basic thesis is that in an Integral age, a more detailed model of spiritual development should consider at least four areas of spiritual growth: states, state-stages, structures, and structure-stages. [27] I focus here in this book on three of these four vectors -- states, state-stages, and structure-stages. I leave a more fully fleshed out explanation of the relationship between structures and structure-stages for volumes 2 and 3 of this series.

The three central chapters of this book explore these particular aspects of spiritual development in detail: chapter 2 focuses on state-stages; chapter 3 focuses on structure-stages; and chapter 4 focuses on states. For now, a brief introduction to these three core elements is useful.

Let's begin with the distinction between state-stages and states. For the purposes of this book, I will refer to one particular type of state-stage that I, following Daniel P. Brown, call vantage points. Vantage points trace the locus of awareness as it moves from a gross, to subtle, to causal, to witness, to nondual identity. This shift in the apparent "source of awareness", and its stabilization, is quite different from the temporary experience of a particular state. States, unlike vantage points, can refer to ordinary shifts (waking, dreaming, deep sleep) or extraordinary shifts (gross, subtle, casual communion/union/ identity). Figures 7 and 8 below point out the initial distinction between vantage points (state-stages of identity) and states by setting them each alongside structures. Figure 7 situates vantage points (horizontal axis) alongside structures of consciousness (vertical axis). Figure 8 situates extraordinary states (horizontal axis) alongside structures of consciousness (vertical axis).

Vantage Points (State-Stages of Identity)

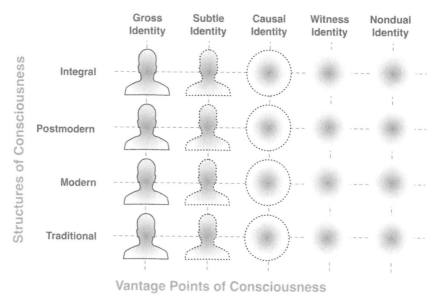

Figure 7: Wilber-Combs Matrix showing vantage points of consciousness (an example of shifts in state-stage identity) alongside structures of consciousness

Figure 7 above shows a Wilber-Combs Matrix with available vantage points of consciousness listed horizontally across the top of the chart. Vantage points represent shifts in state-stage identity as they move from gross identity to subtle identity to casual identity to witness identity to nondual identity. (At a nondual vantage point the word identity can become problematic because there is nothing other than the identity to define it in relation to). Each of these state-stages are available at any of the vertical structure-stages of development (traditional, modern, postmodern, Integral).

Spiritual heroes of the past, such as the Buddha and Christ, attained a specific realization in which the very source of their awareness was no longer confused with an individual and separate-self. In both of their cases, their realization was not a temporary state that simply changed the content or the field of their experience. Rather, in each case, Jesus and the Buddha realized that their deepest vantage point was none other than the very source and ground of existence. It was a recognition that was not dependent on a changing field of experience.

Extraordinary and Ordinary States of Consciousness

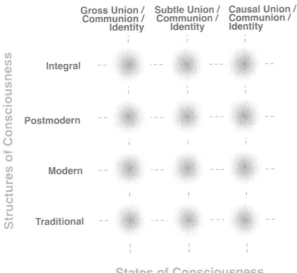

Figure 8:Wilber-Combs Matrix showing extraordinary and ordinary states of consciousness

Instead of listing vantage points across the horizontal axis, figure 8 above shows ordinary and extraordinary states along the top of the Wilber-Combs Matrix. Ordinary states of consciousness are often labeled as gross, subtle, and causal and are usually associated with waking, dreaming, and deep sleep. Over time, however, and with meditative practice, one can develop a capacity to enter into extraordinary states of consciousness associated with gross, subtle, and causal realms virtually at will. Extraordinary state experiences in each realm usually relate to temporary experiences of communion, union, or identity.

Making a clear distinction between vantage points (stabilized state-stages of identity) and ordinary/extraordinary states reveals that one can have any state experience while anchored in any vantage point. (Although this point is implicit in Wilber's notion of *dual center of gravity*, it has not yet been fully elucidated.) Another way of saying this is that no matter how deep of a vantage point one has anchored, he or she will still continue to wake, dream, and deep sleep. For example, let's say someone has a vantage point as the Witness-identity. As the Witness, one has transcended an exclusive identification with his or her personality and time/space; yet simultaneously, experiences still arise as gross, subtle, or causal states. This means that even with a Witness vantage point, state experiences continue to unfold. Similarly, one might find oneself with the recognition of nondual suchness (a nondual vantage point), and then over the course of a few hours, might experience an extraordinary subtle-realm-state experience of luminosity or causal-realm-state experiences of formlessness. The point is that states and vantage points always coexist as two different phenomena and each can be tracked separately. The vantage point represents the source of awareness (the Experiencer) and its various ranges are detailed in chapter 2 according to the work of Brown. States represent the temporary changing field or realm (the Experience) and are detailed in chapter 4.

The distinction between states and vantage points is essential. Shifts in vantage point are the area of spiritual growth that determines one's degree of awakening. Although it is often confused as such, awakening does not indicate a change in one's state of consciousness, but refers more directly to the degree to which one has transcended the confusion of identifying awareness with its more limited vehicles (thought, personality, time/space, individual consciousness).

With all three components elucidated (vantage points, structure-stages, and states), it becomes clear that one may have any vantage point (state-stage identity) at nearly any structure-stage of development, and can develop a capacity to enter into almost any temporary state/realm.[28] Although all three of these elements have a certain degree of interconnectivity, each area of growth develops relatively independently. As Wilber put it in a conversation we had, the various aspects are "linked but not hooked."[29]

When we look at these three components of spiritual development as a triadic matrix of analysis, a much fuller understanding of spiritual potential reveals itself. As we shall see, every event involves an experiencer (vantage point), a mode of experiencing (structure-stage), and an experience (state/realm). And before any of these perceptions, all occurrences are enacted as perspectives. Each of these dimensions of spiritual experience is vital for the articulation of a Great Human Tradition that honors the gifts of the past and sets the foundation for the future.[30]

PART 2:   Deepening Our
          Understanding of
          Spiritual Development

Chapter 2
Vantage Points of Spiritual Awakening

This chapter provides an initial window into our first core aspect of spiritual development: vantage points. Vantage points, as we shall see, refer to the practitioner's "basis of operation" or where awareness seems to source itself in any given moment. Throughout the chapter, I build directly on the work of Daniel P. Brown.

I approach the discussion on vantage points from a faith-neutral perspective. The term faith-neutral means that I introduce a model of spiritual realization that consciously seeks to avoid the trap of cultural or tradition specific biases. It is my hope that this faith-neutral approach corrects for the historical tendency in the West that erroneously used Christian models as a benchmark for validity. In addition to correcting for historical errors, a faith-neutral approach also allows us to access underlying commonalities that hold true across diverse cultures and traditions. Following the lead of Brown, and then building on Wilber's work, I use the term deep structures to refer to these underlying commonalities that show up cross-culturally. Each deep structure remains stable despite the fact that tradition-specific surface features are variegated.[31] This means that, although the stages of vantage point development are constant across traditions (i.e. the underlying deep structures remain in tact) the various ways that shifts in vantage point show up in practice are diverse.[32] Furthermore, not all traditions have esoteric teachings that carry the practitioner through the entire spectrum of vantage point development as a whole.

After establishing confidence in a basic faith-neutral approach, I use the second half of the chapter to look more closely at how three religion-specific examples can help to fill out the model of vantage point development. First, I look at a particular expression of Tibetan Buddhism to demonstrate how the more general model of spiritual

53

realization outlined here can be more greatly refined. Second, I offer an example of spiritual realization from the Tantric Hindu tradition to further support the claim that Brown's deep structures are universal. Third, I take a deeper look at the Islamic tradition to show the most critical shift in identity: the transition from a dualistic vantage point to nondual vantage point. Each of the religion-specific examples provides the reader with a deeper understanding of how universal deep structures tend to translate into surface features. I close the chapter with a brief account of two potential pathologies that can arise with vantage point development.

In both the faith-neutral outline in the first half of the chapter and the tradition-specific examples outlined in the second half, the overall account is not meant to be exhaustive. Rather than offer an extensive and complete study, it is my hope that this chapter will do an adequate job introducing the reader to the importance of vantage point development. At the conclusion of the chapter the reader ought to have a sufficient understanding of how this particular vector of vantage points can be distinguished from the other elements of spiritual development that we shall explore later; namely, the influence of cognitive stages of structural development and the capacity to access gross, subtle, and causal states.

One additional note is worth making before bringing this introduction to a close. Although both Brown and Wilber agree to a large extent in the conclusions they draw, each of them brings quite different approach to the topic. Brown's work is that of a scholar, practitioner, psychologist, and teacher of contemplative development. The differentiations that he has developed are designed to facilitate direct spiritual realization and as such are technical terms with an original source connected to a tradition of practice. (For instance, levels of awareness were discussed in written works by Rechung, a disciple of the great Tibetan master Milarepa, and prior to that were part of a long-standing oral tradition in Tibet.) Wilber's approach, on the other hand, is that of a scholar, practitioner, and philosopher. Consequently, one of Wilber's main interests is how these ideas affect humankind as a whole and how a deeper understanding of these dimensions of spiritual growth might influence and implicate all human beings cross-culturally and across various religious traditions. Although most readers familiar with Wilber's work will already have a general sense for the various aspects of spiritual growth outlined here, it has been my experience that a deeper understanding of Brown's extensive research is of great benefit to those seeking more clarity on the spiritual path. And with this deeper understanding, it is my hope that the reader commits to putting these dimensions of spiritual growth into practice in his or her own direct experience. As these two seminal voices dance together in even deeper harmony, the benefit both bring can be maximized. May this chapter serve such an end.

Event Perspective vs. Mind Perspective

For the purposes of introducing a general outline, I track the cross-cultural comparison of the stages of awakening that Brown conducted between Hinduism, Theravada Buddhism, and Mahayana Buddhism in the 1980s.[33] In doing so, I also articulate some of the ways that Brown's initial research has continued to build since his original ideas were first published.[34]

One preliminary but crucial point Brown articulates is the marked difference between what is called the "event perspective" and the "mind perspective."[35] Notably, this distinction clarifies the difference between the subjective and objective perspectives built into everyday perception. The event perspective correlates to the changing field of experience (the apparently objective aspect of awareness). The mind perspective relates to the source of awareness-itself (the apparently subjective aspect of awareness).[36] Brown explains it in this way:

> The mind can be seen from two perspectives. The practitioner may meditate on the event-perspective of the mind, namely on what arises from (las byung ba) the mind, or may meditate on the mind-perspective, that is, upon what these events depend on (la brten pa), namely the observational point of awareness that stays.[37]

Whereas the event perspective is that which is known, the mind perspective refers to the knower itself. Brown's initial insights between the event perspective and the mind perspective first came during his study with Denmo Locho Rinpoche. Denmo Locho Rinpoche, a Tibetan Buddhist Lama, was former head abbot of Namgyal Monastery in Dharamsala, India.[38] He is currently head of the *dGe Lugs pa* lineage (the lineage of H.H. The Dalai Lama). Since first learning the initial distinctions from Denmo Locho, Brown's clarifications on the two categories of experience have been further derived from his translations of rare Tibetan Buddhist texts. Many of these texts remain unknown to most Western researchers of religious and meditative experience. The distinction between the event perspective and mind perspective plays a crucial role in the model of spiritual development portrayed in this book in helping to distinguish between certain states and vantage points.[39]

As a point of even further orientation, this chapter in particular traces the unfolding changes in the "mind perspective"; the subjective aspect of awareness that signifies where awareness appears to be coming from. In chapter 4, I give more emphasis to what Brown calls the event perspective in my articulation of state/realm access. (Ultimately, however, with the recognition of nondual awakened awareness, both perspectives are known to be an expression of Ultimate Reality).

Let us now turn to the full process of vantage point development in greater detail to see more specifically how spiritual realization actually manifests.

A Faith-Neutral Model of the Five Vantage Points of Awareness

As pointed out in the previous chapter, the terms vantage point and state-stage identity can be used interchangeably. Generally speaking, both "vantage points", as introduced by Brown, and "state-stages" as Wilber uses the term, track the path by which relative reality can be deconstructed to its Absolute base. We turn now directly to Brown's work to obtain a deeper understanding.

In his cross-cultural study of Hinduism, Theravada Buddhism, and Mahayana Buddhism, Brown made several remarkable discoveries. Most significantly, Brown was able to demonstrate that the path of spiritual realization unfolds in a predictable pattern over time.[40] In his own words he explains his research methodology and its results:

> The Yogasutras, Visuddhimagga, and Mahamudra were compared synoptically, stage by stage, to test whether there was an underlying sequence. Each tradition divided the stages of practice differently. Textual outlines of the stages proved an unreliable way to test for common structure.

However, a careful analysis of the technical language used in each text proved more useful. Using this approach it was possible to discover a clear underlying structure to meditation stages, a structure highly consistent across the traditions. The sequence of stages is assumed to be universal, despite the vastly different ways they are conceptualized and described across traditions. This sequence is believed to represent natural human development available to anyone who practices.[41]

Elsewhere, Brown explains the deep structure of the single path to awakening in even greater detail:

The logical order of the one path...is incredible.... Each stage expresses a particular form of de-construction. For example, ordinary attitudes, behaviors, affects and self-images are first deconstructed. Then, thinking is deconstructed. Next, perception is dismantled. While observing the subtle processes behind perception, the point of observation is altered. Next, the temporal nature of information-processing is analysed, and then, dismantled. As a result, the yogi experiences some form of interrelatedness of mind and cosmos. Finally, the activity and observational points that interfere with this interrelatedness are dismantled and enlightenment comes forth. Each of these [ ] stages depicts an episode of structural variance along the path of liberation. The stages are invariant.[42]

Each progressive vantage point described above by Brown signifies a change in the locus of identity or "basis of operation". This unfolds, as Brown explains, through direct observation of how the mind constructs perception. Each new insight into the inner working of perception results in a new observational point. As he writes above: "While observing the subtle processes behind perception, the point of observation is altered." Each time the observation point is altered, Brown describes it as a shift in "vantage point." Let's unpack each of the stages that Brown describes above, one at a time.

According to Brown's cross-cultural model, in the early stages of spiritual practice, prior to any degree of spiritual realization, awareness is confused with thought.[43] That is to say, the locus of awareness or one's vantage point appears to be embedded within a single sphere that cannot be disaggregated from the coming and going of the mental process of thinking. At this level of awareness, the event perspective (thought) and the mind perspective (awareness of the thought) have not been differentiated. Or, to say it another way, at this point thought and the observation of thought are fused.

As concentration deepens, thought elaboration diminishes in frequency and magnitude. When this occurs, it becomes easier to separate thought from awareness. (This becomes particularly obvious in stretches of meditation or contemplation wherein thought ceases and awareness remains.) Using Brown's language, even as thoughts continue to unfold in the field of experience as part of the event perspective, one is now able to recognize that the source of awareness (mind perspective) is something other than thought itself (the event perspective). Brown calls this first level of realization the recognition of "awareness."

Next, as the process of realization continues one begins to recognize that the unique personality with which one normally identifies, including its preferences, attitudes, and desires, are all part of the constructed process as well. Just as we saw above, wherein one is able to move beyond the confines of thought, eventually turning thoughts into objective events of the mind, so too, at this level of awakening, one is able to objectify the personality identity.[44] At this new level of awareness one has dis-embedded identity as it were and shifted awareness to a vantage point beyond any sort of exclusive identification with one's unique personality. Brown calls this level of realization "awareness-itself." Although awareness has now gained enough speed to prevent confusing itself with the contraction of thought and personality, at this stage, awareness is still confined within the common construction of time and space.

Brown's model continues: As spiritual realization deepens even further, the time-space continuum is transcended, dis-identified with, and made an object in awareness. Or as Brown puts it above, "the temporal nature of information-processing is analyzed, and then, dismantled." Brown uses the terms "awareness-in-and-of-itself" and "changeless boundless awareness" to describe the new vantage point beyond time and space. At this level of state-stage identity, one's vantage point does not come and go in time. From this perspective, it is always and only "now" despite the apparent changing of time that continues to unfold.

However, this changeless boundless awareness, the vantage point that Wilber calls the Witness, is still obscured. At the beginning stages of this level of realization, the subject-object duality remains. That is to say, in the experience of reality moment to moment, there still seems to be an individual consciousness (mind perspective) that is observing a field of experience (event perspective). That field of experience appears to be other than the point of observation. The first step at this stage is to employ practices that see through this unnecessary duality.

As duality is deconstructed and as non-duality is established, Brown is adamant in making clear that even with preliminary aspects of non-duality in place this is still not what he would call "awakened awareness." At this level of practice, nondual awareness is still embedded in individual consciousness. In other words, there is still a meditator "doing" the nondual meditation. As practice advances, one must learn to look even into the constructions of individuality. Awakened awareness does not become apparent until this final layer of individual consciousness is deconstructed. Once the final functions of individual mind are seen through as transparent, awareness has the opportunity to recognize its own nature in its most naked state.

Beyond the level of awakened awareness, Brown outlines several additional stages of the path. Although we won't go into too much detail here, each stage is important to mention. Once awakened awareness is accessed there is a process by which one stabilizes the recognition of awakening all of the time. Once stabilization is in place, one can open up a level of awareness Brown refers to as "all-at-once-ness". In the realization of "all-at-once-ness", simultaneous layers and dimensions of reality outside of conventional "point-of-view" are known directly all at the same time. And finally, Brown points to the possibility of opening that which is referred to in the Buddhist context as "the Buddha Bodies". The culmination of all of these levels of realization opening is the capacity for all accomplishing action in multiple realms and times simultaneously for the benefit of beings everywhere.

Caveats and Correlations

It is worth noting that the terms "nondual" and "awakening" is over used in the West. As we shall see below, there are gradations to the type of "nonduality" and "awakening" one can experience. Brown contends that the differences are due, at least in part, to the lack of checks-and-balances in the Western system. Many teachers declare themselves "awake" without the support or critique of a broader lineage stream. For this reason, among others, it is often recommended that the serious student of spiritual awakening find a teacher who is established within a lineage and who is held accountable for his or her actions by a community of peers.

With that initial caveat in place, it is quite useful to understand the dimensions of Brown's work against the backdrop of Integral Theory. Each of Brown's vantage point stages can be correlated with the aspect of the Integral map that Wilber calls state-stages. In the graphic below, I map the correlations:

Correlations between Brown and Wilber

Daniel P. Brown (Vantage Point)	Wilber (State-Stage Identity)
—	Gross
Awareness	Subtle
Awareness-itself	Causal
Awareness-in-and-of-itself	Witness
Awakened Awareness	Nondual

Figure 9: Correlations between Brown's vantage points and Wilber's state-stages of awareness

Although the correlations are clear, it is of vital importance to note again that Brown is careful to explain that nondual awareness is not in and of itself the same as awakened awareness; this is a distinction that Wilber makes in specific writings but one that is often lost in the wider Integral community. For Brown, as I show below in a more refined version of vantage point articulation that we gain from the Tibetan traditions, there are varying degrees of nondual awareness. Each of these layers of non-duality (the first layers of which Brown associates with awareness-in-and-of-itself) correlates to Wilber's state-stage called the Witness. For Brown, only the final refinement of nondual awareness is considered awakened awareness.

For further clarification and correlation, the model below shows both vantage points (Brown) and state-stages of identity (Wilber) as nested spheres.

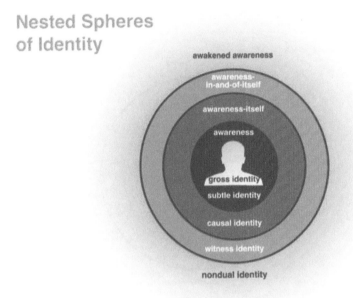

Figure 10: Nested spheres of identity

Similar to the type of development that we will explore in the next chapter with regard to structure-stages, each new vantage point transcends, includes, and penetrates the identity that preceded it. In this way, each subjective sphere of increasing size transcends and penetrates its junior sphere; awakened awareness (the transcendence of individual consciousness), as depicted below in Figures 11 and 12, entails a nondual source of awareness that both transcends but also *penetrates*[45] all lower spheres of awareness.

The model of nested spheres allows us to also depict how

awareness becomes confused with lower levels of identity. Figure 11 offers a pictorial representation of a transformational approach to spiritual realization:

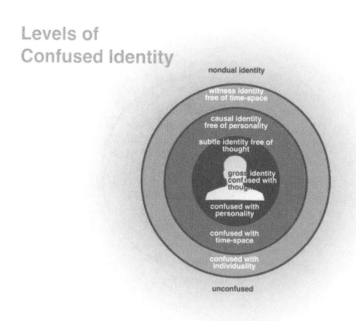

Figure 11: Levels of Confused Identity

Try to follow along using Figure 11 above. Beginning in the center of the spheres, gross identity is confused with both the body and thought. (Here the word "confused" means that awareness suffers from a case of mistaken identity as if it is the same as thought). Moving progressively outward, subtle identity is free of its identification with body and thought but still remains confused by and identified with the personality. Causal identity is free of its confusion with the personality and thought but is still confined within the contours of time and space. Moving outward still, a witness vantage point is beyond the layer of confusion associated with time and space but is still confined by the subject/object duality of individual consciousness. Finally, in the outermost sphere, a nondual identity, or what Brown calls "awakened awareness," is beyond all confusion and rests awake and present as open space. (At this level of practice, one has moved beyond limiting distinctions of subject and object, tacitly knowing that both are expressions of Ultimate Reality).

Another way of viewing vantage points is to imagine that each level of realization or recognition corresponds to a new level of freedom.

Levels of Obscuration and Freedom of Identity

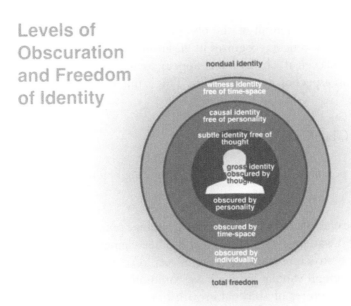

Figure 12: Levels of obscuration and freedom of identity

In Figure 12, each larger sphere transcends and includes the "freedoms" present in its junior spheres. A subtle layer of awareness is free from the obscurations of gross level thought but is still obscured by the subtle clouds of personality. A causal layer of awareness is free from the obscurations of subtle personality and free from gross level thought but still obscured by causal time and space. A witness layer of awareness is free from the obscurations of causal time and space, subtle personality, and gross thought, but is still obscured by individual consciousness. Finally, the nondual base of awareness is recognized as one's original source. From this vantage point, one rests in total freedom without the obscuration of individual consciousness, time, space, personality, or thought. Being free from obscuration we can follow the meaning behind William Blake's so often quoted line in The Marriage of Heaven and Hell: "If the doors of perception were cleansed every thing would appear to man as infinite." Blake points to the perspective when all of the obscurations have been removed. In an instant, awareness recognizes itself. From this newly recognized vantage point, even if obscurations appear to return, they are seen through as an aspect of nondual reality. This is the true liberation.

Points of Clarification

Four points of clarification are worth noting before we proceed further:

(1) As will be elucidated in chapter 3 and 4, vantage points are a unique category of awareness distinct from the other elements of spiritual development (structure-stages and states) explored in this book. For example, although vantage points have common characteristics with the vertical structures of spiritual growth discussed in chapter 3 (i.e. they both follow a similar process of transcendence and inclusion) neither of the two can be reduced to the other. Structural development (e.g. increasing complexity) is always related to the relative self. Vantage points relate to the deconstruction of relative reality to reveal the Absolute base of Reality-itself. Because deeper vantage points penetrate shallower vantage points, all expression in the manifest world comes through the relative self. As a result, realization is conditioned by apparent duality when viewed from the outside in.[46]

In a similar way, we mustn't confuse vantage points with access to various states and realms of consciousness. Whereas the map of vantage point development traces awareness along the mind perspective (the source of awareness), states and realms of consciousness (gross, subtle, and causal) are most often a function of the event perspective (the changing field of experience). That is to say, vantage points track the "knower" whereas states/realms mark that which is "known." As we shall see in chapter 5, one can experience any state/realm from any vantage point.

(2) As each new vantage point is recognized along the spectrum of realization, the shallower vantage point is seen through as transparent but does not cease to exist. That is to say, even as one shifts identity beyond thought (meaning that one moves beyond the confusion and obscuration that are caused by an exclusive identification with thought), the functionality and apparent existence of thought still remains. In a similar way, from an awakened vantage point of nondual awareness, each of the lower vantage points (witness, time/space, personality, and thought) remains open and functioning. This means that appearances of subject and object and the whole manifestation of duality in form do not vanish. In fact, the experience of realization is quite the opposite. All lower vantage points are enlivened with the magnificence of realization and seen clearly as an aspect of the single process that is Reality-itself. Another way of saying this is that each vantage point not only transcends and includes the lower vantage point, but that it also transcends and penetrates each lower vantage point. A realization that fails to fully manifest the functionality and particular skills of a lower vantage point suffers from a state-stage pathology.[47] [48]

(3) Vantage points can be experienced as either temporary or permanent shifts in awareness. When a deeper vantage point is experienced for a brief or extended period of time only to fade again to a shallower level of identity, it is said to be "unstable." When a vantage point has been permanently realized continuously at all times and in all circumstances, it can be said to be "stable." This means that when dealing with vantage point progression, one's "basis of operation" is either stable or unstable at one of five layers of awareness (gross, subtle, causal, witness, or nondual).

(4) Due to the biases created by both preliminary practices and culturally specific perspectives, the experience of each vantage point

shift remains unique even though the deep structure of the path is invariant. For instance, a Buddhist might experience a nondual, nontheistic realization, whilst a Jew might experience theistic insight. The participatory and enactive nature of realization means that we must rid ourselves of the assumption that the actualized and manifest expression of the deepest vantage point (i.e., awakened awareness) is the same across traditions. Evidence demonstrates that it is not. So, rather than assume that all experiences and vantage point shifts will be the same, I follow Brown's lead, who points out that the perspective taken and expectations set at the outset of the meditation itself are built into the experience that results. This means that even if we can determine that a particular individual has recognized awakened awareness, the experience of that nondual vantage point and its resulting expression will be unique.[49] Brown writes:

> Although there is convincing evidence for a single underlying path across traditions, there are different perspectives which can be taken, which in turn result in different experiences during comparable stages along the path.... As a result, the final enlightened mind is different across traditions.[50]

In this light, Brown concludes with a fascinating insight:

> The conclusions set forth here are nearly opposite of that of the stereotyped notion of the perennial philosophy according to which many spiritual paths are said to lead to the same end. According to the careful comparison of the traditions we have to conclude the following: there is only one path, but it has several outcomes. There are several kinds of enlightenment, although all free awareness from psychological structure and alleviate suffering.[51]

Rather than create division, these new discoveries ought to offer us deeper interreligious understanding and have the potential to serve as catalysts for meaningful cooperation across traditions. The Great Human Tradition finds a center or coordination using the single underlying path to awakening as its base, while still preserving the important differences across wisdom streams. (As we shall see in chapter 5 in our exploration of comparative mysticism, this common invariant underlying path is not a pre-given reality but rather an evolutionary emergent laid down over time. As such it does not fall victim to the "myth of the given".) Even with distinct differences in surface features, we now have a consistent faith-neutral model to serve as a touchstone. If there is any hope for an emergence of a single human lineage then the model first laid out by Brown and rearticulated in the first half of this chapter has the power to serve as both seed and source code for trans-lineage coordination with regard to the vector of vantage point development (state-stage identity).[52]

Complementary Examples within Religion-Specific Contexts

With the basic underlying path of vantage points in place, we turn now to the traditions themselves to further flesh out the idea using a few religion-specific examples. Let us also note that the world's great religious traditions are still the only source through which we have access to the sort of practices that can liberate awareness through the various vantage points of spiritual realization. These great teachings represent one of the most remarkable gifts held exclusively by our world's religious traditions, giving us yet another reason why the wisdom streams of the world must be preserved.

The intention of the second half of this chapter is threefold: (1) I offer a Tibetan-specific example to show how a tradition that specializes in vantage point development can help us bring further refinement to our universal model. (2) I offer an example from the Tantric Hindu tradition known as Kashmir Saivism to show yet another context in which vantage points are described. (3) I provide an example from the Islamic tradition, which demonstrates only one major shift in vantage point. This example helps to demonstrate that occurrences of vantage point shifts exist outside of the Eastern context. All three examples show how the core faith-neutral vantage point model can be transcribed according to religion-specific notions. For instance, the Tibetan example offered below uses nontheistic language. In contrast, when vantage points are described using Hindu language and Islamic language they are articulated using theistic terms.[53] Ultimately, all three of the examples below help to shape and articulate the contours of vantage points in a way that is fit for an Integral Age. [54] [55]

Vantage Points in Tibetan Buddhism

In the following example, I draw from the Tibetan Buddhist and Bon traditions to offer tradition specific accounts of how vantage point development tends to show up. The Tibetan Buddhist and Bon traditions offer all five of the basic levels of vantage point development described above by Brown and add to them three levels of refinement of non-duality. Each level of refinement can be thought of as a deeper vantage point of awareness. In total, these refinements help to bring even more nuance to the model of vantage points articulated thus far.

In the first refinement of non-duality (what the Tibetans would consider the shallowest of the nondual vantage points), all events of the mind are viewed as reflective expressions of awareness. This means that awareness begins to view everything as if it were simply another aspect of itself. More often than not, however, this level of practice is conducted through a locus of awareness still packaged in individual consciousness. As such, its speed of recognition is slower. In most cases, during this level of refinement the events of the mind are seen as nondual after they have already arisen.

As one's spiritual realization deepens, the speed of awareness with which one recognizes non-duality quickens. At the second level of refinement, one begins to recognize non-duality simultaneously with the arising of events in the mind. According to Brown, one of the key terms in the Mahamudra tradition to describe this level of practice is *ilhan cig skye sbyor* (Sanskrit, sahaja). It means "arising together" or "simultaneous."[56] Although there are multiple meanings to the phrase (which Brown lists in detail),[57] the most relevant in this context is the way it is used to describe the moment-to-moment realization at this middle range of nondual refinement. Brown describes this level of practice as follows:

From the minds perspective, the extraordinary level of practice invites a remarkable realization about awareness-itself. Awareness-itself begins to seem less and less like the practitioner's ordinary awareness packaged in ordinary patterns of thought or self-representation or even packaged in the practitioner's seemingly unique individual consciousness. When such constructions of mind are cleared away, each seeming moment of awareness-itself is linked to the dharmakaya, the ground or body of awareness saturating all existence. In this sense, each moment of awareness arises together with awakened wisdom. The simultaneous mind is the direct experience of awareness-itself (both the practitioner's seeming individual consciousness and the universal ground of awareness-itself)[58] and the seeming objects of experience arising together as an inseparable pair from the beginning.[59]

The key phrase above is "arises together," marking the simultaneity of the realization that recognizes non-duality with events at the same time as they arise. That means that during this level of refinement the events of the mind are known as nondual as they arise.

In the third and most mature form of non-duality, the realization is "certain." Reality is known as nondual prior to any arising. Awareness is so swift that even before any events arise there is a knowing of the true nature of reality. Brown explains the shift in this way:

> When the conditions of the extraordinary meditation are exactly right, crossing over occurs. A profound shift occurs during which seemingly individual consciousness, and all ordinary experience and all false concepts associated with it, drop away. The vast awareness-space of the dharmakaya becomes the point of observation.[60]

He continues:

> The seeming reality of individual consciousness along with its functions and activities gives way, leaving only an infinite ocean of awareness-space.... Awakened wisdom now comes forth unobstructed, no longer as a brief glimpse or flash but as that which saturates all experience. It has no real support (brten), yet serves as the ground or basis for all experience.[61]

From this aperspectival awareness, the nondual nature of reality knows itself prior to any event that arises. Awakening at this point has come to know the nature of reality with "certainty."

In a beautiful offering of simplicity and summary, Brown uses the Heart Sutra to describe the path of awakening:

gati
gati

paragati
parasamgati
bodhi svaha

Translated as:

Awareness gone beyond thought.
Awareness-itself gone beyond personal identity
Changeless, boundless awareness gone way beyond the convention of time.
Awakened awareness gone way way beyond the constraints of individual
consciousness.
Oh! What a realization!

In synthesizing the wisdom streams of Earth, humanity would be deeply served by taking the Tibetan insights into consideration. The depth offered in relation to the various gradations of non-duality and the simplicity put forth in summarizing texts like the Heart Sutra provide a level of richness seldom matched. The lineages of Tibetan Buddhism will continue to serve humanity well into the future.

Vantage Points in Tantric Hinduism

As we have seen thus far, Brown's original work compared various forms of Tibetan and Theravada Buddhism to an early form of Hinduism as articulated by Patanjali (approximately 200 BCE). To further support Brown's work, we turn now to a much more recent iteration of Tantric Hinduism (approximately 800 CE) known as Kashmir Saivism. The parallels between the deep structures outlined by Brown and the stages of realization articulated in Kashmir Saivism are remarkable. As we shall see below, several vantage points are illuminated clearly and succinctly in the Tantric Hindu tradition.

In the Doctrine of Vibration, Oxford trained scholar-practitioner Mark Dyczkowski explains how the Hindu tradition views the general process of spiritual realization:

The yogi seeking enlightenment must undergo a complete

70

conversion or reversal (paravritti) of perspective. To know as man knows is the very essence of bondage; freedom is to know reality as God knows it. The seeker then finds himself in a new existential situation in which he recognizes his own authentic Being by being as God is. This is achieved by a pure and intense act of self-awareness in which the old mode of understanding reality is dropped in favour of a new and deeper knowledge of oneself as unlimited, infinite consciousness.[62]

The tradition of Kashmir Saivism follows a similar path to the one outlined by Brown and later by Wilber, leading from vantage points of gross, subtle, to causal, to witness, to nondual identity. In a beautiful passage, Dyczkowski explains the process of allowing the depths of awareness to consume the confusion with the gross physical body and thought:

The false identification of the ego with the physical body conditions the power of awareness (citisakti) by generating thought-forms (vikalpa) based on the notion that a difference exists (bheda) between the embodied subject and the extra-corporeal object. These thought constructs constitute the lower order of embodied subjectivity and, to all intents and purposes, its body. The yogi transmutes thought back into its original form as the light of consciousness by burning it in the sacred fire of consciousness (cidagni) inflamed by the contemplative awareness that: 'It is I, the great Lord, Who, as pure consciousness, always shine this as all things'. This inner awareness is the divine radiance (sphuratta) of the rapture of the supreme ego. It is pure Spanda energy, the secret power of Mantra (mantravirya) which burns away the false identification with the body and with it the body of thought.[63]

Dyczkowski then articulates how the path continues as he explains the shift in vantage point beyond thought and personal awareness to a vantage point beyond time. Describing a level of awareness that is ever-present he writes:

This does not mean that the unfolding expansion of

consciousness (unmesa) is an intermittent, transitory occurrence. As the source of all thought, including the notions of past, present and future, it stands outside the confines of time.[64]

In the system of Kashmir Saivism, this vantage point beyond the confines of time is known as turiya (the fourth). Its name is a direct reference to the fact that the ever-present nature of this vantage point is beyond the coming and going of the three major states of existence (waking, dreaming, and deep sleep).

According to the tradition, turiya serves as the launching pad for the final shift in awareness; the shift that dissolves identification with individual consciousness. Dyczkowski writes about this final shift using a metaphor. "[At this stage] the individual ego merges in the pervasive, universal ego, just as the space in a broken jar merges in the space around it."[65] The tradition calls this level of realization turiyatita, meaning beyond the fourth. From this vantage point, one's awareness has moved beyond the subject/object duality of witnessing that existed in turiya, to now fully embrace the entire manifest universe as an expression of its own nondual nature. In a final description of nondual identity, Dyczkowski writes:

> The yogi who perceives that all things are like the limbs of his own body (svangakalpa) plunges in the divine awareness that: 'I am this [universe]' (aham-idam). Bondage is a false identification with the physical body and liberation a true identification with the cosmic body. Thus the split between subject and object is healed the yogi perceives reality everywhere, as an undivided unity (avibhakta) in which inner and outer blend together like the juices in a peacock's egg.[66]

When the inner and outer "blend together," nondual identity is fully actualized.

Comparing the two examples above, it is interesting to notice the vast difference between the nontheistic Buddhist perspective described and the theistic Hindu perspective.[67] Despite the obvious differences in surface features, the commonality of deep structures of vantage points shines through. The comparison between the two shows how a faith-neutral framework serves to unify even when surface features vary.

The Most Fundamental Shift in Identity: Vantage Points in Islam

We can understand the vector of spiritual realization by dividing it up into any number of vantage points. As we have seen above, the faith-neutral model of spiritual realization uses five major vantage points. The Tibetans, with their various levels of refinement of non-duality, add even more. So, with all of these distinctions, which vantage point shift is most fundamental? Classically, in esoteric traditions and mystery schools from around the globe, the most fundamental shift in awareness is one that leads from an identification with the small "self" to identification with the big "Self." It is this reorientation of awareness that takes one from dualistic consciousness to the vantage point (that is no specific vantage point) related to nondual consciousness. Although traditions that include only one major vantage point shift on the path of spiritual development might have less nuance, the teachings remain powerful nonetheless.

Let's look at how this singular and most fundamental shift in identity shows up in the tradition specific context of Islam. Within Islam, esoteric teachings on the various ways that human beings can shift their locus of identity have been most succinctly preserved within the Sufi lineages.

The teachings of Muhyi-d-Din ibn 'Arabi offer a prime example. According to Arabi, a full shift in vantage point from individual consciousness to nondual identity is referred to as a shift into Supreme Identity. According to Arabi, this Supreme Identity is the ultimate form of nondual union existing as "a mutual interpenetration of Divinity and man."[68] When using only two vantage points, we can refer to them as (1) the perspective of the human and (2) the perspective of the Divine, respectively. In our faith-neutral model, the human vantage point corresponds to all dualistic vantage points (thought, personality, time/space, individual consciousness). The Divine vantage point equals the deepest level of awakened awareness.

As with most esoteric teachings, the Sufi lineages outline a path of initiation and inward work that leads one to the full realization of Supreme Identity. In the words of the tradition:

It is by this inward work alone that a being, if capable of it, will ascend from degree to degree, to the summit of the initiatic hierarchy, to the 'Supreme Identity', the absolutely permanent and unconditioned state beyond the limitations of all contingent and transitory existence, which is the state of the true Sufi.[69]

Shifting vantage points, from a human perspective to the Divine perspective, the various principles of development remain intact. For example, as we saw earlier in the chapter, once one's vantage point has shifted to that of a deeper locus of awareness, the shallower identities of personality and thought, and even time and space do not simply vanish. Instead, all junior identities (former vantage points) are transcended and included in a broad embrace of the deeper identity. In theistic terms, although there exists a yoking of God and man, man does not disappear entirely. Burckhardt continues to trace Arabi's perspective along these same lines:

God, as it were, takes on human nature; the Divine nature (al-Lahut) becomes the content of human nature (an-Nasut), the latter being considered as the recipient of the former, and, from another angle, man is absorbed and, as it were, enveloped by Divine reality. God is mysteriously present in man and man is obliterated in God. All this must be understood only from the spiritual point of view, or in other words according to a perspective, not of pure doctrine, but related to spiritual realization.[70]

As described above, although man is absorbed in God, "God is mysteriously present in man." Burckhardt's description of the shift to Supreme Identity hits the mark as he continues:

In the first mode God reveals Himself as the real Self which knows through the faculties of perception of man and acts through his faculties of action. In the second and inverse mode man moves, so to speak, in the dimensions of the Divine Existence, which in relation to him is polarized so that to each human faculty or quality there corresponds a Divine aspect.[71]

As the process unfolds and as the deeper nondual vantage point is stabilized, the Sufis point to the shift in perspective using the terms "perfect man" or "universal man" (al-Insan al-kamil). In all cases, the shallower identity (human perspective) continues even as the deeper vantage point (the divine perspective) lives through it:

> Practically speaking such a man will have his human individuality as his 'external' form [i.e. shallower vantage point doesn't disappear], but in their virtuality and in principle all other forms and all states of existence belong to him because his 'inward reality' is identified with that of the whole universe.... From this it will be understood why the term 'Universal Man' has two meanings which coincide or are distinct according to the point of view adopted. On the one hand this name is applied to all men who have realized Union or 'the Supreme Identity', to men such as the great spiritual mediators and especially the prophets and the "poles" among the saints. On the other hand this name designates the permanent and actual synthesis of all states of Being, a synthesis which is at the same time both an immediate aspect of the Principle and the totality of all relative and particular states of existence.[72] [73]

Building on this point, we might say that when the deepest vantage point is established and shines through the individual self system, anyone of us can become a prophet. We all have the potential to enter into the sphere of divine revelation to share and spread the glory of reality. Accordingly, it is when we live from the Divine perspective that we can share the most significant truths of reality with others. Burckhardt agrees:

> It is to Universal Man, who is at the same time the Spirit, the totality of the universe, and the perfect human symbol, that the epithets refer which are traditionally applied to the Prophet when they are taken according to their esoteric meaning...he is a "messenger" (rasul) because, being in essence Spirit, he emanates directly from God; he is "unlettered" (ummi) through the fact that he receives his knowledge directly from God without the intermediary of written signs.[74]

As we can see, even though the example given from the Sufi tradition offers less sophistication with regards to the number of stages of vantage point unfoldment, it nonetheless offers a powerful message.[75] The inclusion of the one fundamental shift in vantage point, whether we call it a transition from human to Divine or from dual to nondual, is quite clearly of the utmost importance. Any translation of a universal spirituality ought to find a way to include this vital shift from the relative self to the Absolute Self.

Potential Pathologies in Vantage Point Development

Before closing the chapter, I'd like to note two interrelated pathologies that can arise in the development of vantage points. Although we have already touched on several of these, offering just two brief examples here will give us a good idea of the types of problems that all integrally informed spiritual practitioners and their communities ought to make strides to carefully guard against.

Vantage Point Pathology #1: Nondual reductionism. The first pathology, nondual reductionism, occurs when there is a misunderstanding of how awakened awareness actually functions from moment to moment. In some cases, this misunderstanding causes practitioners to ignore the dualistic world. "If non-duality is true" the pathological claim states, "then duality is not true." This is a common confusion between absolute and relative reality that often results from a realization that is more conceptual rather than an authentic and direct knowing. The tendency to retreat into any sort of nondual reductionism is an error. Reality is in fact both dual and nondual. Nondual vision allows one to see reality as it actually is, dualistic vision opens ones heart with compassion to the way things appear to be to "others". Both are necessary. Both are true. The Mahayana Buddhist traditions first explain the significance of this distinction through the doctrine of relative and Absolute truth. In more advanced forms of practice, the Dzogchen tradition introduces terms like the Great Sphere (tiglechenpo). In the tacit realization of Ultimate Reality as the Great Sphere, all of relative reality is seen as a perfect expression of the Absolute. In other words, all of reality is in perfect alignment with Itself and is seen clearly just as it is.

Another way to explain this level of realization is to use the term trans-dual. Non-duality, when properly understood, is in fact trans-dual—it includes both absolute reality and relative reality, non-duality and duality. It is vital that deeply committed spiritual practitioners understand this distinction so as to guard against any sort of nondual reductionism that either denies or bypasses duality. As will be made even clearer in chapter 7, a trans-dual model of realization becomes vital when participating in a framework of conscious evolution in the relative world.

Vantage Point Pathology #2: Disassociation from shallower vantage points. The second but connected pathology directly relates to lived experience moment to moment. As one participates in the co-creation of relative reality from a trans-dual vantage point, shallower identities do not disappear once exclusive identification with them has been transcended. However, such smooth transitions of transcending and including are not always the experience of practitioners. In a more pathological movement through vantage points, shallower identities can be denied, disassociated from, or left unattended. Careful practitioners should be wary of failing to include all the vantage points that have been transcended at every level of practice.

Leaving behind shallower identities creates unhealthy dynamics for others and for oneself. It also leaves room for massive amounts of shadow to flood into one's life. The first and most immediate problem arises as a simple disconnect from reality. For example, if I deny an aspect of one of the shallower identities, or worse see it as illusionary altogether, I fail to honor the relative reality of duality and separation. To be sure, Absolute reality is absolutely real, but relative reality remains relatively real to all those practitioners who have not come to know reality in its most naked form. Out of compassion, one can refine an understanding of the relative so as to be the most perfect guide to help others on the path.

An example helps to clarify the issue: Even if one tacitly knows awakened awareness, he or she still has a unique perspective on the world according to his or her particular gross-body coordinates. He or she still has a particular "point of view". In a similar way, one's perspective is also made even further distinct as a result of the personality (and altitude and typology, etc.). Awakened awareness shines through all of these layers like light shining through a stained glass window. Interacting with others in the relative world happens through the prism of individual personality, physical body, etc. This means that functioning through shallower identities is necessary to engage in the relative world. If a person assumes that the shallower identities of the relative self cease to exist upon realization of the deeper vantage point, there is an obvious disconnect. This type of disconnect can quickly devolve into full moral catastrophe. If this pathology is active, one may be under the mistaken impression that his or her actions are arising from awakened awareness when in fact they are coming from the wants, needs, and desires of the relative "self." This can lead to individuals trying to justify selfish actions through claims of enlightened activity. The Great Human Tradition of which we are all a part, this inheritance of human wisdom across all traditions, will be served most deeply if it recognizes the threat that this potential pathology poses to the legitimization of awakening on a larger scale. Only fully awakened individuals who are fully integrated can affect the type of change we hope to see in the world.[76]

Chapter 3
Structure-stages of Spiritual Intelligence

We can now move on to a second element of spiritual development: structure-stages of spiritual intelligence. A better understanding of how each stage of spiritual intelligence influences the interpretation and enactment of various systems of spirituality is one of the single most important gifts of Integral Theory. It is a topic so critical to our particular time in history that I dedicate the entire second volume of this series to its elaboration and explanation. In doing so, I use volume 2 of this series, *Evolution's Ally*, as a platform to explore evidence for five major waves of spiritual intelligence (magic, mythic, rational, pluralistic, and Integral) within four traditions (Christianity, Islam, Hinduism, and Buddhism). When each wave is understood and presented as a healthy progression of human development, a roadmap is revealed that depicts how our religious traditions might serve as conveyor belts of human evolution.

Because I dedicate the entire second volume to the topic of spiritual intelligence and the various views that each stage enacts, this particular chapter will not overwhelm the reader with excess detail. Rather, my focus here is to paint a picture that portrays the general significance of this vector. (Also note: here in this volume, I treat structures and structure-stages together. In volume 2 and even more so in volume 3, I draw a more refined distinction between the two). Any reader interested in a full and detailed account beyond this single chapter is urged to consult volume 2: *Evolution's Ally* and volume 3: *Earth is Eden*.

A General Introduction to Spiritual Intelligence

The term spiritual intelligence is used in multiple ways and in various contexts. In appendix 1, I offer several examples. Zohar uses the term to refer to the way we access our deepest meaning, purpose, and highest motivation.[77] Emmons defines spiritual intelligence as "the adaptive use of spiritual information to facilitate everyday problem solving and goal attainment."[78] In a yet another distinct way, Cindy Wigglesworth, founder of the international consulting and coaching firm Deep Change, defines spiritual intelligence as "the ability to behave with wisdom and compassion while maintaining inner and outer peace, regardless of the situation."[79] All of these uses have an appropriate context and beneficial forms of application.

Because the definition of spiritual intelligence in this chapter is more particular than the examples offered above, its specificity allows it to serve a unique purpose. Instead of allowing a broad definition of spiritual intelligence, I follow Wilber's lead and define spiritual intelligence only in reference to structural development. The various structural components of spiritual intelligence, as I define it, can be pragmatically determined through the use of a bundle of primary and secondary indicators.[80] These indicators consist of evidence derived from multiple developmental lines, including faith development, cognitive development, ego development, and moral development. In circumstances where evidence for altitude in multiple lines of development is not available, or in those circumstances where a specific assessment can be given directly, Fowler's faith development theory serves as the primary indicator of this vector.[81] I explain all of the details regarding my approach to spiritual intelligence in full in volume 2.[82] I recommend the interested reader explore that volume for a more nuanced account.

Structure-Stages of Consciousness

Within the broad purview of the Great Human Tradition an understanding of the developmental stages of spiritual intelligence is an original contribution of the modern West.[83] Although certain types of developmental stages were certainly known historically in the East, the dimension of structural development (i.e., how structure-stages of interpretation and thinking change overtime and in turn enact different realities) was not fully articulated to the degree we understand it today until the cognitive studies of Piaget in the mid-twentieth century, then later in the 1980s with the blossoming of developmental psychology.

Over the past three decades, developmental studies into structure-stages have demonstrated that human beings can develop increasing structural capacities across multiple intelligences.[84] Harvard professor Howard Gardner originally pointed out seven diverse streams of growth. In his pioneering book *Frames of Mind*, he called them *multiple intelligences*. Gardner was among a string of other developmental researchers who pointed out similar trends. For a multiplicity of reasons, Harvard has been a hotbed for this sort of developmental research, spawning many of today's leading theorists: Kurt Fischer (skill theory), Michael Commons (model of hierarchical complexity), Robert Kegan (orders of consciousness), Daniel Goleman (emotional intelligence). Harvard is also home to the doctoral work of Susanne-Cook-Greuter (ego development) as well as fellow colleagues in my generation, Zak Stein and Katie Heikkinen in what has now spawned developmental testing service (DTS), among many others.

In 1981, James Fowler (who was also engaged in doctoral work at Harvard at that time) picked up on the enormous insight being generated around developmental studies and pointed out that spiritual intelligence, or what he called the "stages of faith," also unfold in a predictable pattern.[85] Fowler's work demonstrates that during the process of natural and healthy growth an individual's lens on spirituality in general and faith in particular moves through a series of stages. Each stage is related to the level of complexity the individual is able to take as he or she relates to issues of ultimate concern.[86] Fowler's research determined that adult humans have the potential to grow and develop through seven structure-stages of spiritual intelligence: primal, intuitive, mythic-literal, synthetic-conventional, individuative-reflective, conjunctive, universalizing.[87] Each progressive structure-stage can be understood as a shift in context as well as a change in the lens through which one *views* reality. (In a more general sense, structure-stages serve a critical function beyond a mere lens of enactment. Structure-stages point to the center of gravity of the relative self-sense. The relative self-sense provides a critical integrating function of healthy ego formation).

As with all developmental sequences, we can demarcate the various views each structure-stage enacts using any number of levels.

As described above, Fowler uses seven stages. Wilber, in his original articulation of the "conveyor belt,"[88] used a five-stage model ranging from magic to mythic to rational to pluralistic to Integral. In other sources, Wilber lists upwards of eleven or twelve stages. In volume 2, I use Wilber's original five-stage approach. (More important than the specific number of stages outlined is the fact that different levels of complexity enact different realities).

Two Ways to Frame Spiritual Intelligence

In volumes 1 and 2, I offer two different ways to frame the structure-stages of spiritual intelligence. Both sets of terms serve to complement Wilber's original conveyor belt model and build upon his basic concept known as *altitude*.[89] As we shall see, certain sets of terms are more appropriate for particular contexts. In addition to more range of choice and possibility in application, the diversification of terms and the varying number of structure-stages used also helps to lessen the chances of erroneously assuming that only one correct metric exists by which to measure spiritual intelligence. There are many.

The metric I use in this volume looks at the way that levels of spiritual intelligence enact religious/spiritual realities according to a scale that ranges from traditional to modern to postmodern to Integral. This terminology is useful for our specific purposes in that it allows us to track individual growth alongside the average modes of spiritual intelligence within historic paradigms. The five-stage model of religious orientation presented in volume 2 (ranging from magic to mythic to rational to pluralistic to Integral) offers a more granular account that meets many of the demands of an academic and scholarly audience. Figure 13 shows how the two models of spiritual intelligence used in volumes 1 and 2 correlate and serve to reinforce each other:

Volume 1	Volume 2	
traditional	magic	**Stage 1**
	mythic	**Stage 2**
modern	rational	**Stage 3**
postmodern	pluralistic	**Stage 4**
integral	integral	**Stage 5**

Correlated Stages of Spiritual Intelligence

Figure 13: Correlating the various metrics used in volumes 1 and 2 to denote the developmental nature of spiritual intelligence

The far right-hand column of figure 13 shows stages of spiritual intelligence as they unfold from the lowest levels of complexity and perspective taking (stage 1) to the highest (stage 5). Because both models divide spiritual intelligence in slightly different ways some of the stages of one model overlap and envelop two of the stages presented in another. For example, the traditional level of development, as shown above in the far left-hand column of the chart, overlaps and envelops both the magic and mythic levels of religious orientation as presented in volume 2. In sum, figure 13 helps to show how multiple language styles and various stage models can be used to meet the same end; both models show the vertical structural development of spiritual intelligence.

A Historical-Social Approach to Spiritual Intelligence

One vertical model of growth useful for our purposes here traces spiritual intelligence as it moves from traditional to modern to postmodern to Integral stages of consciousness. Each of these levels of spiritual intelligence expressed today in individual consciousness (UL) arose historically alongside the corollary shifts in all Four Quadrants. [90] Today, because we are living in world-system where traditional, modern, postmodern, and now Integral levels of consciousness all coexist, there are levels of expression that represent every stage of growth in each of our world's great religious traditions. In other words, there are traditional forms of Buddhism, modern forms of Buddhism, postmodern forms, and integral forms. In a similar way, there are traditional versions of Christianity, modern versions of Christianity, postmodern versions, and Integral versions. Reality is enacted, in part, according to one's level of spiritual intelligence.[91]

Despite the fact that all levels of interpretation are available today, human beings stop along the spectrum of structural growth at different places on the path. Wilber describes each stage of spiritual intelligence as a "station in life."[92] As Wilber correctly puts it, everyone is born at stage one and moves up the ladder of development. Moreover, everyone has the right to stop developing at whatever stage along the conveyor belt that they like.[93] (Most often, arrested development along the spectrum of development is both unconscious and unintentional. People simply aren't aware higher stages are available to them.)

With these preliminary comments in place, let's now look into the basic elements of each stage along with a few examples. Those already familiar with the model presented in volume 2 (magic, mythic, rational, pluralistic, and Integral) will notice the parallels.[94]

Traditional Level of Spiritual Intelligence: At this stage, individuals lean toward literal interpretation of sacred texts and are often distracted with supernatural elements of faith. These individuals give great importance to rites and rituals and may be extremely superstitious. Role and identity are of ultimate concern at this stage. One's main focus tends to be on an absolute "truth" and a puritanical sense of right and wrong. At this stage, a preference for hierarchical structure and order exists even if such structure tends to be oppressive or abuse its power. Individuals at this stage are usually willing to control impulses in exchange for deferred fulfillment (e.g., life after death). Individuals here consider approval of one's own group as extremely important. They are often kept in order through feelings of guilt. In many cases, their identity extends to that of their group, family, or religious community, while seeing the views of those outside the group as either wrong, un-religious, or out of line with the one *straight* path.

Healthy versions of the traditional stage are numerous. For instance, one healthy expression of a traditional stage is portrayed in a classic example of an individual who takes pride in his or her faith. This can be recognized in a Jewish practitioner, who, adhering closely to his or her scripture, believes "he or she is part of a chosen people." The categorization would be true for the Buddhist at this stage who takes pride in the long lineage of practitioners, teachers and spiritual realizers that have come before. Although these examples tend to limit pride to their own ethnocentric sphere (and are therefore limited), such views are not always as troublesome as one might suspect as long as they stay in the range of "healthy." There are millions of traditional religious adherents who continually do good work in the world from a loving heart even while enacting a traditional world. When it comes to action, many of these folks treat others with an open heart, full of true generosity and kindness even while still holding existential judgments.

Unhealthy versions of a traditional level of spiritual intelligence are much more dangerous, exemplified by what we might call religious extremists. Here, ethnocentric beliefs get out of hand and may cause harm to others. These unhealthy versions of traditional belief place one's own racial, cultural, and religious identity above all others. In this category we might refer to the Islamic/Jewish fundamentalists who are willing to commit acts of terrorism in the name of their religion.[95] We might also list Christian fundamentalists willing to bomb an abortion clinic and take the lives of otherwise innocent victims due to a dogmatic set of beliefs. These individuals take their ethnocentrism to an extreme and impose it on others. In each of these cases, individuals have veered away from healthy expressions at a traditional stage and are participating in pathological (unhealthy) variations of enactment.

As development progresses, and as one moves from one stage to the next, it is vital that he or she carries the healthy elements of the previous stage forward, while letting go of older structures that no longer serve. In the example of one transitioning from a traditional structure to a modern structure, it is perfectly appropriate to retain a sense of pride in ones home faith, but any tendencies toward ethnocentrism and superiority ought to be jettisoned.

Modern Level of Spiritual Intelligence: Individuals at this level of spiritual intelligence begin to question and examine all of their existing beliefs. They begin to scrutinize the myths they believed without hesitation at the previous stage, in order to find deeper meaning. For the first time individuals recognize their ability to have their own opinions outside the restrictions allowed by the group or scripture.

Due to the pragmatic and reflective nature of this stage, individuals may become agnostic or atheist, both of which represent healthy expressions of spiritual intelligence at this stage. Individuals at this stage are likely to place a strong emphasis on autonomy, independence, and success. They are usually emphatic about embracing the value of the scientific method, evidence, and *tried-and-true experience.* The tendency to reflect upon their own thoughts and beliefs is common. This means that one moves beyond blind belief in particular religious ideologies to *operate* and improve on them consciously and critically.

One of the examples I appreciate that offers evidence for this stage of spiritual intelligence comes from the work of Bishop Shelby Spong. Spong's work provides a great religion-specific example of a healthy expression of the modern stage. Having moved out of the traditional level of spiritual intelligence, Spong still remains fully committed to Christianity. He writes: "I define myself first and foremost as a Christian believer.... My problem has never been my faith. It has always been the literal way that human beings have chosen to articulate that faith." A representative of a modern stage of growth, he has transcended the inadequacies of the traditional version of Christianity. In response to the tenets of Christianity held dogmatically and absolutely by traditional fundamentalists, Spong writes:

> Today I find each of these fundamentals, as traditionally understood, to be not just naive, but eminently rejectable. Nor would any of them be supported in our generation by reputable Christian scholars.
>
> Scripture is filled with cultural attitudes that we have long ago abandoned and with behavior that is today regarded as immoral. Concepts such as virgin birth, the physical resurrection, and the second coming are today more often regarded as symbols to be understood theologically than as events that occurred in literal history. The substitutionary view of atonement has become grotesque, both in its understanding of a God who requires the shed blood of human sacrifice as a prerequisite for salvation and in its definition of humanity as fallen and depraved.
>
> If these things still constitute the faith of Christian people, then Christianity has become for me and countless others hopelessly unbelievable. Surely the essence of Christianity is not found in any or all of these propositions.[96]

Healthy versions of modern consciousness, like Spong's, can expand across all religious traditions. Healthy versions can also arise in contexts where religion is abandoned all together. As mentioned above, agnosticism and atheism, when they are achieved as a result of self-authorship (i.e., after growing out of a traditional environment), are most often expressions of this level of development.[97]

Like all levels of development, modern consciousness can also be taken to its extremes and can show up in unhealthy ways. Rather than simply transcending a traditional level of consciousness, an extreme modern orientation may try to rid the world of all lower levels of religious expression altogether. I like to use the new atheists (Dawkins, Harris, Dennett, Hitchens) as an example of a group of individuals who have taken atheism to an extreme.[98] Although at times only trying to be provocative, these social theorists, in the guise of secular humanism, take atheism to its furthest reaches and actually call for the abandonment and abolition of all religious traditions. This violent position lacks the nuance of even a basic developmental understanding. If a developmental perspective were embraced, Dawkins, Harris, Dennett, and Hitchens would see clearly that there are modern, postmodern, and Integral versions of religion that can live side by side their modern claims. Furthermore, a developmental perspective shows us that each person on the planet begins the journey of spiritual intelligence at "square one".[99] As a result, traditional ways of thinking are a valuable and irreducible stage in human growth.

As transition occurs from a modern to postmodern structure, it is important that the practitioner retains the healthy sense of self-reflexivity and skepticism that emerged at this stage.

Postmodern Level of Spiritual Intelligence: Individuals at this stage begin to realize that issues don't have to be black and white. They become comfortable with and may even enjoy the embrace of paradox, claiming that all traditions are simply different perspectives of one ultimate reality. The religious pluralism expressed from this stage moves beyond mere tolerance as expressed in the modern stage to now actually fully embrace other religious traditions for their inherent value. Individuals at this postmodern level of spiritual intelligence begin to recognize the cultural embeddedness of their own religious and spiritual beliefs. As a result, they begin to search out other spiritual systems. They search not with a desire to convert those of other faiths (as might be the case at a traditional level of spiritual intelligence) but in order to take other perspectives, to find out how another's view may be able to supplement their own.

Healthy versions of this level of spiritual intelligence understand the relative nature of perspectives. As a result postmodern individuals know that dialogue is one potent solution to creating shared meaning and mutual understanding. Most efforts at interreligious dialogue stem from this stage of spiritual intelligence.

I like to use the Hindu sage Ramakrishna as an example of this structure of spiritual intelligence, despite the many traditional elements of his life in other lines of growth. Ramakrishna understood that there were certain basic truths in all religious traditions. He even understood that many of these truths could supplement his own understanding of the divine. Following this intuition, Ramakrishna not only practiced his own path of Hinduism but also engaged in Christian and Islamic practices to demonstrate that holding the polarities of different traditions is actually complementary rather than contradictory.[100] Other healthy expressions of this structure-stage can be found in the Islamic Sufi tradition in the mystical works of Rumi and Hafiz.[101]

Unhealthy versions of this level often slip into extreme positions of relativism and even nihilism.[102] Because this level of spiritual intelligence understands the relative nature of reality, some expressions of this stage conclude that reality has no meaning at all. In subtler forms of expression, individuals at this stage might claim that no universal spirituality exists (ultimately, stepping into a performative contradiction wherein their own claim that no universals exists is in itself a universal claim). In its most extreme versions, this level of spiritual intelligence can combine with other lines of intelligence at pre-conventional levels to justify immoral and unethical actions. [103]

As transition occurs from the postmodern stage of spiritual intelligence to the integral stage, the practitioner is served well by maintaining an understanding that a plurality of perspectives can provide an enriched understanding of reality.

Integral Level of Spiritual Intelligence: Having taken the perspectives of other religious traditions, supplemented their beliefs, and uprooted their own worldview from the limiting perspectives of their own culture (to whatever degree possible), individuals at an Integral level of spiritual intelligence begin to find a sophisticated yet simple orientation. My colleague Clint Fuhs calls this Second Simplicity; (Distinguishing this simplicity that rests on the other side of postmodern complexity from the first type of simplicity that arises at more traditional levels of growth).

Those at an Integral stage have found a center within themselves with regard to their own personal beliefs, yet find that they can move seamlessly into a trans-lineage space that transcends and includes their own native system of thought. Often this level of spiritual intelligence begins to include some degree of vantage point development. (At higher Integral stages of spiritual intelligence, vantage point development is required.) As vantage point development comes online, reality (or even God) is actively and consciously viewed through first-, second-, and third-person perspectives.

Most fundamentally, the Integral stage of spiritual intelligence recognizes the importance and value of all preceding levels. For example, an Integral level sees that the postmodern altitude served as a filter to neutralize all dominating tendencies. Passing through the postmodern level ensures oppressive tendencies will not resurface when healthy, natural hierarchy returns at the Integral stage. In its fullest expression, an Integral level of spiritual intelligence would not only try to include all three vectors of spiritual intelligence outlined in this book but would also be able to make each of the distinctions operational for the benefit of all.

Father Chris Dierkes' successful attempt to unite Eastern Orthodox and Catholic theology using an Integral lens is a perfect example of this stage of spiritual intelligence. Dierkes' groundbreaking book, *Indistinct Union: Integral Christian Mystical Theology and Practice*, includes the use of vantage points (reaching into nondual identity), states (exploring the changing fields of experience in the mystical Christian path), and levels of spiritual intelligence (explaining that each structure-stage interprets the tradition and the experiences they have according to their developmental lens). He even includes an orientation to God that includes first-, second-, and third-person perspectives. Other examples of Integral levels of spiritual intelligence can be found in the work of Sally Kempton (Hindu Tantra), Father Thomas Keating (contemplative Christianity), and Daniel P. Brown (Mahamudra and Dzogchen teachings of Buddhism). The list of others natively `applying the Integral lens is ever increasing.

Because the emergence of the integral stage is so new, the various healthy and unhealthy expressions are not yet obvious. As post-integral stages emerge, we can all rest assured that the limitations of this stage will be made clear.

The Goal of Structural Development

The intention and purpose of any Integral leader employing

the model of spiritual intelligence within the context of spiritual growth is two-fold: First, horizontally speaking, the goal is to make every individual as healthy as possible at whichever level of development they are in. This means increasing the relative degree of health at whatever appropriate stage of development. In a religious context this usually translates into helping individuals lean more towards moderate views and away from forms of extremism that might be potentially harmful. The second goal of an Integral leader is to help set the conditions for vertical transformation up the conveyor belt of development through increasing stages of complexity. More specifically, this means that an Integral leader must know how to best provide the circumstances that will help someone at a traditional level of development begin to move vertically towards a modern orientation of faith. Along these same lines it also means helping a postmodern practitioner grow into Integral expressions of spirituality, and so on.[104] As a whole, spiritual intelligence is best understood when both horizontal and vertical dimensions of growth are taken into account.

Toward a Second Enlightenment

Before closing the chapter, I'd like to make a few comments from the perspective of the Great Human Tradition by examining the collective implications of embracing a developmental model of spiritual intelligence.

As stated in this chapter's introduction, certain approaches to spiritual intelligence are more useful than others depending on the context and the particular purpose of the application. For the type of broader historical and social approach I set forth here, the best language style to use is the paradigmatic approach following stages that range from traditional to modern to postmodern to Integral. In this particular case, the correlations between the stages of individual growth and the historical stages of the evolution of consciousness make it easier to draw connections.

From the perspective of the Great Human Tradition, most of humanity has today, quite unknowingly, entered into a *Modern Endarkenment*; a new Dark Age of sorts.[105] The term Dark Age was initially recorded in 1602,[106] in reference to a period of time in the Middle Ages, following the fall of the Roman Empire, wherein Europe was perceived to have undergone economic and cultural deterioration.

Although it's true that spirituality flourished during this time, the dominate mode of religiosity was at a traditional level of development. In this particular world-sphere there was a predominance of mythical and magical thinking. Among other things, this meant limited self-authoring in individuals and often literal interpretations of scripture. The Church, as it stood in its peak of strength, held a dominating influence over political, social, and religious matters. The cruelties it inflicted in the name of religion served as catalysts to set the stage for the transformation into modernity. The full shift into modern consciousness in Western culture, marked by the revolutions that brought rationality and science to the forefront of thinking, signified the end of the Dark Age and the entrance into the European Renaissance. Historically, we mark this as a major cultural transition (LL) between traditional and modern consciousness as it emerged in combination with advancements in the other quadrants.

Now, as we find ourselves on the other side of the Western Enlightenment, reason and rationality are abundant. The triumphs of the European Renaissance have made their way around the globe and have penetrated almost every culture on the planet. We can generally agree that the benefits brought by the transition into modernity are tremendous and ought to be preserved. From the democratization of the masses to the shifts in modern medicine and technology, many of the advances of modern culture are undeniably positive. These, as Wilber and others have called them, are the dignities of modernity.

On the other hand, some of the advancements of modernity have been devastating. From the perspective of spirituality, the shift into an age of reason came with its own set of faults. On a whole, we might say that the enlightenment of modernity produced its own form of spiritual *endarkenment*. As advances in rationality were made, connection to Spirit was ostracized as irrational (a classic pre/trans fallacy). This meant, as Wilber notes, that although reason was liberated, the majority of spiritual traditions became isolated and frozen at a mythic level of development.[107] Today, the spiritual *endarkenment* that was first set in motion during modernity and then strengthened in postmodernity still casts its shadow over most of the Western world.[108]

As Wilber points out in *Integral Spirituality*, the first step to correcting the cultural pathology is to understand the development of spiritual intelligence within its historical and socio-political context. During the traditional (premodern) era, the average level of spiritual intelligence in culture matched the level of consciousness offered in the majority of religious institutions. This means that most individuals held a traditional level of spiritual intelligence and most institutions had a center of gravity at a traditional stage. In the West, after the Enlightenment, culture and society made a major shift from a traditional level of consciousness (in the UL and LL) to a rationally based modern orientation (in the UL and LL). Because the shift in consciousness and culture from traditional to modern had much to do with breaking the dominating stronghold of the Catholic Church, the transformation led many to reject all things spiritual instead of only the traditional versions of spirituality. Wilber accounts for the process of what I call the modern endarkenment beautifully:

> In correctly spotting the immaturity of the notion of a mythic god—or a mythic [traditional] level of the spiritual line—[Western intellectuals] threw out not just the *mythic level* of spiritual intelligence *but the entire line* of spiritual intelligence. So upset were they with the mythic level, they tossed the baby of the spiritual line with the bathwater of its mythic level of development. They jettisoned the [traditional] amber God, and instead of finding [modern] orange God, and then [postmodern] green God, and [Integral] turquoise God, and indigo God, they ditched God altogether, they began the repression of the sublime, *the repression of their own higher levels of spiritual intelligence.* The intellectual West has fundamentally never recovered from this cultural disaster.[109] [Wilber's italics]

Wilber calls this a level/line fallacy.[110] The entire line of spiritual intelligence was erroneously confused and conflated with a particular stage of spiritual growth. Rather than simply transcending the stage of traditional spiritual consciousness that culture had outgrown, cultural leaders abandoned the entire spiritual endeavor altogether. This means that for many people, rather than allowing spiritual intelligence to move onto modern forms of expression, they rejected all forms of spirituality. Even as the average mode of consciousness in the culture evolved from a traditional to modern level of development in all other lines of growth (releasing cognitive intelligence, emotional intelligence, and moral intelligence to pursue truth at a rational stage), spiritual intelligence was abandoned and left frozen at a mythic level of development.[111] Wilber writes:

In order for the higher levels in the spiritual line to be recognized and allowed, the spiritual line itself needs to be recognized and honored. Both religion and science are perpetuating this cultural LLF [level/line fallacy] and this epidemic fixation at the mythic [traditional] level of spiritual development.... The de-repression of the sublime, the de-repression of the developmental line of spiritual intelligence, requires many things, but one of them, which we have been emphasizing, is to possess an orienting framework that allows and encourages a more spaces view of the role of both science and spirituality in the modern and postmodern world.[112]

Today, spirituality still suffers from the wounds inflicted by modernity (not to mention the later thrashing imparted by postmodernity).[113] In many cases, spiritual intelligence is still stunted at a traditional level of development. Much of humanity is divided with the ways they have navigated this spiritual trauma. Many individuals who have allowed the majority of their consciousness to pass through the modern rational stages of development abandon spirituality altogether because the traditional forms in which it is available no longer meet the requirements for higher stages of development. Those who are unwilling to abandon spirituality find themselves in an even more peculiar situation. All of their other lines of intelligence (e.g., cognitive, moral, and emotional) have developed beyond traditional levels, yet their spiritual intelligence still clings to an outdated, prerational level of religious orientation. Whether one has abandoned spirituality or allows it to persist, frozen at an earlier stage, the psychograph of an average individual at a modern level of development alive today can be reconstructed as follows:

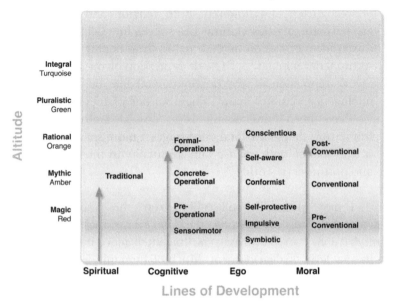

A Modern Psychograph
with Stunted Spiritual Growth

Figure 14: A modern psychograph showing stunted spiritual growth represented by a traditional lens of interpretation at a mythic altitude.

As shown in figure 14, the typical modern individual in the graph above has cognitive, ego, and moral development that has been liberated to fully express itself at a modern stage of development, yet his/her spiritual intelligence still remains *endarkened* at a traditional level of development.[114] (A similar graph, showing stunted spiritual growth at a traditional level, could be drawn for an individual at a postmodern level of development as well.)

The content in this chapter as well as the entire second volume of this series provide the foundation to rejuvenate spiritual intelligence allowing it to move through the steel ceiling of traditionalism. With this deeper understanding, the pathologies of modern and postmodern consciousness can be healed and spirituality can again take its rightful place in the lives of human beings. If it is true that spiritual intelligence can exist in healthy forms at modern, postmodern, and Integral stages of development, then the recognition of the Great Human Tradition sets the stage for humanity to lift itself out of the pathologies of the modern shadow. If it is true that there are rational versions of spiritually that can exist alongside modern science and reason based on evidence and experience, then the Modern Endarkenment is nearing its end.

A better understanding of the stages of spiritual intelligence can rejuvenate religion and spirituality catalyzing a new En-light-enment or "Age of Light" around the globe. This time however, the second renaissance, or what might be called the "second enlightenment," will not be limited to the Western world alone. The second enlightenment is a global awakening to the importance of modern, postmodern, and Integral levels of spiritual intelligence. The capacity for higher levels of spiritual intelligence helps human beings shift into world-centric and even kosmo-centric levels of development. Understanding spiritual intelligence gives us the opportunity to transform our world's religious traditions into vehicles of evolution. And perhaps most significantly, a shift into modern interpretations of religion gives rational segments of humanity access to spiritual teachings about vantage point development that would otherwise be discarded in their mythic forms. Such dreams are only possible to the degree to which the application of an Integral model of spiritual development can be successfully understood and operationalized.

Chapter 4
States of Spiritual Cultivation

In chapter 2, I used the term vantage points to signify state-stages of increasing depths of identity. Each vantage point shift signifies a loosening of exclusive identification with a shallower identity and the establishment of a deeper and more inclusive level of subjectivity. In short, I referred to this vector as "the knower." In chapter 3, I used the term "spiritual intelligence" to signify the various structure-stages of psychological growth and how each of those stages contributes to what I called the view or "lens of knowing."[115] In this chapter, I point to a third element of spiritual development called "states". Whereas chapter 2 focused on the "knower," and chapter 3 on the "lens of knowing," this chapter makes reference to "that which is known." In other words, using the terminology introduced by Brown, chapter 2 focuses on shifts in the "mind perspective" whereas this chapter focuses most poignantly on the "event perspective." An exploration of states, as I define it, includes both intentional access and spontaneous experiences in multiple realms of consciousness (gross, subtle, and causal).

Similar to the intention I've held in the previous three chapters, one of my main goals here is to provide a catalyst that sparks further Integral inquiry. In no way are the speculations here meant to be exhaustive or definitive. With that said, however, I do think that this chapter, to the degree to which it helps more clearly distinguish between vantage points (state-stages of identity) and states, offers an important step in the comprehensive study of spiritual development. When the difference between vantage points and states is clearly defined, it is more obvious that spiritual realization, involving a shift in subject, is ever-present regardless of the states that arise in the objective field of experience. This important differentiation prevents

97

the spiritual practitioner from confusing spiritual realization with spiritual states. Spiritual realization (through shifts in vantage points of awareness) leads an experiential understanding of absolute reality and, as a result, the end of everyday unhappiness. Spiritual states have substantial heuristic and evolutionary value but always arise as part of relative reality.[116]

In this chapter it will become clear that state/realm access and vantage points development represent different categories of spiritual development.[117] In doing so, I offer this third element to set the foundational framework for the synthesis of the Great Human Tradition.

The Objective Aspect of Experience

Much of this chapter follows Wilber's original work and builds upon the foundation of Integral Theory that he has spent so many decades nurturing. Simultaneously, I unpack and expand upon many ideas that have only been hinted at by Wilber. For heuristic purposes, I speak about states in reference to two aspects: (1) realms and (2) objects (both interior and exterior). Let me begin by outlining some of the basics of this chapter before I dive into the specifics. Here are a few guiding principles:

(1) We are always in a state. States, in the way I use the term, represent the basic objective field of experience and can be either ordinary or extraordinary. States point to what is happening in experience (this also includes formless states where the field of experience is simply a void wherein no form arises whatsoever).

(2) States are often associated with a particular realm. Realms (gross, subtle, or causal) are the containers that hold various kinds of states. Each state/realm correlates to a particular patterning of the interrelated categories of consciousness (attention, thinking perception, affect, self-system, reality-sense, and time/space organization).[118] Ordinary states like waking, dreaming, and deep sleep are associated with the vibrational frequencies of the gross, subtle, and causal realms, respectively. In a similar way, extraordinary states like the ones most often highlighted by Wilber such as nature mysticism, deity mysticism, and formless mysticism also correspond to gross, subtle, and causal realms, accordingly.[119] (It is important to note, however, that wakefulness

can be taken into all states).

(3) Realms and states contain objects and events. Objects and events can be exterior or interior to awareness. Both interior and exterior events are most obvious in the gross and subtle realms because they arise as various forms.[120] In the causal realm events are formless.

(4) Objects are enacted by perspectives. Because Wilber's Four Quadrants/ Quadrivia exist for all sentient beings regardless of their realm (honoring the fact that there is an increasing subtlety of quadratic differentiation as one moves from gross to subtle to causal), one can relate to any object that arises in a realm by way of what Wilber simplifies as *identity, union,* or *communion.*[121] Relationships of identity, union, and communion are, in many ways, analogous to the enactment of an object by way of a first-, second-, and third-person perspectives.[122]

(5) All states and objects are enacted through participatory co-creation according to the specific AQAL constellation of the particular individual having the experience. Unlike most postmodern approaches to participatory enactment,[123] Integral co-creation includes the influences of the Four Quadrants as well as all of the elements of the AQAL matrix.[124] In particular, this means that Integral co-creation, like postmodern theories of "participatory" co-creation (e.g., Ferrer), recognizes that objects are enacted by way of culture, social influences, linguistic matrices, historical considerations, as well as gender and identity concerns. However, Integral participatory co-creation goes beyond the more common postmodern expressions to also include an invaluable understanding of developmental levels (both individual and collective) and an understanding of vantage point realization. Among other things this means (as Wilber has rightly pointed out) that because developmental progress enfolds previous paradigms, each new higher/ deeper level rightly passes judgments and corrects shortcomings of previous levels. This occurs through a process of creative emergence and in service of what might result in greater virtue and goodness (or at the very least, correctives that intend to create less "torment," as Wilber calls it).[125] The common postmodern version of co-creation often leaves this important dimension of enfoldment out. I'll address this particular note more fully in chapter 5, but it is worth keeping in mind here as notions of events, objects, and states are introduced.

(6) Conscious and controlled access to specific realms and states can be cultivated. Consciously shifting realms and states can be cultivated through endogenic or exogenic catalysts. That is to say that one can consciously enter into a particular realm or state through internally trained practice

such as meditation or contemplative prayer (endogenic catalysts) or via external means (exogenic catalysts) through working with plant medicines, or use of other external mechanisms like electronic brain stimulation; bi-neural beats; brain-hemisphere-syncing music; drumming; or isolation tanks (among countless others). Consciously shifting states and realms can lead to philosophical and spiritual insight, increased motivation and purpose, individual and collective healing, ethical maturation, and, at times, can have profound heuristic benefits.

Some of the notes above are self-explanatory. Others need more unpacking before their implications can be fully digested. Again, I'll save point 5 above for the next chapter as it is more fitting to discuss the process of *Integral participatory enactment* in the context of all three elements (state-stages, structure-stages, and states) at once.
Let's move on together to the details of spiritual states so that we can deepen our understanding of this final vector of spiritual development and its role as a foundational element of the Great Human Tradition.

Unpacking States and Realms

Realms are the containers. States are the various changes in the field of experience that arise in those containers.

We are always in some sort of state. States are an ever-present part of our experience. State experiences, whether ordinary (e.g., waking, dreaming, or deep sleep) or extraordinary (e.g., nature mysticism, deity mysticism, or formless mysticism) tend to represent an alteration in the field of experience.[126]
As many thinkers of the past have clearly taken note, it is helpful to ground our understanding of states and realms in simple everyday experience so as to not get lost in some sort of conceptual abstraction. A narrative example is useful to help deepen our basic understanding together: In a single twenty-four hour cycle of the day, all human beings pass through at least three very broad, ordinary states of consciousness. Every day the field of our experience passes from waking to dreaming to deep, dreamless sleep. Each of these shifts in consciousness represents what the pioneering researcher Charles Tart called *discrete states of consciousness (DSoC)*.[127]
Generally speaking, the three major categories of states

of consciousness (waking, dreaming, deep sleep) arise in a different vibrational container, a different realm. The waking state most often arises in the gross realm. The dreaming state arises in the subtle realm. The deep dreamless sleep state arises in causal realm.[128] (It is important to note, however, that there are variations of waking, dreaming, and deep sleep that can arise in realms other than their primary association. For instance, in lucid dreaming one is waking in the subtle realm).[129]

Extraordinary States

Gross, subtle, and causal realms each contain specific types of extraordinary states.

Scores have been written about the topic of extraordinary states of consciousness.[130] The Tibetan Buddhists, for instance, speak of three special states of bliss, luminosity, and non-conceptual stillness that often arise in one's field of experience during the process of meditation.[131] All three states, according to the Tibetans, can be seen as distractions on the path to a full realization of an awakened vantage point. In the Christian tradition, states of bliss, union, and communion are often described. The intense state experiences that unfold within shamanistic cultures described in the second half of this chapter provide yet another example of how states have showed up both historically and how such states continue to play a role in contemporary spiritual experience.

Notable researcher and transpersonal psychology pioneer, Stanislav Grof is careful to point out a specific category of state experiences that can serve both healing and heuristic purposes. He calls the category of states *holotropic.* According to Grof, "this composite word [holotropic] literally means 'oriented toward wholeness' or 'moving in the direction of wholeness' (from the Greek *holos* = *whole* and trepein = moving toward or in the direction of something)."[132] I like Grof's categorization and adopt it accordingly.

Grof draws on his forty years of research to further distinguish the category of holotropic states. He names some of the specific characteristics that tend to arise during these types of experiences:

In holotropic states, consciousness is changed qualitatively in a very profound and fundamental way, but it is not grossly impaired like in the organically caused conditions. We

typically remain fully oriented in terms of space and time
and do not completely lose touch with everyday reality. At the
same time, our field of consciousness is invaded by contents
from other dimensions [realms] of existence in a way that
can be very intense and even over whelming.... Holotropic
states are characterized by dramatic perceptual changes in
all sensory areas. When we close our eyes, our visual field
can be flooded with images drawn from our personal history
and form the individual and collective unconsciousness. We
can have visions and experiences portraying various aspects
of the animal and botanical kingdoms, nature in general, or
of the cosmos. Our experiences can take us into the realm
of archetypal beings and mythological regions...."[133]

Although these extraordinary states can indeed cause significant
variations in a whole range of emotions, Grof believes that "by far
the most interesting insights that become available in holotropic states
revolve around philosophical, metaphysical, and spiritual issues."[134]
He writes: "We can experience sequences of psychological death and
rebirth and a broad spectrum of transpersonal phenomena, such
as feelings of oneness with other people, nature, the universe, and
God...."[135]

Just as gross, subtle, and causal realms correlate to the major
ordinary states of waking, dreaming, and deep sleep, so too each realm
also correlates to particular types of extraordinary and holotropic
experience. Wilber, for example, often signals out three types of
extraordinary states (while simultaneously acknowledging a plethora
of additional possibilities). The three types of states most often noted
by Wilber are experiences of nature mysticism, deity mysticism,
and formless mysticism.[136] Each state clearly fits Grof's criteria for a
holotropic state and are worthy of being labeled as such. In his book
Integral Spirituality, Wilber offers a clear and simple definition of each
type of extraordinary state:

One of the ultimate peak experiences in any realm is to
be *one with* the phenomena in that realm. To experience a
oneness with all phenomena in the gross-waking state is
a typical nature mysticism. To experience a oneness with
all phenomena in the subtle-dream state is a typical deity
mysticism. To experience a oneness with all phenomena

(or lack thereof) in the causal-unmanifest state is a typical formless mysticism....[137]

In other words, Wilber points out correctly that each realm (gross, subtle, and causal) can be the container for a particular type of extraordinary experience. In this case, the gross realm is associated with the extraordinary experience of nature mysticism or what I call a *union state* with all gross form. The subtle realm is the container for extraordinary experience of deity mysticism, or what I call a union state with subtle form. Finally, the causal realm is the container for the experience of formless mysticism, or what I call a union state with the formless. (The term union here refers to one of the three ways that objects are enacted in a given event. More on this below.)

Various extraordinary states almost always refer to experiences that are temporary. Wilber calls these temporary experiences *peak experiences*. When the experiences last for longer periods of time (days, weeks, months), Wilber calls them *plateau experiences*.[138] In both cases (peak and plateau), the experiences have a specific duration. Precisely because there is a moment in which they come into the stream of time, there is a corresponding moment at which they leave. In his now classic volume on extraordinary states of consciousness, *Varieties of Religious Experience*, William James uses the term *transient* to refer to this particular quality of state experiences.

Just as all human beings wake, dream, and deep sleep (ordinary states), cross-cultural research has shown us that there are particular qualities within extraordinary state-experiences that exist regardless of one's tradition or cultural background. As I cite in appendix 1, some of the earliest research attempted to categorize religious and spiritual experiences across different cultures according to common qualities. Approaches, like those of Stace, point out that extraordinary states often demonstrate unitive and noetic qualities. Sometimes these experiences are coupled with a sense of transcendence of space and time, a deeply felt positive mood, and paradox.[139] [140]

Realms Contain States; States Contain Objects and Events

Whereas I use the term *realm* to describe the energetic or vibrational container for experiences, and states to point to the ever-changing field of experience that arises in those containers, each state is often populated with specific objects and events. Both objects and events can arise as exterior or interior phenomena. (Refer to the footnotes for a more detailed account of objects and events in realms using Wilber's Four Quadrants and 8 Zones.)[141]

Taking our examination of objects and events one step further, Wilber again correctly explains that one's relationship to any object, event, or occurrence in the objective aspect of experience can be that of identity, union, or communion.[142] Another way of saying this is that one co-creates an experience depending upon the perspective taken to enact it (first, second, or third person). Because the process of enactment necessarily requires an apparently separate subject and object, state experiences of identity, union, and communion are enacted by those identities shallower than nondual identity. [143] (This means that even with a nondual vantage point, the lower spheres of causal, subtle, or gross identity can still enter into state experiences.)

Three Basic Types of States: Identity, Union, Communion

The working definitions I'll use to explain identity, union, and communion experiences are subtle but distinct. Making sure these definitions are coherent allows us to work with state experiences in an Integral context with even greater clarity. Here's one way to distinguish between the three types of enacted experiences:

"Identity" State Experience. When the term identity is used with reference to an object it means that in a given moment in time, a particular aspect of awareness arises simultaneously as non-different than an object as it appears. In an identity experience, all distinctions between subject and object dissolve.[144] Such an experience is enacted using a first- person perspective.

An example helps to further illustrate the point. In Tibetan Buddhist practice, for instance, if one is living from a nondual vantage point (awakened awareness), he or she may still invoke a practice that enacts the form of Avalokiteshvara at a subtle level of mind. This enactment can be done from a first-, second-, or third-person perspective. If enacted from a first-person perspective, one remains in awakened awareness while simultaneously allowing shallower levels of mind to arise as the deity. This means that even while awareness stays anchored in a deeper vantage point (e.g., nondual), a shallower identity (subtle) arises as the deity form itself. Because of the trans-dual nature of awakened awareness, the view of naked reality is never lost. This kind of deity state practice can invigorate a massive amount of energy as well as the potential for positive manifestation in the world.

"Union" State Experience. Union implies a unification of two things that are fundamentally different. In a union experience, a subject and object unify and merge but there is still a trace of duality that continues to mark their difference on the subtlest of levels. A Christian mystic for example may have a union experience with God. This experience is a complete "marriage" or coming together of the self and the Great Other. However, even though this union is complete, a subtle duality still exists.[145] The Christian often finds union with God but does not usually find a state of identification as God (I'll discuss this in the next chapter with regard to what Brown calls the "biasing perspective"). A union experience is most often related to enacting a second-person perspective of love or devotion and following that experience to its fullest intensity.

"Communion" State Experience. A temporary experience of communion is enacted when an object arises in awareness as clearly separate than the perspective perceiving it. To be aware of an object is to commune with it. In a communion experience, the particular object is clearly noted and observed in the objective field of experience but is clearly distinct from the subject perceiving it. In shamanistic trance, when working with a particular plant medicine like ayahausca, an individual may experience visionary patterns in new dimensional realms. All of these would be variations of a subtle-realm experience of communion. A communion state-experience is most often enacted in a third-person perspective.

In short, we can think of each of these extraordinary state experiences as follows: An identity state experience is when a level of mind *arises as* a specific object in awareness. A union experience is when an aspect of awareness *merges with* a particular object but there remains a subtle distinction of duality. Finally, a communion experience is when an aspect of awareness *arises in observation of an object*. For heuristic purposes, I've divided these categories up cleanly. I suspect that, in reality, many of these experiences can slide from one category to the other, and that these boundaries are not so hard and fast. The distinctions between identity, union, and communion do, however, provide a bit of clarity as we continue to find better ways to map states. (Elsewhere, I speak of these 1st, 2nd, and 3rd person experiences using the terms *identity*, *entity*, and *energy.* See my edited volume *The Coming Waves* for more detail).

Cultivating Vision into Realms and States

With the foundational definitions in place to establish what I mean by use of the terms realms and states (and all the variation therein), let us now take a look at how one might grow over time in this third element of spiritual development. In other words 'What does it mean to develop intentional access to various realms and states?'.[146]

Intentional access to both states and realms can be cultivated in two different ways. First, access can be cultivated through internally generated practices. When state and realm access is generated *from within*, I use the term *endogenic* (endogeny = an action or object coming from within a system). Alternatively, access to states and realms can be induced through stimulation from some type of an external source. When states are catalyzed *from without* I use the term *exogenic (exogeny* = an action or object coming from outside a system). With regard to endogenic catalysts, I focus below primarily on practices like meditation and contemplative prayer. With regard to exogenic catalysts, I limit the study to the ways that working with particular psychoactive substances can create realm and state shifts. Future study holds plenty of room to explore other catalysts for state and realm access (e.g., external brain stimulation, psychoactive visual stimulus, isolation tanks, bi-neural beats). Additional approaches could all find their appropriate home and be included in any robust Integral approach.[147]

Endogenic Catalysts

Historically, the most common endogenic catalysts used to induce holotropic states and to open up multiple realms of existence are meditation and contemplative prayer. Meditation in its simplest definition is an internal technology designed to focus one's awareness on either the mechanisms of the mind and its faculties of attention or on particular aspects in the field of experience. Contemplative prayer, along a slightly different vein, often consists of a type of internal, mental, discursive consideration of a particular topic. Although some types of meditation focus on the deconstruction of mind and its particular faculties of attention and tend to lead to stabilized vantage point realization, there are other forms of meditation that give more emphasis to the field of experience. These experience-based meditations along with various forms of contemplative prayer have been successfully used for centuries to induce profound shifts in both states and realms.

As mentioned earlier in this chapter, when particular types of meditation and prayer are practiced that involve contemplation and visualization of particular forms, such effort can lead to experiences of temporary shifts in identity, union, and communion. These extraordinary state experiences may involve lights, images, and intense emotions, and in some cases may also include interactions with what appear to be separate entities. Meditations and contemplative prayers without form or visualization can lead to profound experiences of silence, clarity, stillness, and bliss. Clearly, there can be heuristic benefits to all of these types of states.[148]

Let's dive deeper into one particular example so as to add a further element of depth to the discussion.

Intentional Access to the Subtle Realm

Some forms of meditation have the capacity to train individuals to enter directly into the subtle realm from the gross realm while awake. Both the Buddhist and the indigenous Bon traditions of Tibet have specific meditation practices to invoke subtle and causal realm access. Often these practices are referred to as yogas of dream and sleep.[149] In both traditions the practice of particular meditations is designed to cultivate a continuity of unbroken awareness, including the process through which one enters into dreaming and deep-sleep states. In Western terminology, when wakefulness is maintained during the transition into the dream state it is analogous to what some call a WILD, or a wake induced lucid dream.[150] The particular techniques offered to induce WILDs can be compared to specific forms of Eastern meditation. Because the concept of lucid dreaming is likely more familiar to many of the readers of this volume, I'll take the example of lucid dreaming a bit deeper. I refer all those interested in more traditional forms of Buddhist and Bon practice to the work of Tenzin

Wangyal.[151]

We have seen together already that the dreaming state is best associated with the subtle realm. In this light, to be lucid or aware that one is dreaming while in the midst of a dream is to be conscious in the subtle realm. WILDs involve a process by which no continuity of awareness is lost between gross and subtle states.

The most astute Western research to date on lucid dreaming has been conducted at Stanford University.[152] Head sleep-researcher Stephen LaBerge writes the following about the significance of lucid dreaming: "Empowered by the knowledge that the world they are experiencing is a creation of their own imagination, lucid dreamers can consciously influence the outcome of their dreams. They can create and transform objects, people, situation, worlds, and even themselves. By the standards of the familiar world of physical and social reality, they can do the impossible."[153]

For many, these extraordinary experiences of being conscious and aware while in the subtle realm can be life changing. As LaBerge and his team at Stanford have shown, lucid dreaming can have radical long-term positive effects on peoples' lives. In reference to his own research, he writes:

> Lucid dreams can be extraordinary, vivid, intense, pleasurable, and exhilarating. People frequently consider their lucid dreams as among the most wonderful experiences of their lives.... If this were all there was to it, lucid dreams would be delightful, but ultimately trivial entertainment. However, as many have already discovered, you can use lucid dreaming to improve the quality and depth of your life...You can learn from your dream experiences just as much as from your waking life experiences.[154]

The fact that these experiences have value is obvious. Furthermore, according to LaBerge's research, "there is no doubt that lucid dreams produce real effects on our brains and bodies.... [In addition,] there seems no doubt that the dreams are as real as real can be, according to the subjective point of view of the dream." This brings us then to one final but interesting point worth bringing to the table before closing this section.

We know that lucid dreams are subjectively "real." However, one of the most controversial questions, at least within the current dominant Western paradigm, is whether or not these realms of existence represent an ontological and/or objective reality outside of the subject perceiving them. Are the dreams just as real as our waking state in the gross realm?

A definitive answer to this question is outside the scope of this book, but Laberge's research into a phenomenon called mutual dreaming, in which the same lucid dream is shared by two or more people, may shed light on the inter-subjective validation needed to make such conclusions.

In reference to mutual dreams Laberge writes:

Accounts of "mutual dreaming," (dreams apparently shared by two or more people) raise the possibility that the dream world may be in some cases just as objectively real as the physical world. This is because the primary criterion of "objectivity" is that an experience is shared by more than one person, which is supposedly true of mutual dreams. In that case, what would happen to the traditional dichotomy between dreams and reality?[155]

In another account, LaBerge continues the analysis and explains what the implications might be if mutual lucid dreaming is accepted more broadly as fact:

These [mutual dreams] are the perplexing experiences in which two or more people report having had similar if not identical dreams. In some of these cases, the reports are so remarkably alike that one is almost compelled to conclude that the dream sharers appear to actually have been present together in the same dream environment. If this does occur, it would imply that at least under certain cases the dream world and likewise the dream bodies within it could possess some sort of objective existence.[156]

As state and realm access is developed in more and more individuals, I speculate that the number of accounts reporting mutual lucid dreaming will continue to rise.[157] As such discoveries slowly make their way into our shared consciousness, conscious access to the subtle realm may very well become part of our common everyday reality.

Shifting Realms and States through Exogenic Catalysts

Whether derived from traditional spiritual sources (e.g. meditation and contemplative prayer) or from Western scientific methods (e.g. practices for lucid dream induction), endogenic catalysts are certainly not the only way that one can enter into various states and realms of existence consciously and intentionally. Exogenic catalysts (i.e. those catalysts that spur state and realm shifts *from without*) have also been quite prominent historically throughout the globe.

Although there are multiple exogenic catalysts that can help induce state and realm shifts, the most common methods have often involved specific forms of dance, drumming, chanting, and, in many cases, through working with psychoactive "medicines". I'll narrow my focus to the last category so that I can report some of the latest Western scientific findings in relation to several of these medicines.

The types of holotropic states that Grof and Wilber have both pointed to throughout the chapter can be catalyzed through working with a whole variety of psychoactive substances both natural and synthesized. The most common substances used to induce state and realm shifts include plant-based psychoactives such as ayahuasca, salvia divinorum, mescaline, psilocybin mushrooms, and amanita muscaria (fly agaric) mushrooms, as well as synthesized psychoactives such as MDMA (ecstasy), lysergic acid deithylamide (LSD), and dimethaltryptomine (DMT).[158] To take our study deeper, I'll turn to a few academic considerations describing how two of these psychoactive chemicals have been shown to open up multiple realms and states.

Ayahuasca and DMT

Ayahuasca was first described in an academic context by Harvard ethnobotanist Richard Evans Schultes in the 1950s.[159] Ayahuasca, or Yage as it is sometimes called, is a brew made from two distinct plants (usually a mixture of the caapi vine and the leaves from a variety of particular plants containing the active chemical DMT).[160] If either of the two plants are consumed on their own, no psychoactive effects will result. However, when the two plants are combined, the active chemical DMT is released and is absorbable by the body. The results can be astonishing if proper set and setting are established.

Historically, ayahuasca was used for its medicinal and healing capacities (both physical and psychological) as well as its compelling capacity to open multiple realms of reality. It was almost always consumed within a religious context during sacred ceremony and under the guidance of a trained shaman. The same context and commitment to sacredness remains true for many modern spiritual practitioners still working with the medicine today. In the United States, the Santo Daime and the União do Vegetal churches (both syncretic traditions that combine Christian and South American indigenous elements) have successfully solicited legal exemption from laws prohibiting the consumption of substances containing DMT.[161] Since 2006, precedent has been set to protect their right to ingest ayahuasca as part of religious ceremony under the Religious Freedom Restoration Act.

In appendix 1, the reader can find the reports of Micheal Harner, a Western Anthropologist who broke through a major research barrier when he began participating in medicine ceremonies rather than merely observing from the outside. In his reports, he describes several instances of working with ayahuasca in sacred ritual with an indigenous tribe of the Amazon. He writes that "for several hours after drinking the brew, I found myself, although awake, in a world literally beyond my wildest dreams.... transported into a trance where the supernatural seemed natural." Using the Integral map introduced thus far, we can speculate that the supernatural world that Harner speaks about is in fact an extraordinary state experience in which the vibrational frequency, or what we might call "realm/dimensional center of gravity," has shifted to the container of the subtle realm.

Early accounts like those of Harner have inspired other Westerners to continue the research outside of ritual and instead in a controlled laboratory setting in hopes of pinning down just what is happening during these intense other-worldly experiences. Dr. Rick Strausman, at the University of New Mexico, is one particular person who has conducted recent scientific studies of DMT, the active ingredient in ayahausca.[162]

Strassman's studies, also mentioned in appendix 1, show us that there is no doubt that DMT can produce extraordinary shifts in state as well as what I would call a profound capacity to access multiple realms. Strassman explains the immediacy and the intensity in the onset of a DMT experience:

In our volunteers, a full dose of IV DMT almost instantly

elicited intense psychedelic visions, a feeling that the mind had separated from the body, and overpowering emotions. These effects completely replaced whatever had occupied their minds just before drug administration.... Effects began within seconds of finishing the 30-second DMT infusion, and people were fully involved in the psychedelic worlds by the time I finished clearing the intravenous line with sterile saline 15 seconds later.[163]

Strassman conducted the standard tests to determine the effects of the substance on the brain, heart-rate, blood pressure, and other vital areas of medical interest. He also tracked particular neurotransmitters in the brain to see how the substance effected brain chemistry. Interestingly, he noticed major changes to the chemicals released in the pineal gland. Consequently, as a result of multiple factors, he suspected that certain forms of DMT were naturally produced and secreted from the pineal gland itself, and may very well be one of the key neurochemicals that correlate to mystical experience.[164]

Out of all of the experiences reported by Strassman, including classic mystical experiences of union, the most strange and intriguing events related to consistent contact with beings and entities in what appeared to be other dimensional realms. Many of these experiences would fall under the category of *communion* state experiences, as I have defined them here in this chapter. Strassman writes with some hesitation, recognizing the stigma surrounding such conversation in our Western culture:

> I continually feel surprise in seeing how many of our volunteers "made contact" with "them," or other beings. At least half did so in one form or another. Research subjects used expressions like "entities," "beings," "aliens," "guides," and "helpers" to describe them.[165]

As strange as this may seem, Strassman readily acknowledges that "contact" with beings quite obviously challenges our modern Western worldview: "It may be that I have such a hard time with these stories because they challenge the prevailing worldview, and my own. Our modern approach to reality relies upon waking consciousness, and its extensions of tools and instruments, as the only ways of knowing. If we can't see, hear, smell, taste, or touch things in our everyday state of mind, or using our technology-amplified senses, it's not real. Thus, these are non-material beings."[166]

As he tries to make sense of these reports, all of which were generally consistent across different individuals and multiple contexts, Strassman tries to keep an open mind as he juxtaposes our modern Western worldview with that of many native and indigenous cultures. He writes: "In contrast [to our own Western view], indigenous cultures are in regular contact with the denizens of the invisible landscape and have no problems with straddling both worlds. Often they do this with the aid of psychedelic plants."[167] Wrestling with the reality of the evidence and his own rational scientific background, Strassman seems to be applying a trans-rational level of cognition (at least at times).

Note: Although Strassman's point above about the normalcy of such realms and beings in indigenous cultures is an important one, it is critical that we also take into consideration the Integral distinction between prerational and trans-rational thought. A prerational lens takes the world as it is without the capacity to take a third-person perspective and reflect critically on its beliefs and without the need for verifiable evidence. A trans-rational perspective requires inter-subjectively verified truth claims and insists on performing the injunctions that can provoke them. Unlike the merely rational orientation, however, a trans-rational lens remains open to infinite possibilities beyond the mere positivism and a reliance on the mere waking state in the gross realm.

Regardless of how we consider the ontological status of these types of entities and even if we are set on maintaining a purely rational level of thinking, there is no doubt that DMT has the power to induce massive realm and state shifts. Because the experiences are real from the subjective point of view at minimum, such holotropic states can have lasting positive influence and significant value to all those who experience them. Seen in this light, spiritual cultivation in service of realm and state access is something well worth pursuing.

Let's look at one more example of an exogenic catalyst.

Psilocybin

The psilocybin mushroom, sometimes called a magic mushroom, is yet another example of a powerful exogenic catalyst used to induce extraordinary state experiences. Historically, the psilocybin mushroom was used among particular Central and South American tribes (among others). Like the ritual use of ayahuasca described above, these native spiritual traditions ingested mushrooms as part of their sacred ceremonies.

Modern research into the power and potential of the mushroom was first introduced to popular culture by Valetina and Gordon Wasson in the mid 1950s. Valentina was a Russian immigrant to the United States and a practicing pediatrician. Gordon was a well-respected New York banker and vice president of JP Morgan & Co. Together, feeling adventurous and inspired by tales that they had heard, they journeyed to Mexico to sit in a sacred ceremony with a native tribe. Upon their return, they were asked to write an article for *Life* magazine about their experience.

It was through the *Life* article, that many Westerners heard about the power of the magic mushroom for the first time. Wasson explains the noticeable changes in state that opened as the mushroom's effects began to take hold:

> The visions were not blurred or uncertain. They were sharply focused, the lines and colors being so sharp that they seemed more real to me than anything I had ever seen with my own eyes. I felt that I was now seeing plain, whereas ordinary vision gives us an imperfect view; I was seeing the archetypes, the Platonic ideas, that underlie the imperfect images of everyday life. The thought crossed my mind: could the divine mushrooms be the secret that lay behind the ancient Mysteries? Could the miraculous mobility that I was now enjoying be the explanation for the flying witches that played so important a part in the folklore and fairy tales of northern Europe? These reflections passed through my mind at the very time that I was seeing the visions, for the effect of the mushrooms is to bring about a fission of the spirit, a split in the person, a kind of schizophrenia, with the rational side continuing to reason and to observe the sensations that the other side is enjoying.[168]

Wasson spent the remainder of his life studying and writing about the magic mushroom.

In appendix 1, I mention the Marsh Chapel Experiment, or what is more commonly known as the "Good Friday Experiment." This now infamous study, conducted by Walter N. Pahnke under the supervision of Timothy Leary and the Harvard Psilocybin Project showed that psilocybin can indeed help to catalyze extraordinary state experiences. After attending a church service under the influence of psilocybin, nine out of ten students from Harvard Divinity school who took part in the experiment reported some sort of religious experience while 30 to 40 percent reported experiences that qualified as "complete" mystical experiences.[169] Despite these remarkable results, shortly after these early studies and in part as a result of negative publicity involving recreational drug use of other psychedelics like LSD in the years that followed, almost all research into the potential role and use of entheogens/psychedelics in the United States was abolished.[170]

Today, it seems that the tides are turning once again. After nearly a twenty-five-year moratorium on the academic study of psychedelics, studies are once again being approved by the United States government. One of the most recent studies of psilocybin was conducted at Johns Hopkins University in 2006. Like "the Good Friday Experiment" that took place at Harvard over four decades earlier, the objective of the Johns Hopkins study was to determine whether or not psilocybin had the potential to "occasion" spiritual and religious experiences. The study, in short, delivered staggering results, affirming the hypothesis that psilocybin can indeed provide a kind of access key to extraordinary holotropic states.

A few significant details regarding the Johns Hopkins study are worth noting. According to the published research,[171] nearly 20 percent of the participants reported that the experience was the single most spiritually significant event of their life. Approximately 57 percent reported it was among the top five most spiritually significant experiences of their life. Two months after the study, 79 percent of the participants reported increased well-being or satisfaction; friends, relatives, and associates confirmed this. They also reported a decrease or complete absence of symptoms for anxiety and depression:

> The present study shows that, in some people under some conditions, psilocybin can occasion experiences that are rated highly valued. This seems a likely mechanism underlying the long-term historical use of psilocybin and other hallucinogens such as DMT within some cultures for divinatory or religious purposes.[172]

In addition to the positive outcomes, the facilitators are quick to note that the sessions were not all entirely carefree. Even given the careful settings and selection process, eight of the thirty-six volunteers did experience at least some period of anxiety/dysphoria during the session. When these negative states arose, "psychological effects were readily managed with reassurance."[173] (I mention this simply because one can imagine how easily such experiences might get out of control in a setting that lacks the same sort of careful attention that was put into the Johns Hopkins study. It is important for me to highlight that this chapter as a whole is not meant to be a recommendation to or endorsement of working with entheogens like psilocybin or ayahuasca. May it instead serve as an informed presentation of what might be possible in the future as we continue to deepen our collective inquiry together.)

Even with important caveats and warnings in place, the types of broad-ranging positive conclusions reported in the double-blind psilocybin experiment are enough to make even the strongest skeptic think twice about the need for future research to further uncover the power and potential of what many native traditions rightly call medicines. All in all, as our capacity to understand and control adverse effects deepens, studies like those conducted at the University of New Mexico and Johns Hopkins provide valid proof of the fact that some exogenic catalysts can indeed be used to facilitate conscious access to multiple states and realms. Such experiences can have a positive influence and may very well serve significant heuristic, transformative, and evolutionary ends.

Implications of Consciously Shifting Realms and States

The argument could be made that intentional access to states and realms is not as valuable as the transformation that unfolds in the other two aspects of spiritual development (state-stages and structure-stages). For instance, we've already learned the value of understanding structure-stages and state-stages. Higher levels of spiritual intelligence through structure-stages will give us more complex lenses through which we can enact the realities necessary to address our global problems. In addition to problem solving, higher levels of spiritual intelligence will also allow us to liberate our world's religious systems from traditional to modern and eventually postmodern and Integral orientations.

The advantages of spiritual realization through deeper vantage points of depth are equally as important. Spiritual realization gives individuals the tools needed to end everyday unhappiness by coming to know Absolute reality as the very base of awareness. In place of constant dissatisfaction, one can stabilize a perspective whose source of awareness is nondual, ever-present, and always-already content. In today's world of massive suffering and depression, liberation through spiritual realization is clearly needed. [174]

What, then, might the implications be if we explored spiritual cultivation of states with an equal degree of sincerity? Like spiritual realization of deeper vantage points and the development of higher structures of spiritual intelligence, I speculate that the category of spiritual states could have profound implications for our understanding the world and how we make sense of it. Let me highlight just three of the breakthroughs that could result if state/realm access were to be taken into account as a real possibility for all of humanity.

(1) If intentional access into realms and states were taken seriously, we could collectively begin to live and honor multiple levels of reality. Our current socially accepted maps of reality include the gross realm and its waking state as the single and only valid realm of reality. As access to states and realms increases (whether access is induced through meditation, contemplation, entheogenic plants, or some other means), they will continue to be inter-subjectively verified. As this occurs, we can more broadly begin to recognize that there are multiples levels of reality, all of which are equally valid dimensions of this vast kosmos. We can also begin to accept that each level of reality has the potential for learning, transformation, healing, and evolution. Imagine, briefly, the first people that Galileo tried to convince about the vast world of stars and galaxies that existed if they only looked through his telescope. Those first few onlookers would surely think that he was mad. What Galileo was explaining to them simply didn't fit within their accepted paradigm. Pioneers exploring intentional access to multiple states and realms of existence today face a similar task. The new "telescopes" are the endogenic and exogenic catalysts explained above (e.g., meditation, contemplative prayer, plant medicines). Those who look through these new "telescopes" see firsthand that one can learn how to enter into various realms and states at will.

(2) If intentional access to realms and states were taken seriously, we could begin to take advantage of the tremendous benefits available in states and realms outside

117

of the usual gross realm. Because many of the laws of reality shift as one's awareness shifts through different realms, the capacity and potential for new insights, healing, and individual and collective evolution are enormous. As just one example, those well skilled in lucid dreaming and others who have experience with various entheogens have already tasted some of the benefits of accessing the subtle/ causal realm at will. (I suspect, at the very least, massive karmic metabolizing and shadow work can take place in these states and realms.) Shifting into this sort of a multi-realm or multidimensional worldview is sure to have reverberating effects in every area of human life.

(3) If intentional access to realms and states were taken seriously, we would have to reconsider many of the beliefs within indigenous and native cultures that modern Westerners discard. Many indigenous cultures, often as a result of drumming, dancing, and plant medicines, demonstrate a high degree of spiritual cultivation of states and vision into realms. Additionally, intentional access to realms and states was not only the practice of isolated individuals. Perhaps even more importantly, at this critical juncture in history at the dawn of an Integral Age, these realms and states were opened up by collectives, simultaneously, as part of sacred ritual. What if there was more to learn from cultures at a magic level of structural development than we had previously suspected? What if there is a recapitulation of a magic level of development at what Wilber might refer to as second or third tier? What if there truly are subtle beings and entities that have an ontological existence in and of themselves? Fully noting that most indigenous cultures enact a magic/ premodern world, what would these realities look like when enacted by an Integral practitioner or group. (It would be a grave error to confuse state/realm access with a particular level of development. Just as Wilber speaks of a level/line fallacy such an error could be considered a state/level fallacy. Not all *Magic* is *magic.* In other words, not all magic relating to subtle-realm influence on gross-realm reality/miracles/ psychic phenomena is restricted to a magic structure-stage.)

If any one of the above implications represents a valid and plausible position it would mean that we are on the precipice of a major transformation. I suspect there may be relevance in all three.[175] If states are to be looked at seriously, important distinctions will have to be in place between prerational and trans-rational thought.[176] Historically, ideas related to multiple realms have almost always been the domain of prerational thought. For example, as Grof correctly points out, prerational religious traditions all took for granted the fact that there were other realms of reality (e.g., the Christian heaven).[177] The entrance of the rational paradigm and the overreach of science into the other value spheres destroyed all possibilities of any reality other than the waking state in the gross realm.

With regard to access to multiple states and realms, the baby was thrown out with the bathwater. Instead of preserving any of the truth that might exist in state and realm access (as much as they can be verifiably tested through specific sets of injunctions), it was confused with a prerational level of consciousness and discarded by rational thinkers. A trans-rational Integral post-metaphysics may very well have the capacity to explain multiple realms of existence based on injunctions and inter-subjectively validated truth claims without any of the prerational or premodern baggage. In all of our discussion about realms and inter-dimensional realities, it is vital that we are clear about the differences between these types of prerational and trans-rational distinctions. It will be through our shared discussion over the coming years and decades that we might gain more clarity about this potentially important element of spiritual development.[178]

Chapter 5
The Spiritual Development Cube

Let us now turn to discuss the three elements of spiritual development altogether. For visual reference, I show how state-stages, structure-stages, and states all interact in a graphic I call the Spiritual Development Cube.

Below, I'll first introduce the cube itself. Then I'll offer several examples of how using the Spiritual Development Cube can bring a deeper sense of clarity to our understanding of spiritual unfolding. After providing several variations of the graphic to help further elucidate the model, I'll also offer two practical examples. These examples use the Christian tradition and the Tantric Hindu tradition as centerpieces to show how the three-vector model can help us prevent the common conflation between vantage points and states. At the close of the chapter, I'll show how both the Spiritual Development Cube and, more specifically, how the cube and the entire AQAL matrix can be used to build the case for an Integral post-metaphysics. It is my hope that the model outlined in this chapter, or some variation thereof, might truly help move us toward the full realization of our Great Human Tradition.

Spiritual Development Cube

The Spiritual Development Cube provides a graphic model that shows the various ways that vantage points, structure-stages (views), and states interact and influence each other. Just as the original Wilber-Combs matrix allows us to map what Wilber calls states and structures using a two-vector axis,[179] the Spiritual Development Cube supports Wilber's vision while providing an extra layer of analysis. Rather than conflating states and vantage points into a single category (as one might do when working with the classic two-vector Wilber-Combs matrix), the figure below expands all three vectors to show how all interact together in a single graphic.

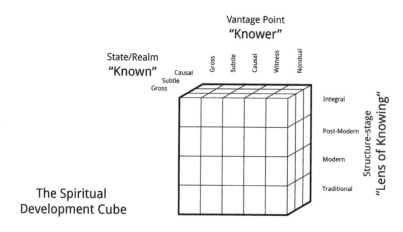

Figure 15: The Spiritual Development Cube

In figure 15, the horizontal x-axis represents the vector I call vantage points. Across the top of the graphic vantage points are labeled from left to right as gross, subtle, causal, witness, and nondual. Recalling chapter 2 we called this vector the "knower." A gross vantage point is equal to what we referred to as awareness coming from a source that is confused with thought. A subtle vantage point is equal to awareness coming from a source beyond thought yet still confused with personality. A causal vantage point is equal to awareness coming from a source beyond personality yet still confused with time/space. A witness vantage point is equal to awareness coming from a source beyond time/space but still confused with individual consciousness. Finally, the nondual vantage point (in the way I use it) is equal to awakened awareness, coming from its original source without confusion or obstruction. In chapter 2, all of these vantage points are framed using the work of Daniel P. Brown and I point out that there are varying levels of nonduality, only the last of which can be considered *awakened awareness*.

The vertical y-axis labeled on the right-hand side of the graphic represents structure-stages of development, in chapter 3, I call this the "lens of knowing." When this topic was introduced, I used several different metrics to measure structural development as it relates to spiritual intelligence. One option is to use the altitude markers of magic, mythic, rational, and pluralistic Integral as I do in volume 2 of this series. A second option, and the one I choose to represent in the graphic above, shows increasing levels of complexity as they unfold from traditional to modern to postmodern to Integral structures and beyond.

The z-axis, labeled in the top left-hand corner of the graphic, refers to state/realm access (gross, subtle, causal). In chapter 4, this vector is referred to as "that which is known." States can be extraordinary, ranging from various experiences of communion, union, or identity with particular objects, or might simply refer to ordinary states like waking, dreaming, and deep sleep. The use of this vector can also point to the fact that these experiences often arise specifically in gross, subtle, or causal realms (i.e., access to the state of lucid dreaming arises most commonly in the subtle realm). In both cases, whether this vector refers more specifically to the states or the particular realms, the z-axis represents those events most often described in terms of what is arising, changing, and passing away in the objective field of experience.

Advantages of Using the Spiritual Development Cube

There are several immediate advantages to using the Spiritual Development Cube. First, a three-vector model allows us to more carefully pinpoint an individual's specific degree of spiritual development at any given point in time. A few examples will help to illuminate the point.

Let's say, for example, one has stabilized a subtle vantage point (awareness comes from a source that is no longer confused with thought but is still confined within the vantage point of the personality). Let us then suppose that this person enters into a state of formless mysticism (causal union). Finally, let's say that this person has a vertical center of gravity at a traditional stage of development. Accordingly, this vertical center of gravity tells us that he or she will use a traditional lens of spiritual intelligence to interpret and explain his/her spiritual experience. An expanded variation of the Spiritual Development Cube allows us to show precisely where this experience can be mapped with a clear distinction between structure-stage, vantage point and state:

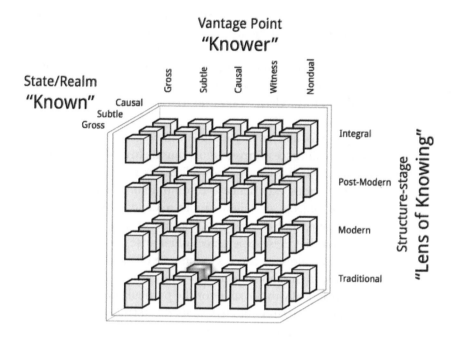

Figure 16: A subtle vantage point, a traditional structure-stage of spiritual intelligence, and a causal state of union

Notice above that there is a box highlighted in the second column from the left using the horizontal x-axis. This demarcation signifies a subtle vantage point (the subjective sense of where awareness is "coming from"). Next, notice that the box is highlighted on the first level of the vertical y-axis. This marks a traditional structure-stage of development. The structure-stage of spiritual intelligence signifies the "lens" through which any experience will be interpreted/enacted. Finally, notice that the box is highlighted in the third row along the z-axis. This shows the particular state/realm into which the individual has temporarily gained access. In this case the person had an experience of a causal state/realm. The label to the left of the graphic on the z-axis reads "Causal Union" to signify the specific type of state experience. Depending on one's preference of terms, this label could also read "formless mysticism." (I've selected the term "causal union" to maintain consistency.)

If we were using a classic Wilber-Combs Matrix with only

two vectors we would have to choose between showing the individual's vantage point and structure-stage or state and structure-stage. That is, the two-dimensional matrix would either show a subtle vantage point alongside a traditional structure-stage of development or a causal state alongside a traditional structure-stage of development. In either case, the two-dimensional matrix leaves out a critical piece of information that the Spiritual Development Cube can account for.

Let's look at a second example using the Spiritual Development Cube to track a different type of spiritual experience. Take the scenario of a businessman similar to Gordon Wasson described in chapter 4. Let's assume that this individual functions with a vertical center of gravity in everyday life, and at a modern (rational) level of structural development. Let's imagine further that this particular person holds a state-stage center of gravity at a gross vantage point (thought is assumed to be the source of awareness). Finally, let's say that this person is invited to participate in a sacred ceremony with a native tribe wherein all the members ingest psilocybin mushrooms. Imagine next that the individual has an experience of nature mysticism (gross union). We could map his or her experience using the Spiritual Development Cube as follows:

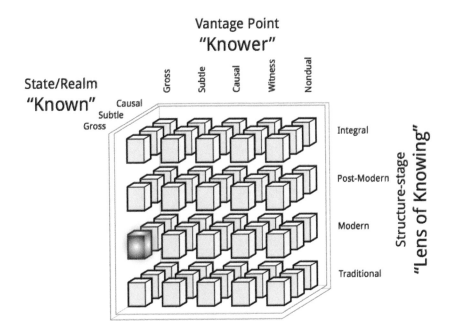

Figure 17: A gross vantage Point, a modern structure-stage of spiritual intelligence, and a gross state of union

The graphic above shows a gross vantage point, living though a modern lens of spiritual intelligence, enacting a spiritual experience of gross union. Let's again breakdown our mapping step by step:

Tracing the horizontal x-axis we see the box highlighted in the first column from the left signifying a gross vantage point. The vertical y-axis helps us to locate the individual vertically in the second level at a modern stage of structural development. Finally, the highlighted first row in the z-axis shows us that the individual has had an experience of gross union (or what we often call nature mysticism). Again, the three-vector model allows us to directly pinpoint the experience in a way that a two-vector model simply cannot.

Let's take one more example to show why the three-vector model might have an advantage in certain circumstances over a two-vector model that collapses vantage points and states together into one category. Let's say someone has a shift in vantage point without any major change in state. Imagine a person who is functioning from an Integral level of structural development and a causal vantage point (awareness consistently beyond confusion or contraction with personality and thought). Next, imagine that during the normal waking state this person has a temporary dip in awareness to a nondual vantage point without any of the objects in the field of experience changing. We could map the experience as follows:

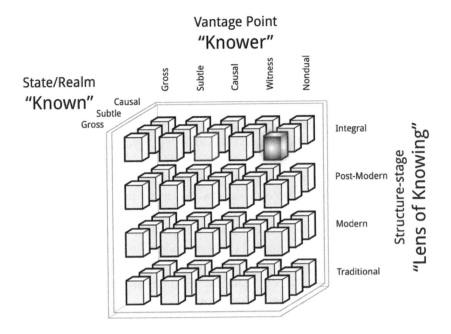

Figure 18: A temporary dip in vantage point from causal to nondual while in the gross realm, waking state

In the graphic above, notice the lighter lines in the third column from the left highlighting the causal vantage point box. These lighter lines indicate the individual's normal vantage point. The shaded box in the far right column indicates the temporary experience of a deeper nondual vantage point. The three-vector model allows us to show that an experience of a deeper vantage point does not always mean a dramatic change in state. In this particular case, the shift to a nondual vantage point collapses the subject and object duality but does not alter the forms that arise within that sphere of non-duality in any way. Everything remains just the way that it is.

More generally speaking, this means that although the source of awareness has shifted, such a change in vantage point may or may not include dramatic changes in the field of experience. (This becomes a vital realization on the path. True progress comes when one can stabilize an awakened vantage point regardless of changes in state/realm.)

If the distinctions made in this book hold any truth, further exploration will be the work of Integral religious scholars for decades to come. For now, all those interested in additional graphics and potential configurations are encouraged to consult the book's endnotes. [180]

Using Only Two Vectors to Map Spiritual Development

Once we have clearly disaggregated Wilber's meta-category of "states" to fully include the distinction between shifting vantage points (state-stages of identity) and intentional access to states/realms, we can again return to examine any two vectors side by side using only a two-dimensional matrix. Using two vectors prior to a three-vector differentiation can be confusing as it conflates two unique dimensions of growth. Using two vectors after a three-vector differentiation can bring us the simplicity needed to zoom again to examine specifics of a situation in a simpler way. Let's look at the available combinations. (Pay careful attention to the x-, y-, and z-axes. They are fluid depending on which two vectors are being compared.)

First let's compare structure-stages and extraordinary states. This sort of comparison gives us a variation of the classic Wilber-Combs Matrix:

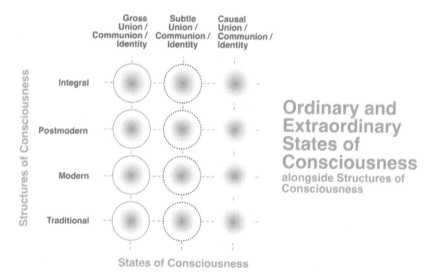

Figure 19: Ordinary and extraordinary states of consciousness alongside structures of consciousness

In the graphic above the vertical y-axis represents structure-stages of spiritual intelligence (changes in the lens of interpretation) and the horizontal x-axis represents specific categories of extraordinary states (changes in objective the field of experience). As stated in Wilber's initial articulation of the Wilber-Combs Matrix in his book *Integral Spirituality*, an individual will interpret their particular state experience through their specific lens of structural development.[181]

Second, we can compare structure-stages and vantage points:

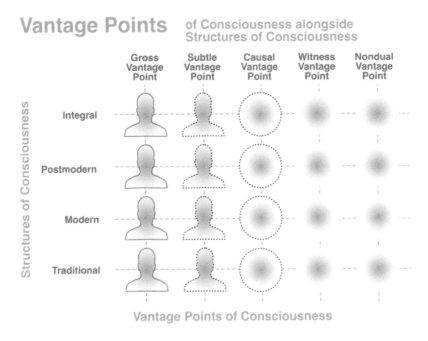

Figure 20: Vantage points of consciousness alongside structures of consciousness

Here, the vertical y-axis points to the structure-stage of spiritual intelligence (i.e., the changing lens of interpretation) and the horizontal x-axis represents the vantage point (i.e., the shifting source of awareness). To be sure, the Wilber-Combs Matrix is used at times to portray this particular interaction as well. More precisely, the graphic above is used by Wilber to show what he calls "dual-center of gravity."

The distinctions made in chapter 2 (vantage points) and chapter 4 (access to states/realms) show the vital difference between "where awareness is coming from" and "what awareness is experiencing."

Making these important distinctions first in a three-vector model and then returning again to only two vectors helps to further support Wilber's original model while simultaneously bringing even greater clarity to the field of Integral religious studies and Integral spirituality.

Finally, as a third option, and a unique contribution of this book, we can also represent a two-vector model that compares vantage points to states. A graphic showing vantage points and extraordinary states would look like the following:

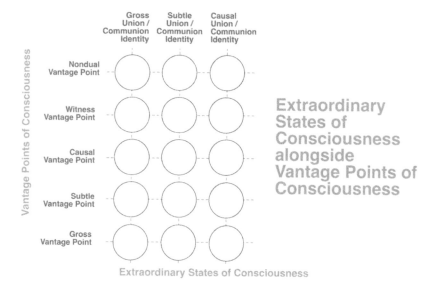

Figure 21: Extraordinary states of consciousness alongside vantage points of consciousness

Previously, as stated above, vantage points and access to states/realms were not clearly disaggregated. As a result they have not yet been compared on this sort of two-vector model. In figure 21, the vertical y-axis represents vantage points of increasing depth. The horizontal x-axis represents shifts in state.[182]

Examining the vectors of states and vantage points side by side reveals a few interesting discoveries about the differences between them. Below I list some of the reasons why an advanced Integral scholar might want to ensure that these two categories are seen separately:

(1) Most extraordinary states arise and develop independently from vantage point shifts. Access to states isn't required for development

of deeper vantage points. Conversely, deeper vantage points are not required for access to states.[183] (However, as we've noted, these dimensions are not "hooked," but they are "linked".)

(2) Spiritual liberation depends entirely on the vantage point one is sourcing awareness from in any given moment. This is true regardless of the state.[184] A deeper understanding of the fact that vantage points and states are separate vectors teaches us that the freedom inherent in spiritual realization is not related to or dependent upon any changing phenomena.

(3) All vantage points transcend, include, and penetrate the shallower identities. This is not the case with access to states.[185] The states listed across the horizontal x-axis are usually mutually exclusive. For example, an extraordinary state of subtle communion does not normally also include a state of gross union. Similarly, a state of causal union (formless mysticism) does not also include an experience of subtle and gross union (deity and nature mysticism).[186] However, I suspect that in deeper practice one can open gross, subtle, and causal realms all at once.

(4) Finally, because one's vantage point coexists with shallower identities (i.e., a deeper vantage point transcends, includes, and penetrates shallower identities), any of the extraordinary states shown in the x-axis above can be experienced whilst one has stabilized any vantage point. Regardless of one's stabilized vantage point, the shallower identities stay active and continue to enact subject-object duality wherein states continue to arise. This means that even while anchored in a nondual vantage point (void itself of subject-object duality), shallower identities (witness, causal, subtle, gross) are all still active and in duality. As a result, any shallower identity can enact a subject-object relationship of communion, union, or identity in gross, subtle, and causal states.[187]

Offering one further example to illustrate the last point listed above will help ground the concepts in actual experience. From the perspective of a nondual/trans-dual vantage point the apparent subjective and apparent objective aspects of awareness are non-different. As such, the idea of a change in state according to subject-object co-creation doesn't exactly make sense. From this trans-dual vantage point everything is the "same taste" of awareness. However, to assume that states no longer arise would be an error. Changes in realm and state do continue to unfold.

I use a simplified two-vector model comparing vantage points and states to make the point. As shown in figure 23, it is not the nondual vantage point itself but rather one of the shallower identities that enacts a particular state experience. Let's look at it graphically and then I will elucidate.

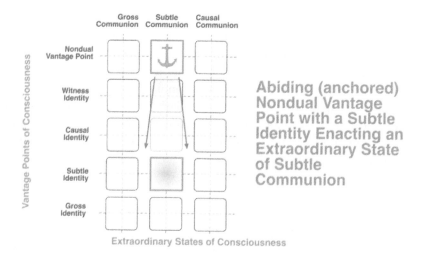

Figure 22: Abiding nondual vantage point with subtle identity enacting an extraordinary state of subtle communion

The graphic above shows an example of a person whose awareness is anchored in nondual vantage point while a shallower level of awareness enacts an extraordinary state experience of subtle communion. If this person were a Christian, the subtle experience might be a vision of Jesus. (In this case, however, the subtle form of Jesus would arise as non-different from the awareness appearing to observing it.)

Notice the "anchor" in the top row of the vertical y-axis and the second column of the horizontal x-axis. This anchor signifies a person who is living from a nondual vantage point. In addition to the anchor, the outline of the box is highlighted in the subtle identity row (y-axis)

under the column of subtle communion (x-axis). This highlighted box shows that the active subtle identity is responsible for enacting the subject-object experience of communion.[188] If we continue with our Christian theme, one might therefore describe the graphic as depicting a nondual *vantage point anchor*, living through an active subtle identity that is enacting an extraordinary subtle state experience of communion with Jesus. Although Jesus arises as non-separate from the perspective of the nondual anchor, Jesus remains "apparently" separate from the perspective of the subtle identity.

Examples like these allow us to point to the truly trans-dual nature of awakened awareness. The trans-dual vantage point transcends, includes, and penetrates all of the dualistic identities and can easily accommodate and incorporate continued experiences in relative reality. From the standpoint of realization, nothing is left out and everything is gained. As we saw in chapter 2, this means that individual consciousness, time and space, personality, thinking, and all of the relative world do not go away upon awakening to full spiritual realization. Rather, as both Brown and Wilber have put it before as they draw from the Tibetan tradition, all of duality is viewed as "ornaments" of awakened awareness.

Bringing Greater Clarity to Comparative Mysticism

In the second half of this chapter, I would like to unpack two key ideas that help us to build upon the notion of the Spiritual Development Cube to further show how understanding its three vectors can bring greater clarity in an Integral age. To do this, I first show how an element that Brown calls a "biasing perspective" generates differing surface features of spiritual experience within diverse traditions. Then, after establishing the logic of surface features, I show how a fuller understanding of participatory enactment can be portrayed from an Integral perspective in a way that honors both modern and postmodern critiques of spirituality.

Biasing Perspectives

One of the keys to Brown's early research into the stages of spiritual development is to show that the deeper sequence of meditative stages holds true even though the surface features of experience at each of those stages can be quite different across traditions. To show this, Brown's original research demonstrates that experience will always be enacted according to the particular philosophical training built into the culture and tradition within which the meditator is practicing. Brown explains his concept of a biasing factor further in the following excerpt:

> While the order of stages [deep structures] is fixed, the actual experience of each stage [surface features] varies significantly across the three traditions. This is because each tradition introduces a biasing factor through preliminary philosophical training. Philosophical training fosters a distinct perspective in each of the respective traditions. This perspective, in turn, influences the approach to meditation, but more importantly, affects the nature of the meditative experience itself.... These perspectives are more than conceptual biases because they represent something intrinsic to the acquisition of human knowledge. Since perspectivism is therefore unavoidable in meditation, as in any other mode of inquiry, except perhaps in the initial moment of enlightenment, each of the descriptions of meditation experience in the respective traditions is valid, though different.[189]

Biasing Perspectives in Christian Mysticism and Hindu Tantra

When we pay careful attention to the difference between vantage points and states we find that Brown's concept of a biasing perspective plays an important role in determining which aspect of awareness is emphasized. In the next few pages I expand on Brown's concept to show that some traditions (particularly those with an outward theistic orientation) tend to give preference to the unfolding changes in the objective field of experience (i.e., fluctuations in state). While other traditions (typically those with a preference for an inward orientation) tend to focus more on the changes that occur to the subjective aspect of awareness (i.e., shifts in vantage point). These perspectival differences between giving reference to the "mind" perspective vs. the "event" perspective aren't hard and fast in the literature, but I do think that when we add such distinctions to the obvious culturally constructed aspects of spiritual experience, we can begin to answer why some surface descriptions from mystics of varying traditions can sound so different.

If we speculate as to why these preferences for either the objective field of experience or the source of awareness came to be in the first place, the answer seems rather obvious. Maps of spiritual development in theistic traditions develop either through a direct relationship with God (enacting a second-person perspective) or in contemplation about God (enacting a third-person perspective). Both of these orientations "set up" awareness from the very beginning so that attention is given to the changing field of objective experience. (For where else would God be?) This is quite a different biasing perspective than one that might come from an orientation wherein attention is put on the mind or the Self from a first-person perspective.

Ultimately, this new understanding teaches us that although two traditions might track stages of spiritual growth along similar deep structures (e.g., gross, subtle, causal), some might preference changing vantage points as they move through gross, subtle, causal, and nondual, while others might track the changes in the objective states as they move from gross to subtle to causal forms of union, communion, and identity with particular objects and events. Any Integral perspective ought to know how to distinguish between the biasing perspectives of various traditions and, as a result, track spiritual growth accordingly.

Let me offer two examples to ground the point about perspectival bias and to demonstrate how it shows up in the traditions. I'll begin with an example from the Christian contemplative tradition and then contrast it with an example from the Hindu Tantric tradition.

In her book *Mysticism*, Evylyn Underhill maps several stages of spiritual development as they unfold through stages according to a Christian biasing perspective. This means that not only will spiritual events be enacted accordingly to the culture and traditional teachings of Christianity but each event will also likely be enacted from either a second- or third-person perspective (union or communion) because of the outward orientation toward God. In other words, a Christian spiritual path will often focus on the changes that arise in the objective field of experience.

Underhill's map of spiritual development fits the hypothesis.

In her research, Underhill lists the stages of spiritual growth as: awakening, purification, illumination, dark night, unification. Although the subjective sense of self certainly goes through transformation, greater emphasis is given to the external objective side of awareness in each stage. Accordingly, each stage of growth shows consistently deeper access to the various realms of experience. Let's take a closer look.

The first two stages, including the processes she labels "awakening" and "purification," relate to adjustments in the objective field that arise in relation to gross-level thoughts and various objects of internal contemplation. Her third stage, illumination, deals with the changes that arise in the objective field of experience in the subtle realm during prayer or meditation. Most experiences here fall under the category I call "subtle communion" in chapter 4. Her fourth stage, dark night, is most closely related to changes that arise in a causal state during which nothing whatsoever arises and an individual is left in what is often described as the "Cloud of Unknowing."

Finally, in the final stage that Underhill calls unification, the individual soul and God unite in a "sacred marriage." It is important to remember, however, that in mystical traditions that hold a biasing perspective that relates to God as either the great "Thou" (second-person) or great "It" (third-person), the highest stage of realization is often not a shift to the "vantage point" of God (first-person) but rather one of union. Often this means a joining of the soul and God in an experience of complete union and not the realization of a nondual vantage point.[190] Underhill agrees with Ruysbroeck's perspective. She draws on it as she explains that her final stage of unification does not mean that one's identity *is* God. She writes: "Yet, the creature does not become God, for the union takes place in God through grace and our home-ward turning love: and therefore the creature in its inward contemplation feels a distinction and an otherness between itself and God."[191] (Now that we know vantage points and states can coexist, it is interesting to consider what a nondual vantage point in conjunction with a state of unification might be like.)

A second brief example from the Tantric Hindu tradition of Kashmir Saivism gives us a map against which we can juxtapose Underhill's work. Although objective changes are certainly mentioned and described as different levels of reality are "conquered," the main thrust of Columbia professor's Somadeva Vasudev work in the teachings of Malinivijayottaratantra traces the subjective aspect of awareness through seven vantage points. Vantage points are tracked along a subjective orientation to show that each new realization leads to a deeper level of identity. He refers to these vantage points as the "seven perceivers" and sometimes as the "seven experients." At the beginning of the meditative path in Kashmir Saivism, the "first perceiver" is totally identified with the body. The Malinivijayottaratantra calls this level of meditation the *sakala-experient*. Clearly this vantage point is closely related to the gross vantage point (awareness is confused with body and thought). In Vasudev's work, vantage points continue to deepen step by step through gross, subtle, causal, and witnessing vantage points until the final stages of meditation wherein the meditator is no longer exclusively identified with the body, sensory perception, the faculties of the mind, or even individual consciousness. Instead, at this final stage, awareness is first and foremost experienced as vast and infinite and the entirety of manifest existence exists within it. At this level of awareness, all of the normal operating systems of the mind have been dismantled and the meditator resides as what the Malinivijayottaratantra calls the *siva-experient*.[192] When the *siva-experient* is recognized as the source of awareness, it is equal to what we have been referring to as a nondual/ trans-dual vantage point.

In both the Christian and Hindu examples above, the stages of realization described in the tradition move from gross to subtle to causal levels of experience. The difference is that each approach is influenced by the biasing perspectives built into the philosophical training of the tradition. The Christian tradition, oriented first and foremost toward a second-person God, biases the objective field of experience (event perspective).[193] The tradition of Kashmir Saivism, oriented ultimately to the realization of one's true Self, gives preference to the subjective side of experience (mind perspective). Although this hypothesis is in only its nascent form, I suspect that this trend will hold true across other traditions as well. It is my hope that this deeper understanding of biasing perspectives in relation to the perspectival enaction in general and the distinction between vantage points and state/realm access in particular will begin to bring even more clarity to our attempts at comparative mysticism. (For an interesting case study that makes the hypothesis even more complex, see the example of Meister Eckhardt in the footnotes.)

Integral Participatory Enactment[194]

A second relevant topic in comparative mysticism needs to be highlighted before we close this chapter. Scholars often debate as to whether some "common core" mystical experiences are shared across traditions. In the West, we see arguments for deep structural similarities by scholars like William James and Walter Stace and, more recently, Houston Smith, Ken Wilber, and Daniel P. Brown.[195] Yet other scholars, Katz and Ferrer among them, argue that spiritual experiences are not universal.[196] They argue instead, as we shall see below, that claims to universal commonalities fall victim to modernist assumptions about some sort of fixed pre-given reality.

Because so much of the work in this book is aligned with Wilber and Brown and claims that there are indeed universal deep structures to the spiritual path that are the same across traditions (even as surface features continue to be different), the concept needs to be teased out so that the critiques of scholars like Ferrer and Katz can be adequately addressed. (For those less interested in this sort of academic, post-metaphysical justification, feel free to skip ahead to the next chapter.)

We'll first start with a few initial notes from Brown's work to set the tone and will then proceed to include some of the critiques of other scholars more directly. I'll close the chapter with several examples of how Wilber's line of thinking (which I follow closely) navigates the territory of critiques in a way that honors the type of postmodern nuance that Katz and Ferrer point to, while also allowing for a fuller, deeper, and wider Integral embrace.

In one of his early works Brown points out a prominent topic of debate in comparative mysticism:

> Anthropologists and historians of religion have been puzzled by the commonality in religious symbolism across cultures. For example, how is it that a similar experience of mystical light is reported by people of such different cultures and times as an eskimo shaman, a Tibetan Buddhist yogi and a Christian mystic? [197]

Answers to such questions from a predominantly modern era of scholarship suggested such experiences came from either some "ideal form" of reality or from some sort of cultural diffusion. Ideas that point toward a solution that is dependent on some ideal form assume that there is some sort of pre-given objective reality "out there" waiting to be uncovered. Those more prone to cultural diffusion theories suggest that the mystical experiences are similar because the experiences were transmitted from person to person and shared broadly across cultures. Brown comments on some of these early theories, showing that neither is very appealing:

> Eliade explains these similarities in terms of ideal patterns which periodically manifest themselves in particular historical forms. Adherents to a diffusion theory of anthropology might explain these similarities in terms of one or more points of cultural migration.

Neither of these approaches has been very successful.[198]

Instead of falling victim to these modern hypotheses, Brown draws on the very best of modern and postmodern scholarship and works his way beyond both while including their important contributions. In the following quote, notice how Brown manages to point toward the common underlying structures of perception to explain why experiences might be similar in different contexts:

> The concept of stage-specificity and level-specificity may be a viable alternative in the comparative study of religion. The "sacred" knowledge of religious experience may only be available in certain states of consciousness, induced by ritual and other means. For any discrete state of consciousness, the very interrelation of the categories of consciousness—attention, thinking perception, affect, self-system, reality-sense and time/space organization—may determine forms of knowledge regardless of culture. The eskimo shaman, Tibetan yogi and Christian contemplative may share common symbols of mystical light not because of cultural contact or some ideal pattern, but because they have induced a similar discrete state of consciousness, in which perception occurs as the experience of light. [199]

Even here in his early work, Brown points to the possibility of an underlying deep structure that might exist across traditions and cultures. As Brown suggests above, discrete states of consciousness might be universal according to the particular interaction of the various modes of perception, etc. To reiterate Brown's point, an experience of light might very well be related to a shift of perception that opens specific "forms of knowledge regardless of culture." In the language we have used thus far, we could say that certain shifts in perception open up access to the subtle realm. This "container" that we call the subtle realm and the extraordinary states of luminosity that can arise in it are available to all cultures and levels of development, and are accessible from any vantage point. With this line of thinking, we can base access to realms on particular interactive categories of perception that we all share as part of what it means to be a human being, rather than needing to depend on some sort of universal form that is pre-given. From this point of view, we understand that worlds are brought forth when certain dimensions of perception are seen through and rearranged.

Looking more specifically at the critiques, we notice that scholars like Katz are critical of claims to universal structures because experience is always "mediated." In other words, according to Katz constructivist approach, experience cannot be divorced from the matrix of linguistic and cultural factors in which the individual having the experience is embedded. Katz writes: "The experience itself as well as the form in which it is reported is shaped by concepts which the mystic brings to, and which shape, his experience."[200] As such, Katz argues, universal principles are simply inaccessible. In other words, this means that because the linguistic and cultural matrix of "mediation" is always in effect, and because this matrix will always result in a particular construction of reality, access to any sort of universal structure is impossible. (A form of LL reductionism.)

Almost thirty years ago, Brown was already intuiting an Integral level of development. Brown's approach included both linguistic and cultural concerns (in the LL), like that of Katz, as well as postulating the existence of deep universal structures (in the UL). First he explains the way he includes the constructivist aspects of mystical experience:

> Searching for common comparative categories for states of consciousness, need not however, negate the great culture-particularity of such experiences. For example, Wallace has studied the vast cultural differences in response to comparable dosages of hallucinogenic drugs in a subject

in a Western experimental laboratory and a member of an American Indian peyote cult. He believes that states of consciousness are "culturally patterned" so that not only their expression but the actual experience of the state may be different in different cultures.

Brown then goes on to show that simply because the experiences are culturally enacted doesn't exclude the fact that the experiences themselves are also part of inherent deep structures. He writes:

> Both positions, no doubt, contain some truth. A scholar of religion might search for common discrete states of consciousness behind religious experiences, while also identifying the unique culture-particular patterning of those states.[201]

Including both perspectives, Brown was one of the first researchers in the early 1980s to show the cross-cultural deep structures of the meditative path while simultaneously including the important point that all experiences will be conditioned by a biasing perspective.[202] From Wilber's Integral view, Brown was already intuiting the fact that the Four Quadrants tetra-arise.

An AQAL Approach to Comparative Mysticism

With Brown's insights in place as an initial framing, we can dive in to see more specifically how an Integral scholar might address issues in comparative mysticism using an AQAL (All Quadrants, All Levels, All Lines, All States, and All Types) approach. As Wilber so often articulates, an AQAL analysis argues first and foremost that "everyone is right." While maintaining this axiom, an AQAL approach also acknowledges that every view is also partial. (This, of course, holds true for my own Integral analysis.) An integral perspective that is driven by a hermeneutic of generosity, principles of nonexclusion, enfoldment, and enactment, and a careful consideration of what Wilber calls the "calculus of torment" (enacting the solution that causes the least pain), allows us to honor and respect the great thinkers that have come before us. [203] Rather than undervaluing the insights of earlier scholars due to their modern proclivities that now might be seen as partial, and rather than some sort of ego-glorification that is in the end only self-serving, an Integral scholar holds earlier perspectives in a loving embrace and honors them for everything that they bring to the table. The Integral scholar knows full and well that many of these earlier orientations provide critical lower rungs on a ladder that lead to higher levels of understanding.

In this light and in the context of comparative mysticism, Wilber's Integral framework allows us to include the important elements of constructivist scholars like Katz, but it simultaneously helps us to avoid the forms of postmodern reductionism to which scholars of his ilk far too often fall victim. Using the Integral model, we can allow for the existence of both universal structures (i.e., deep structures) and the fact that each of those deep structures will be brought forth according to the particular differences that arise in the AQAL matrix (i.e., surface difference).

For starters, an Integral analysis notes the fact that the Four Quadrants (introduced in chapter 1) are always at play. With this realization, we understand from the very beginning that of course, there are elements of Katz's strict constructivist argument that are accurate and true. Experience is mediated in certain ways by the cultural and linguistic matrices of which we are most certainly a part. This is information gained through inclusion of the LL quadrant.

However, an Integral analysis doesn't stop there. Including, the other three quadrants prevents us from reducing everything to culturally specific and culturally determined causes (Quadrant Absolutism). Accordingly, we acknowledge that social and systemic conditions in the LR quadrant also play a role in influencing the enactment of a given experience. In a similar way, we understand that in the UR quadrant there are certain elements, like the EEG readings of specific brain states or interactions of particular neurotransmitters, that will remain constant and universal across cultures as the exterior correlates to interior experiences. (See the work of Newberg in appendix 1).

Finally, and perhaps most importantly for our work here, including the UL quadrant we are able to acknowledge that our subjective experience includes underlying, and invariant structures, vantage points, and states. This means that there are invariant structures of consciousness (increasing lenses of complexity) that humans move through regardless of culture. There are systematic ways that vantage points can be revealed along a shared spectrum of spiritual depth.

There are shared containers of experience (realms) within which particular types of experience can arise (states). All of these deep structures in the UL quadrant are universal regardless of culture. As such each category helps us to more clearly define the Great Human Tradition. Taking all four quadrants together, we avoid reductionism while still allowing the fact that reality is enacted. Enacted not just in a simplistic postmodern way that includes differences in culture, linguistic matrix, and the like (in the LL), but enacted in a way that also acknowledges multiple levels of reality according to structures, vantage points, and states/realms (UL), as well as systemic and social influences (in the LR), and biological/neurological factors (UR).

Participatory Enactment

A second type of critique is sometimes made of models that assert universal deep structures. It is here within the context of this second criticism that the brilliance of the Integral lens truly begins to shine. Some brief historical context is helpful before diving into the issue fully.

For most of modern history, claims to a universal spiritual path have been asserted. These claims are often associated with perennial philosophers like Huxley and Lovejoy who contend that reality is composed of some variation of "the great chain of being." Jorge Ferrer is one scholar in particular who brings a strong critique against perennialists.[204] Among other things, he argues that because perennialism necessarily posits a pre-given reality it (1) falls victim to what Wilfred Sellars called "the myth of the given" and (b) preferences certain spiritual insights (i.e., nondual) over others. To this point Ferrer writes:

> Assuming a pre-given ultimate reality, perennialism regards the variety of contemplative goals (unio mystica, moksa, sunyata, theoria, nirvana, devekut, kaivalyam, etc.) as different interpretations, dimensions, or levels of a single spiritual ultimate. Then, while ecumenically claiming to honor all those truths, perennialism consistently grades spiritual insights and traditions according to how closely they approach or represent this pregiven spiritual reality (e.g., nondual traditions over dual ones, monistic over

theistic, impersonal over personal, etc.).[205]

Always employing a hermeneutic of generosity and love, one of the first things any Integral scholar would point out in regards to Ferrer's critique is that just as religious traditions are brought forth according to the developmental level of the person enacting them, so too interpretations of the perennial philosophy are brought forth according to various developmental levels. This means that there is not just one version of the perennial philosophy but that there are as many interpretations as developmental levels. Modern versions of the perennial philosophy, along with postmodern versions and Integral versions, are fully allowed to exist as stations of interpretation. However, to confuse one level of interpretation with another or to confuse one level of interpretation with the whole of it is a grave error. In almost all of Ferrer's work (at least in the pieces I have seen) instead of using his postmodern lens to critique a postmodern interpretation of the perennial philosophy, Ferrer uses his postmodern lens to correct a modern version of universal claims. Instead of recognizing that interpretations of the perennial philosophy continue into postmodern, Integral structure-stages and beyond, Ferrer confuses its modern variation with the whole of its universal claims. This is a classic level fallacy. If Ferrer was to tackle a postmodern or Integral version of perennialism he would have no luck finding the same modern mistakes.

With this developmental clarity in place, an Integral scholar would quickly agree with Ferrer's work regarding participatory spirituality "as far as it goes." The modern variation of the perennial philosophy, like nearly all modern epistemologies, does indeed fall victim to the "myth of the given." As such, Ferrer's postmodern corrections, when applied to modern interpretations of the perennial philosophy, hold weight and are valid. A similar type of critique of early modern interpretations of the perennial philosophy can be found in Brown's work as well. Brown explains that his conclusions "are nearly the opposite for that of the stereotyped notion of the [modern] perennial philosophy according to which many spiritual paths are said to lead to the same end." As we shall see below, when Brown's notion of a biasing perspective and the entire AQAL matrix are taken into account in the context of an evolving and emergent universe, an updated version of the perennial philosophy does not claim a pre-given reality but rather one that has emergent deep structures that are enacted through participation, transcending and including aspects of

Ferrer's position that are useful, while jettisoning those aspects that do not apply. This means that the arrows that Ferrer shoots end up missing the mark when the perennial philosophy is enacted by a postmodern or post-postmodern lens.

How does a post-postmodern version of the perennial philosophy avoid falling victim to postmodern critiques? Proceeding with our hermeneutic of generosity and care, an Integral perspective includes Ferrer's desire to ensure we allow for experience to be participatory while simultaneously ensuring that certain universals stay valid through a more developed form of enactment. As such, the most fundamental point to consider is that a post-postmodern version of the perennial philosophy does not posit a pre-given reality. From this deeper and wider Integral view, it is quite clear that spiritual experience is not discovering a pre-given reality but rather that the reality is coevolved through participatory engagement overtime. In other words, reality is a process that is both creative and generative while it simultaneously builds upon the past.

Wilber explains this process brilliantly through his concepts of "kosmic grooves" and "kosmic habits." Each new unfolding in the universe is a composition of historical habit and emergent novelty. Wilber sometimes calls these dimensions "karma and creativity." This means that overtime kosmic habits have built up, and have begun to erode deeper grooves in the Kosmos. These grooves exist today not because they were set in an ideal form in some sort of *a priori* fashion (as modernists would have it) but because they emerge in time and are co-created through participation. This means that today, the stages of development from magic to mythic to rational to pluralistic "appear" pre-given not because they are uncovered and somehow laid down prior to creation but rather because they have become deep grooves with morphic fields. Following this line of thought, any updated version of spiritual claims to universals ought to point out, as Wilber does eloquently, that there is a greater degree of freedom in those grooves that are new and fresh (Integral) than in those grooves that are deeper (mythic). This means that at the very leading edge of evolutionary consciousness, there is an astonishing amount of freedom. At this leading edge, the interior and exterior of individuals and collectives synchronistically enact a co-creative reality that has never existed before. Just as these patterns hold true for emergent structures that now "appear" pre-given, similar occurrences have arisen over time with regard to vantage points and access to states/realms.

With Ferrer's first concern that all perennial philosophies assert a "pre-given reality" now adequately addressed, let's examine his claim that perennial philosophies preference certain insights (i.e., Eastern claims to non-duality) over others. Let's look again at Ferrer's main critique. He writes:

> Hierarchical arrangements of spiritual insights.... heavily depend on the assumption of a universal and pregiven spiritual ultimate relative to which such judgments can be made. To put it another way, these interreligious judgments make sense only if we first presuppose one or another version of the Myth of the Given, and/or the existence of a single noumenal reality behind the multifarious spiritual experiences and doctrines. Whenever we drop these assumptions, however, the very idea of ranking traditions according to a paradigmatic standpoint becomes both fallacious and superfluous. Do not misunderstand me. I am not suggesting that spiritual insights and traditions are incommensurable, but merely that it may be seriously misguided to compare them according to any pre-established spiritual hierarchy.[206]

As we saw above, it is true that modern approaches to perennial philosophy depended largely on a pre-given reality and, as such, are rightly dismantled by a postmodern critique. However, this is not the case when we include versions of the perennial philosophy (or any other philosophy claiming universals) that emerge from higher structures of consciousness.

This brings us directly to Ferrer's second concern regarding hierarchical arrangements of spiritual insights. (In dismantling the first half of Ferrer's argument above, Ferrer's platform for concern around judgment falls away. The establishment of kosmic grooves in time, rather than eternal and outside of time, provides the backdrop against which experience can be judged and ranked. In service of a full articulation, I'll address notions of "ranking" in one more sweep in order to make sure it is clear how universal claims can be entirely legitimate.) A deeper, wider, and more evolved articulation of the perennial philosophy does not assert a pre-given reality outside of time. It can instead show that spiritual realities have emerged *in time*. Because these realities have emerged in time, some of them have laid deep enough grooves that they "appear" to be invariant because of history. These apparently invariant deep structures provide the backdrop against which we can today pass judgments on which levels of realization are more advanced than others.[207] Using this logic, we can clearly see that nondual realizations transcend and include dualistic ones. Understanding kosmic grooves and using the Four Quadrants we can see that there is a natural hierarchy (or holarchy) of what Wilber calls "enfoldment" in specific areas of spiritual development in all of our world's traditions. I'll offer several examples.

With regard to structures (view), we see that interpretations that are rational/modern transcend and include interpretations that are expounded using a traditional mythic or magic lens. These are differentiations that evolved in time. Each new structural emergent grew out of the previous. Today, because these grooves have been laid down over time, they appear to be invariant, whereas the leading edge is only now emerging. In a similar way, if one has realized a vantage point beyond time (ever-present witness) then this means that as long as conditions are healthy such a realization is also beyond confusion with thoughts or personality. Each deeper vantage point transcends, includes, and penetrates the shallower identities. These vantage points progressively opened up over time, in time. They now appear as invariant state-stages, not as a result of a pregiven reality but because of emergent kosmic grooves. Trained access to states and realms hold the same patterns of enfoldment. An individual will normally gain full access to the subtle realm prior to gaining full access to the causal realm, etc. (It is worth noting that at least with vantage points and states these dimensions might in fact be part of a pre-given reality laid down in involution, however, with a post-metaphysical approach, we don't need to lean on the metaphysical baggage to make it true. So whether or not they are or are not pre-given is irrelevant. We can prove the same point in support of universal, invariant deep structures without the need for these types of broad metaphysical claims.)

As long as we look at specific areas of growth in specific contexts (i.e., vantage point development, structural development, or intentional access states) we can accurately show how traditions line up against each other (see appendix 2). Again, to reinforce the point above, this is done not against some pre-given background as a modernist might claim but rather against the emergent background of evolutionarily co-created kosmic grooves.[208] In this way, we can indeed pass judgments and rank the insights of the traditions, But we do so from within the same "worldspace" or "horizon" in which the assertions originally arose. Per usual, Wilber articulates the process of Integral analysis from this level with elegance:

> The integral claim is simply this: we accept ALL of [Ferrer's] type of pluralistic approach, *as far as it goes*. Of course you start with a caring hermeneutic within the horizons of that which is acceptable to the Other. Of course you do not attempt to impose meta-narratives on the Other that the Other would not impose on itself. Of course caring dialogue is the beginning of any sort of dialogical understanding. Of course there are a series of multifocal, heterogeneous discourses that cannot be meta-narrated. Of course hermeneutic enactments are grounded in participatory intersubjectivity and not intra-personal empiricism. In this academic day and age, *all of that truly goes without saying*.[209]

Following this line of thought, we see that an Integral approach introduces a form of post-postmodern participatory enactment, that honors Ferrer's position as far as it is accurate but then also transcends it in a deeper embrace. Wilber writes:

> With the dialogical cooperation of participatory subjects sharing the hermeneutic of their worldviews within the horizon of their own self-understanding (thus avoiding metanarratives), we follow these worldviews over time and space; we do a genealogy *from within* the unfolding waves. That helps all parties mutually trace a dialectic of historical unfolding, watching both the good news and the bad news of any unfolding wave of intersubjectivity, subjectivity, objectivity, and interobjectivity—which are simply the dimensions vibrating from within the horizon of enacted, co-created worldviews.... Both new differentiations and new dissociations; both new integrations and new fusions; both new expanses of increasing care and compassion; and new ways to be mean and shallow, all unfold to the hermeneutic, dialogical eye once it is cut loose from a stagnant hermeneutic of de facto stationary pluralism and set free to roam the halls of history, time, genealogy,

unfolding, temporality. Far from a static flatland horizon of fixed and rigid authentic ultimates, which does not honor the Other but cripples the Other in its temporality, the dialectical, dialogical, genealogical hermeneutic honors the Other as it sees itself unfolding over the ever-surprising new horizons of a flowering, flourishing, effervescent, historically anchored world.[210]

When analysis is conducted in this way, using an Integral approach, we are able to pass judgments openly, honestly, (without trying to hide them in performative contradiction as most postmodernists do), while engaging those judgments with as much compassion as possible.[211] Wilber points to the ways in which the inclusion of history and evolution allows us to see clearly that judgments are not only a natural and *true* part of the evolutionary process but also *good* and *beautiful*:

In short, pluralism plus history is genealogy. The greatest of the postmodernists all knew this, and whether they saw history as obscuring Being or releasing Being, they all intuited the basic fact that history passes judgments, from within, on its own self-enacted worldviews—how else could the postmodernists themselves (correctly!) condemn patriarchy, slavery, female oppression, and so on? Of course genealogy is capable of passing judgments! Of course slavery and freedom are not two equally valid spiritual ultimates![212]

In an analogous fashion, of course the beauty of *liberation into the whole of unbounded reality* as a nondual vantage point is not an equal spiritual ultimate to and being exclusively identified with a shallower sense of awareness! Of course absolute realizations and relative realizations are not the equal. The former is radical trans-dual freedom the latter is dualistic confusion! This is not a pre-existing claim but an emergent evolutionary reality available to every human being today in a way that appears universal and invariant.

It shall only be through this type of vital Integral discernment that the future will be created in all its goodness and freedom, fully possible for all.

Summary

This chapter not only introduced the three-vector Spiritual Development Cube (state-stages, structure-stages, and states) but also gave several examples of how it might be used and implemented. In the second half of the chapter I showed how the maps provided by Brown, Wilber, as well as the ones offered in this book, suggest universal deep structures while simultaneously acknowledging and accounting for postmodern concerns. I'd like to take a moment to summarize this second half so that its major points can be continually digested.

With a deeper Integral understanding, the universal claims I make in this book do not fall victim to the "myth of the given." Nor do they rely on any sort of metaphysical assertions. The approaches discussed here are indeed participatory in nature but simultaneously go beyond common postmodern participatory claims to include important Integral distinctions; namely, the fact that participatory enactment is an AQAL affair (Wilber) and that cross-cultural, invariant deep structures of meditative practice can indeed be tracked across cultures (Brown).

As Wilber helped us to clearly outline, these deep common structures are not some sort of pre-given reality, thus falling victim to the myth of the given, but are rather inherited kosmic habits that arise as evolutionary emergents. That is to say, even if early structures, and vantage points "appear" to be pre-given when they manifest today, they are actually more like morphic spiritual grooves that have been laid down over time. The longer the deep structural groove has been around, the deeper it cuts. The deeper the groove cuts, the less freedom for variance exists. The less freedom for variance, the more these grooves appear to be pre-given when looking back at the possible tracks of developmental unfolding available to humanity right now. This means that hierarchical ranking judgments can indeed be made against various spiritual insights in particular contexts around particular content precisely because they can be compared against the backdrop of deep grooves that have been inherited through evolutionary time.

This long-term, "deep time" vision allows us to see that at the leading edge, in those circumstances wherein grooves have not yet been laid, creativity and potentiality is at its maximum. It is here at the leading edge of vantage point development and structural development that the involutionary manifestation is enacted in real time. Spirit reaches down into causal potential, which reaches down into the subtle ideation, which then reaches down into its manifestation of pure creativity, all in the flash of a single instant. This dynamic is the key to the type of conscious evolution I introduce in chapter 7. This is our destiny as human beings.

Deep structures, thus described, allow us to resurrect the use of developmental paradigms (through vantage points, structures, and the cultivation of states/realm access) while simultaneously holding carefully and addressing the important critiques of the postmodern scholarship. Successfully articulating this sort of post-postmodern, universal, cross-cultural map offered in the first three vectors of spiritual development sets the stage for an Integral age.

PART 3: The Great Human Tradition
in an Integral Age

Chapter 6
Magnetizing the Great Human Tradition

With the details of an Integral framework explicated, we can now begin to analyze the importance of this kind of work. Why is spiritual development important? What are the implications of a deeper understanding of vantage points, structure-stages, and states? Is there any heuristic or pragmatic value in having a better understanding of how spiritual development unfolds? If the Integral model can indeed describe spiritual experience and development in a way fit to serve the Great Human Tradition, what are the benefits we might expect? Here, in chapter 6, I use an Integral lens to highlight several of the positive benefits that are likely to emerge if Integral Theory were adopted and applied to help individuals and collectives orient more fully toward our shared spiritual potential.

In this chapter, I examine some of the immediate ways that an Integral model of spiritual development might bring value to both personal and collective spheres. As we shall see, a better understanding of spiritual development and the emergence of the Great Human Tradition that it serves to liberate resurrects latent potentials for prosperity, happiness, and transformation both individually and collectively.

Why Is Understanding Spiritual Development Important?

It is true that maps are not replacements for practice. However, better maps can and do lead to better navigation of unknown lands. Just as a traveler in foreign territory will have better luck reaching the destination with a more accurate map, so too will a spiritual practitioner be more prepared for the journey if he or she has a foundational theoretical understanding of the path. When these foundational elements are more fully understood and articulated, we have a real opportunity to synthesize the wisdom streams of planet Earth into a single, trans-lineage human tradition. For these reasons alone, understanding spiritual development is vital to both our current well-being and our successful transition into a better future.

Beyond successful navigation and the emergence of a truly universal understanding of spirituality, applying the Integral model to spiritual growth has the potential to lead to other important personal and collective benefits. Individually, spirituality can help to increase human happiness and well-being. Collectively, a clearer model of spiritual development has the potential to catalyze positive social transformation.

Individual and Collective Benefits of Understanding Vantage Points (State-Stages)

As awareness shifts (or, more accurately, *appears* to shift) to a source beyond the vehicle of personal identity, one is significantly released from the confines and restrictions of everyday unhappiness that tend to result from the unfulfilled desires, wants, and needs of the personality. This release from unhappiness leads to the realization of an identity that is always already satisfied and content.

Just as a clearer articulation of vantage point development will enable individuals to benefit through increasing each person's potential for happiness, humanity as a collective stands to benefit as well. An improved understanding of vantage point development will enable the systemic changes needed to better usher individuals through the stages of spiritual realization from gross identity, to subtle identity, to causal identity, to a witness identity, to a nondual identity. When individuals, all living beyond an exclusive identification with the egoic personality, come together in a shared commitment to creating the future and healing the structures of the past, the stage is set for a truly enlightened culture to emerge.

With a deeper appreciation of vantage points, the positive potential for collective transformation is nearly endless. In the public sphere, nonreligious and appropriately secular teachings that take a psychological approach to human possibility are likely to emerge.

Using these secular teachings, public and private schools might begin to design curriculums that not only help children to "grow up" (through the stages-structural development) but also to "wake up" (through the stages of identity shift that result from vantage point development).[213] In the religious sphere, leaders across various traditions might begin to include teachings about vantage point development in weekly sermons, offering contemplative practices from their own traditions to help individuals progress through the various identity shifts.

Major roles in political and economic spheres are also likely to change when a deeper understanding of vantage points finds even more solid footing. As more leaders experience and value shifts in identity away from an individually oriented awareness and into a nondual vantage point, the boundary between self and other will begin to dissolve—in its place, a desire to do what is best for the whole naturally begins to emerge. This means that political and economic leaders who have transcended their own ego and personal identification to significant degrees are likely to curb decision-making based on their own short-term financial or electoral aspirations. Instead, they are likely to make decisions based on the type of long-term thinking that is in the interest of their company, country, and/or planet as a whole. In his book, *Not-Two Is Peace,* spiritual teacher Adi Da moves along similar lines as he explains what a world, based on "prior unity," might look like. (We will explore several specific examples along these lines later with regard to what I call the Bright Alliance.)

Individual and Collective Benefits of Understanding Spiritual Intelligence (Structure-Stages)

A more complex understanding of spiritual development allows us to see how the particular structural lens and context through which we *view* reality affects what we are able to see. A change in context often correlates to a change in worldview along a developmental spectrum.

One easy way to incorporate an understanding of spiritual intelligence is through the use of three different types of strucutral shifts: (1) egocentric to ethnocentric, (2) ethnocentric to world-centric, and (3) world-centric to kosmo-centric. These shifts are all part of a developmental process. In each shift, the meaning that individual derives from one stage is transcended by the new. Just as with all healthy developmental sequences, even as the new stage emerges, the core elements of the previous stage remain intact and are included. For instance, as one moves from egocentric to ethnocentric, healthy care and concern for oneself, developed at the egocentric stage, remains. Only now, egocentric desires are recontextualized within a larger worldview. The same is true for each subsequent contextual stage. In some cases, an experience of a change in context may be so powerful that an individual's life purpose can be transformed. A change in developmental context that also aligns with a change in purpose and direction in an individual's life often results in a significant increase in everyday happiness.[214][215]

In the collective sphere, a better understanding of spiritual intelligence will allow us to liberate religious interpretation beyond its traditional forms. One of the most exciting clarifications made first by Wilber and continued in my own work (see volume 2 – *Evolution's Ally*) is that an Integral understanding now allows us to instigate a rejuvenation of spirituality so that new and more mature forms of spiritual intelligence can exist alongside rationality and science. With an improved understanding of the stages of spiritual intelligence and the various levels of religious orientation, we have the opportunity to resurrect spirituality, returning it to a prominent and respected place in modern society. New versions of spirituality (based on evidence and injunctions at a rational stage, cross-cultural analysis at a pluralistic stage, and intuitive pattern-recognition at an Integral stage) can and ought to exist alongside a scientific paradigm. The fact that many of today's spiritual systems, already equipped with multiple technologies for human happiness, have been relegated to the sidelines is nothing less than a cultural disaster. Once religion and spirituality are released from their mythic and magic baggage, we can start to design collective systems that better value the role of spirituality in everyday life. The model of spiritual development expounded in this book creates the conditions for us to update religious traditions to meet the requirements of current modern, postmodern, and Integral worldviews.[216][217]

In sum, if these higher stages of spiritual intelligence are embraced, we will be poised to exit the spiritual void in which we now find ourselves. If successful, we will move from our current paradigm wherein there exist only limited expressions of mature spiritual intelligence and into an age wherein spiritual intelligence is liberated to help guide our decisions and direction.

It is my contention that a true second enlightenment cannot

fully manifest unless we include both reason and spirit side by side. This means that a second enlightenment is not something of mere history, associated with the renaissance, but also something that we can all help to create today and into the future. The Great Human Tradition liberates spiritual intelligence up the spectrum of development to allow us all to consciously engage in creating a future rich in values and potential. With a full recognition of spiritual intelligence, we have the opportunity to bring light into our current dark age.

Individual and Collective Benefits of Understanding States

Spiritual systems contain within them technologies to help individuals generate positive orientations to their experience. Gratitude, compassion, humility, and integrity are all qualities that can be cultivated and nourished through spiritual technologies. (All of these qualities can, of course, be nourished without spirituality as well.) In more extraordinary scenarios, spiritual technologies help to cultivate states that dramatically transform one's field of experience. One can gain the capacity for *vision* into and experience of fields of pure love or bliss, or similarly, complete stillness, void of disturbing or agitating thoughts.[218] As we have seen, these states can also include incredible experiences of gross, subtle, and causal communion, union, and identity. Each of these states has the capacity to enhance human life.

Along similar lines, vision, extending from gross to subtle to causal, allows individuals to begin exploring multiple realms of existence. When vision is no longer limited to the gross waking experience, lucid dreaming, lucid sleeping, and exploration of the various subtle and causal realms of existence become common experience. As state and realm access is cultivated, one gains new sources of happiness heretofore yet unrealized. The potential of penetrating into multiple realms of reality simultaneously or at will provides nearly infinite possibility.

Collective benefits are also likely to result on multiple levels in proportion with greater state cultivation. As a clearer and more comprehensive understanding of states of experience increase, new technologies are sure to emerge that base their models on a multidimensional reality. It is likely that some of these technologies will include new capacities to help shift experience through gross, subtle, and causal realms.

Some models that employ state and realm technology, like *Theory U* developed by MIT lecturer Otto Scharmer, are already gaining momentum within both academic and business institutions. Scharmer's model induces a new mode of collective problem solving. By taking groups through a cycle of states, tracking from gross to subtle to causal back to subtle and back to gross, the *Theory U* process results in emergent solutions that come from exposure to alternate states.

It is also likely that cultivation of states will result in a transformation of our shared views about reality. As new realms of experience are legitimated by more people, the accepted lens of reality is sure to expand. That means that our current models of existence that tend to include only one realm of experience (gross), are likely to broaden to include subtle and causal realms of experience as well. Not only will these changes in experience (in the Upper Left) mean advances in technologies that tap subtle and causal energy (in the Upper Right), but it may even mean that we begin to live consciously with shared values (Lower Left) and social systems (Lower Right) in multiple levels of reality at once. Coming to articulate the Great Human Tradition, using the three vectors of spiritual development as its base, could lead us in this direction.

In summary, the benefits of understanding spiritual growth are poised to impact both individual and collective spheres.

The Benefits of Understanding and Encouraging Spiritual Development

Vector of Spiritual Growth	Individual Benefits	Collective Benefits
Spiritual Realization (state-stages)	Shift beyond Exclusive Identification with the Ego	Enlightened Culture
Spiritual Intelligence (structures)	Shift in Context and Purpose	Transcendence of the Modern Dark Age
Spiritual Cultivation (states)	Shift in Quality of Experience	Expansion into Multiple Realms of Reality

Figure 23: The individual and collective benefits of understanding and encouraging spiritual development through a three-vector Integral lens

Figure 23 helps to summarize and correlate the three elements of spiritual development with the various areas of individual and collective benefit that is to be expected if each domain is fully honored.

Chapter 7
Evolving Together

As we have seen, understanding the differences between state-stages, structure-stages, and states lays the foundation for a deeper recognition of our Great Human Tradition. In addition, coming to know and stand in our trans-lineage river of human wisdom provides a possibility for all of us to unite in the active participation of what has come to be called "conscious evolution". This chapter continues to take our discussion out of the UL quadrant and further into a full quadrant contemplation.

The Two Streams of Conscious Evolution

The term *evolution* is used in many spiritual circles today. Often, however, individuals fail to clarify the type of evolution to which they are referring. Depending on the cultural matrix you find yourself in, you may hear the terms "the evolution of consciousness" among friends and community. Or perhaps even you may be guilty of saying colloquially that "[he or she] is really evolved." One point addressed implicitly thus far, but worth noting explicitly, is an important distinction between two general types of evolution: (1) the evolution of complexity and (2) the evolution of identity.[219] I call these the *path of creativity* and the *path of remembrance*, respectively. The evolution of complexity refers to the creative emergence of relative reality in time as structure-stages are laid down by the leading edges of consciousness and culture. The evolution of identity refers to the path by which the individual self traces its way back up the involutionary ladder to discover identity as the Absolute Self. We'll look at the evolution of complexity and its relationship to the Great Human Tradition first.

Evolution of Complexity

Up until this point, most of the discussion regarding evolution has centered on an UL approach. I begin here with the inclusion of a few other quadrants to balance out the general view of evolution. In its most common usage, the term evolution usually refers to the development of biological species over time that result from Darwin's proposed theory of natural selection. With this understanding, species are understood to have emerged over the course of millions of years here on Earth. Over the course of time, as life progressed from eukaryotes to multi-cellular life, to animals and eventually humans, evolution was directional. We see clearly that evolution moved from levels of less complexity to greater complexity, as well as from levels of less organization toward greater organization.[220] For example, it takes more complexity and self-organization for the emergence of a dolphin than it does for the emergence of a jellyfish. Each stage of emergence is a creative step into novelty.

As Wilber has so brilliantly articulated in his book *Sex, Ecology, Spirituality,* the same patterns of evolution (increasing complexity and increasing self-organization) hold true for external systems and modes of production (LR) as well. For example, foraging humans existed before humans who based their sustenance on horticulture. Horticultural societies existed before agrarian cultures. Agrarian cultures emerged before industrial societies, and industrial societies before information networks (see figure 24 below), etc. Again each new stage is a creative step forward that builds upon the past.

Every new level of systemic emergence represents a greater capacity for self-organization that transcends and includes the levels of evolution that preceded it. In a similar way, each new level of complexity depends (at least in part) upon the lower structure for its sustenance and survival. This means that each stage is both whole in itself and simultaneously part of a larger whole.[221] [222] Wilber follows Arthur Koestler's lead and uses the term holarchy to describe this phenomenon of nested hierarchies. A holarchy is a natural hierarchy composed of holons. A holon is both whole in itself and a part of a larger whole.

These same external processes of biological evolution (UR) and systemic evolution (LR) have correlates in the internal spheres of existence. Consciousness and culture also move through similar progressions of greater and greater complexity, greater creativity, and greater levels of self-organization. As I have articulated, spiritual intelligence (UL) progresses through structure-stages of increasing capacity (from magic to mythic to rational to pluralistic to Integral). Each new stage builds on its predecessor. Cultural complexity in the LL evolves in a similar way.[223] In short, the evolution of complexity occurs in all Four Quadrants; relative reality terta-evolves. Figure 24 below offers Wilber's graphic representation of the multiple domains of evolution. Today, pioneers at the leading edge push forward into new levels of novelty in all Four Quadrants. This is the evolution of complexity. This is the path of creativity.

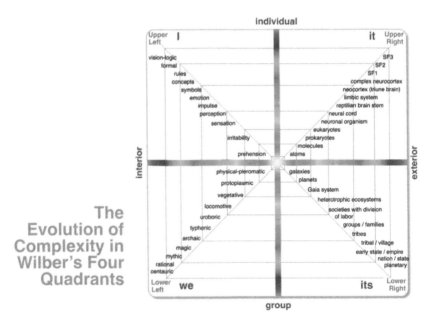

Figure 24: The evolution of complexity in Wilber's Four Quadrants (adapted from Wilber's *Sex, Ecology, Spirituality*)

An understanding of the evolution of complexity through structure-stages is one of the fundamental truths uncovered by the West. Seeing tetra-evolution as a comprehensive whole through all Four Quadrants at once (shown above in figure 24) is one of the gifts we inherit from Wilber. The evolution of complexity through the Four Quadrants is important and ought to be acknowledged in any Great Human Tradition.

Evolution of Identity

The term evolution is also used in a second and distinct way. In addition to describing the evolution of complexity, the term evolution can also refer to the evolution of consciousness as it moves through the series of vantage points to greater and greater depths of awakening. As one evolves from a smaller, individual sense of self to a larger, all embracing Absolute Self, I call this the evolution of identity. Each new vantage point of identity deconstructs as aspect of relative reality.

When properly understood, the evolution of identity retraces the path of involution back to its unitive nondual source. In the evolution of identity, subjectivity shifts from gross to subtle to causal to witness to nondual unbounded wholeness.[224] [225] Each new vantage point transcends, includes and penetrates the shallower identity. This means, as we have seen, as identity shifts beyond its exclusive identification with the ego, the ego doesn't cease to exist, rather it is simply made an object of awareness that is then included within a new sphere of subjectivity. Like the evolution of complexity, the evolution of identity is also holarchical in nature.

Healthy and Unhealthy Evolution

Each type of evolution has healthy and unhealthy forces of eros and agape that influence it. It is helpful to distinguish the difference between these forces that we can better comprehend what constitutes healthy and pathological variations of evolution. A graphic helps to visualize these important nuances. Figure 25 below shows both types of evolution, as well as the healthy and unhealthy versions of eros and agape that influence each.

Two Types of Evolution
Healthy and Unhealthy Eros/Agape

Type of Evolution	Healthy Eros	Healthy Agape	Unhealthy Eros	Unhealthy Agape
Evolution of Complexity through Structure-Stages (Altitude)	Higher Levels of Transcendence, Creativity, and Self-Organization in Relative Reality	Responsibility for Sustaining Lower Structures	Transcendence Without Inclusion and Care for Lower Structures	Regression/ Devolution
Evolution of Identity through State-Stages (Vantage Points)	Deeper Levels of Transcendence through the Deconstruction of Relative Reality to its Absolute Base	Compassion through Conscious Self-Contraction	Transcendence Without Penetration through Shallower Vantage Points	Unconscious Self-Contraction

Figure 25: The two types of evolution and their corresponding healthy and unhealthy Eros and Agape

Healthy eros in the evolution of complexity influences the movement to higher levels of creative emergence and self-organization. Unhealthy forms of eros in the evolution of complexity transcend current structures but fail to preserve the important aspects of the lower structures.

Healthy agape within the evolution of complexity is the perpetual movement to preserve and nurture all that has come before. This may include the various ways to heal and mend broken aspects of lower structures. Unhealthy agape within the evolution of complexity is a movement from greater levels of complexity and self-organization to lesser. When unhealthy forms of agape are present we call it regression or devolution.

Healthy eros in the evolution of identity is the movement of identity to deeper and deeper levels of transcendence. This process unfolds as the self begins to deconstruct relative reality to its absolute base. Unhealthy forms of eros in the evolution of identity is a movement that successfully transcends shallower levels of identity (e.g., state-stages identified with thought, personality, time/space), but fails to affirm lower identities as relatively real. Another way of saying this is that in unhealthy forms of eros in the evolution of identity, deeper vantage points fail to penetrate lower identities (gross, subtle, causal, etc.). This can result in the type of nondual reductionism discussed in chapter 2.

Healthy forms of agape in the evolution of identity allow the process of involution/self contraction to unfold consciously. (The vow of the kosmic bodhisattva.) An awakened individual who has mastered the capacity for conscious self-contraction anchors awareness in a nondual vantage point (or the highest vantage point that he or she has attained), then allows his or her lower levels of mind to contract through the process of involution without getting lost and deluded by the apparent successive unfolding of dualistic identities. It is through allowing all lower identities to be open that an awakened being can serve most effectively in the dualistic world. This force is driven by compassion to serve in relative reality. Unhealthy influences of agape result in unconscious self-contraction. This is like falling down the involutionary ladder into relative reality. When unhealthy forms of agape are present, relative reality is mistaken as absolute reality and liberation is lost. (This is the condition of most of humanity.)

The distinction between the evolution of complexity and the evolution of identity is critical for a deep understanding of the Great Human Tradition. Far too often, as we'll see below in the discussion on conscious evolution, the term evolution is used to refer to both of these types of development without distinction.[226]

Together

How do we consciously evolve through complexity and identity together? How can we support each other and mutually enrich the path of creativity and the path of remembrance as a community?

A "We" Line of Development

Gardner's concept of multiple intelligences and Wilber's notion of lines of development suggest that we each have different levels of structure-stage development across different capacities. One might be highly cognitively developed but poorly morally developed. Or one might have a high level of moral intelligence but a low level of kinesthetic intelligence. Thus far in this book, we examined structure-stages with reference to spiritual intelligence (chapter 3). I speculate that alongside the spiritual line of intelligence there is also a brand-new line of development just breaking the surface of consciousness at this particular time in our evolution. I call it a "We" intelligence. Just as we can train other lines of intelligence to increase our skills and capacities, the "We" line of development is something that we must train through collective engagement in order to be more aware of its various dimensions.

In his various writings, Wilber makes the point clear: "the "We" (or Lower Left Quadrant) has always existed." So it is important that we ask: "What makes this sort of "We" intelligence different now at this time in history? What makes this particular area of growth an evolutionary emergent?" In my opinion, what is occurring now, and what I point to when I speak about a "We" intelligence is not just the fact that a "We" exists, vis-a-vis Wilber, rather I point to the fact that we are only now gaining a self-reflective capacity to be self-conscious of the "We". Each of us has a different internal barometer that allows us to sense into a "We" space. This internal barometer develops in each of us at a different rate. I mark this self-reflective, conscious awareness of the "We" as its own line of development. Eventually, future research, both experientially and empirically will let us know such a speculation is valid. [227]

The Levels of "We" Space

Ideas surrounding "We" intelligence can be taken a bit further. Building upon aspects of both individual and collective development, we can begin to examine the emergence of several different levels of We-space.[228] Now, let us be clear. A "We" does not have a dominate monad that progresses through stages in the same way that an individual self might move through structure-stages. However, it is true to say that each of these levels of We-space can be *intentionally generated* by a group of individuals practicing together. Such an act of conscious generation can be learned over time as members of the "We" increase their level of "We" intelligence.   Notice below that the first two stages of We-space are impersonal, the second two stages are personal, and the last three stages are transpersonal:

1. Conventional We-space Individuals share a common experience. (Think: fans at a football game or attending a lecture.)

2. Impersonal We-space Individuals share common values and engage with each other, but the conversation stays in the third person about an object. (Think: an Integral salon.)

3. Interpersonal We-space Individuals meet together on a personal level. This may often entail sharing personal stories. In these exchanges one can experience therapeutic healing and deep levels of intimacy. (Think: group therapy.)

4. Transformational We-space Comparable to a classic spiritual community, this level's "We" engagement is focused on individual transformation. Sometimes this takes the form of a focus on individual awakening. (Think: the classic Buddhist sangha.) In other forms at this level of "We," individuals focus on the cultivation of members' highest potential. (Think: golden shadow.)

5. Awakened We-space All members have done enough individual transformation that they can enter into awakened awareness (the deepest vantage point). From this perspective a group of people can look around the room at each other in full recognition that there is one awareness moving through each of them. This is the first level of *transpersonal* We-space.

6. Evolutionary We-space All members can rest in awakened awareness and simultaneously engage with each other through their unique perspectives, acknowledging what Andrew Cohen calls "natural hierarchy" in an inter-subjective. This allows for an amazing emergent dimension of creativity in which all members can begin to constructively explore and create reality from a perspective that is truly trans-dual (dual and nondual at the same time). The focus is on following the thread of conversation and action and building upon it. As the process of co-creation/co-construction is learned, individuals literally feel as if they are creating the future in real time, together.

7. Kosmic We-space[229] This level of "We" requires individuals functioning from not only awakened awareness as their vantage point but also from the highest view (third-tier levels of structural development). In this type of "We," individuals sit together as the Divine and literally download the future all at once. Rather than stage-by-stage progression of creation, as was experienced in the Evolutionary-We, here, in the Kosmic-We, Supermind[230] bends time and the basic laws of developmental dynamic no longer function here in the same way.

If we desire the healthiest community possible, it is recommended that we engage in each of these levels of We-practice together. The reason these distinctions are so vital is precisely because there are different practices used to enter into each level of "We." Depending on the type of "We" that a group wants to create, certain elements ought to be emphasized. In an advanced community, all levels would be online and functioning simultaneously. The key to the conscious creation of any type of We-space is shared intentionality. (This very theory was the seed impetus that led Christina Vickory, Bill McCart, and I to found the WePractice community; an inter-subjective practice group now functioning in cities throughout the United States.)

Aspirations and Cautions with Regard to We-Engagements

When individuals align wholeheartedly under a single vision, together, the sum total of their collective gifts are liberated in service of the whole; a spontaneous impulse arises to offer one's particular gifts as sacrifice to the greater vision. This type of collective liberation re-contextualizes everything: we no longer strive solely to amplify ourselves in worldly success, but because we see it as a moral obligation to develop our talents to their fullest capacity in the hopes that they might serve the larger vision. In serving that larger vision we begin to create a new culture consciously.[231]

We have seen powerful examples of collectives in the past and many of us, for good reason, hesitate to take seriously a vision that suggests total surrender to a higher "We." When most of us think of grandiose visions of commitment, we envision popularized cults, where followers appear to live in mental prisons void of self-reflectivity. In these forms of collective cohesion, the "We" consciousness unconsciously informs all decisions; the power of the collective has usurped each individual's agency.

The radical new forms of trans-personal communion are different. Levels of evolutionary We-space and a kosmic We-space allow each individual to join in communion while simultaneously preserving agency. Evolutionary Enlightenment teacher Andrew Cohen explains the yoking of autonomy and communion in this way:

> What I'm trying to teach is a form of intersubjective nonduality, in which individuals are able to come together

in seamless communion beyond ego while also experiencing no limitations on their own individual autonomy. The autonomy does not inhibit the communion, and the communion does not inhibit the autonomy; instead, the autonomy and communion exist simultaneously in a context of natural hierarchy.[232]

In other words, unlike the surrender to communal vision that has led to cult tragedies in the past, an Integral perspective preserves each individual's autonomy while still allowing for a deep and rich communal experience. Cohen's practice leading groups of people into this sort of collective engagement "beyond exclusive identification with the ego"[233] gives him a powerful and unique perspective.

Cohen explains the preservation of autonomy elsewhere in this way: "The normal boundaries of the false self fall away in an experience of profound communion, and miraculously, a new kind of autonomy that is inherent in our own higher development is released."[234]

Unlike other forms of group cohesion that tend to drop the power of the collective below the threshold of consciousness, an experience of a true evolutionary We-space, as described by Cohen, ensures that inter-subjective power is constantly maintained in consciousness. In an experience of this kind of "We," surrender to the collective vision only exists as long as one consciously chooses it. At any point in time, one can pull back to individuated autonomy, leaving the conscious connection to the group. (This is quite the opposite of a traditional mythic version of surrender, wherein autonomy is lost and the "I" stays perpetually surrendered to the "We" unconsciously).

How is it possible that these levels of trans-personal We-spaces can emerge now but didn't prior to this particular point in the evolutionary process?[235] Let me be clear. It is very likely that at least some forms of awakened We-space unfolded historically. This could arise in any we space where there are several individuals awake to a nondual vantage point. However, higher levels of We (evolutionary and kosmic) are unlikely to have emerged. Applying our developmental vector of spiritual intelligence helps to examine the question a little deeper.

An experience of the higher levels of transpersonal We-space (i.e., evolutionary and kosmic We-spaces) likely require that an individual's consciousness has progressed through modern and postmodern levels of awareness to more Integral levels of complexity. At these higher stages, the individual ego has learned to differentiate itself from the conformist mentality of the group. Strong levels of individuation preserve autonomy and agency. This impulse toward self-reflexivity is born at the modern stage of individual development (e.g., Fowler's individuative-reflective faith development).[236] Prior to this level of structure-stage development there would not be a strong enough capacity for individual self-reflexivity and the individual would likely mold to the whims of the collective.

Something profound occurs when a group enacts nondual awareness, and allows it to pour through a well-developed individual with a high level of structural development. When the inter-subjective is engaged from this perspective in a shared context of evolution, the potential for true conscious evolution together is released.

It is important to recognize that even if individuals in a group all share a nondual vantage point each manifestation of individuality brings something different to every "We" of which it is a part. More than just a different perspective, each individual brings unique talents, skills, and shadow. This means that although the shared vision of the collective may very well be impersonal, as Cohen often articulates, the actual engagement and implementation of that vision is and can only be radically transpersonal (it transcends and includes the personal). This individual and personal side of realization is the very basis for what Cohen calls "natural hierarchy."[237] (Note that although this level of engagement includes the personal, it is far from interpersonal or transformational levels of We-space.) The process deepens if each individual can hold nondual identity with the Absolute while simultaneously embracing the relative uniqueness of each individual. In such instances the autonomy of the individual is supercharged rather than surrendered, because now it is plugged into and supported by a larger "We." I refer to the fact that every "We" is different given the unique constellation of participants with the term "Unique We".

In the few times that I have been fortunate enough to have the right conditions for an evolutionary We-space to emerge, what astonished me most was that a new form of trust solidified between the individuals involved; a kind of trust that feels fundamental to the type of cooperation needed for global problem solving in the twenty-first century.

The Bright Alliance

A broader and deeper understanding of the dynamics of transpersonal levels of We-space and conscious evolution can be brought together to offer a possible vision for our planetary future. Imagine individuals coming together to form a transpersonal We-space not just at a local or regional scale but on a planetary scale. Imagine that this trans-personal We-space included representatives from the major cultural and wisdom traditions of the world. Imagine that this group of individuals agreed upon several universal vectors of spiritual development and elected the appropriate representatives to lead according to their all-vector development.

This would mean that a diverse group of individuals with a high level of state-stage development, structure-stage development, and state/realm access could lead the planet in a new direction and advise on global affairs. Each could agree to help implement these three aspects of spiritual development within their own cultural streams. Each could develop *dual conveyor belts* within their respective lineages to help usher humanity through state-stages and structure-stages. If such group of trans-lineage practitioners could truly come together in service of the goodwill of humanity, we might actually, for the first time, be able to align our planetary purpose under the direction of a true Bright Alliance. The starting point, to make room for the possibility for such a group to emerge, is to first acknowledge our single Great Human Tradition and the possibility for evolution and health in all dimensions of humanity's potential.

No matter how awake or developed one individual might be, a single human being on the world stage can be easily ignored. However, if a group of enlightened leaders stand unified together, in full trans-dual awakening, articulating a prophecy from a trans-rational structure-stage, in contact with support from multiple states/realms, such an effort could not be ignored. Some have postulated that the next Buddha is the sangha and that the second coming of Christ is the collective. An Integral understanding of spiritual development makes the realization and manifestation of this sort of vision entirely possible.

Chapter 7 - Evolving Together

Chapter 8
Integral Realization

In this final chapter, I begin to articulate what I believe it would mean to embody a truly Integral realization of spiritual development both individually and collectively. In doing so, it is my goal to also simultaneously symphonize several of the ideas laid out in the past seven chapters.

After first providing an initial exploration into the idea of embodying an Integral realization, I'll explore several of the key features of an Integral approach to spiritual practice that can be referred to using a series of four phrases: "Wake Up, Grow Up, Clean Up, Show up." I then offer a vision for the future and a few suggestions of what it might mean if we were to update our world's great religious traditions with the insights offered in this book to form one single Great Human Tradition. Finally, I conclude with a brief discussion on Integral ethics and something I playfully call the Integral rapture.

Embodying an Integral Realization: All Vector, All Quadrant Awakening

Using the model offered in this book, we recognize that an Integrally informed spiritual practice and the embodied realization that manifests as its fruition has at least three goals: stabilization of a trans-dual vantage point; perpetual development of higher structure-stages; and the intentional access to all states and all realms. In this sense, by focusing on the three features listed above, an Integrally informed spiritual practice seeks an all-vector awakening.

An All-Vector Spiritual Practice

Without substantial firsthand experience in the three core elements discussed in this book (state-stages of spiritual realization, structure-stages spiritual intelligence, and cultivated access into states/ realms) it might not yet be clear to the reader how one might actually integrate each of these three dimensions into spiritual practice. In this light, I offer two examples of how all three of these aspects of development can be trained within a single holistic practice. I'll preface the examples by saying that for those just beginning on the path, the illustrations may appear a little advanced. If this is the case, just sit with the examples and keep an open mind to the possibilities they represent. For those already more advanced with their practice, it is my hope that the examples will give a taste of how an Integral orientation can help to catalyze advanced practice that takes one beyond the myriad of beginning introductory exercises currently filling the spiritual marketplace.

In the first example, I'll focus on the relationship between vantage point practice and state access as one moves through natural cycles of waking, dreaming, and deep sleep. In the second example, I'll point to one of the possible ways that state and realm access can begin to unfold as a constant acquisition of awareness and how such a cultivation relates to the stabilization of deeper vantage points. In both cases, structure-stages serve as the lens of knowing and determine the objects that are enacted in any given experience.

In our initial example, let's consider the relationship between a trans-dual vantage point and subtle state/realm access. As we have seen, lucid dreaming is one example of conscious access to the subtle realm. Although the onset of regular lucid dreaming during the sleep cycle can be an outward sign of stabilized identity beyond exclusive identification with thoughts and personality (causal identity), the experience of lucid dreaming itself should not be confused with or reduced to vantage point development in and of itself. The two vectors develop independent of each other. This means that one could presumably develop the capacity for lucid dreaming (conscious access to the subtle realm) without developing a stabilized vantage point deeper than personality. (The many examples of individuals learning to lucid dream using the techniques offered by LaBerge is just one citation of individuals lucid dreaming who seemingly do not have a causal vantage point). Although, deepening vantage points may lead to state and realm access, state and realm access does not necessarily lead to deeper vantage points of identity. (One could lucid dream for years and still confuse identity with his or her thoughts/personality.)

Even though each vector is distinct, development of each aspect can be combined in complementary fashion in an advanced Integral spiritual practice. Cross-culturally, we have examples of how vantage points and state access can be combined. Both the Buddhist and Bon traditions of Tibet have specific practices to invoke subtle and causal state access. These practices are sometimes referred to as the "yogas of dream and sleep".[238] In both traditions, the practice of particular meditations are designed to cultivate a continuity of unbroken awareness as the natural cycles move from waking to dreaming to deep sleep. The objective in both lucid dreaming and lucid deep sleeping is not simply to remain awake and aware. Presence is not an end in itself, but rather a means to a deeper end. In the yogas of dream and sleep the objective is to maintain wakefulness so that one can continue meditation practice beyond the waking state and into the night. Tezin Wangyal, founder of the Ligmincha Institute and lineage holder in the Tibetan Bon tradition, writes:

> Eventually we develop a continuity of awareness that allows us to maintain full awareness during dream as well as in waking life. Then we are able to respond to dream phenomena in creative and positive ways and can accomplish various practices in the dream state. When we fully develop this capacity, we will find that we are living both waking and dreaming life with greater ease, comfort, clarity, and appreciation, and we will also be preparing ourselves to attain liberation in the intermediate state (*bardo*) after death.[239]

Access to the subtle and causal realms is, according to the definition set out in this book, a property of one's state cultivation. Once the practitioner gains intentional access to various states/realms, the traditions encourage a combined practice that engages both states and vantage point training at the same time.[240] This means that one's practice of nondual vantage point stabilization can continue into dream and sleep. Wangyal explains the goal of a subtle- and causal-realm practice where vantage point training is emphasized. His distinctions help to differentiate the Tibetan Bon and Buddhist spiritual practices from mere conscious access to the states as described in Stephen Leberge's work on lucid dreaming. Wangyal writes:

> I am teaching these things because so many people in the West have an interest in dreams and dreaming, and in dream work [e.g. Leberge]. Usually this interest is psychological; I hope by presenting these teachings that dream world might progress to something deeper. Psychological dream work may create more happiness in samsara and that is good, but if full realization is the goal then something more must be done. [e.g. nondual vantage point training must be combined with state/realm access.] This is where sleep yoga is particularly important. It is fully at the heart of the practice of the Great Perfection, Dzogchen, which could be summarized thus: every moment of life—waking, dreaming, and sleeping—abide in pure nondual awareness. . .this is the essence of sleep yoga.[241]

Whether practices are done to enter into the subtle realm for mere state experience (creating more happiness in samsara, as Wangyal puts it), or for more specific forms of meditative practice like those Dzogchen techniques described above (i.e., to anchor nondual awareness at all times and throughout all realms/states), there is no doubt that some capacity for realm and state access has the potential for positive influence on the practitioner's life. A holistic Integral training fully considers the three aspects of spiritual development set forth in this book. An informed integral practitioner understands that a well-rounded spiritual development requires both trained access to states/realms as well as a stable realization of the deepest nondual vantage point while in those realms.

A second example of access into states/realms and vantage point development combined into a single practice is useful. At even more advanced levels of spiritual practice even the cycles of dream and sleep become less reified. According to some wisdom streams, all realms begin to open up at once. This means that during the waking state, one begins to fully open the subtle realm, not just in the sense of subtle energies but in a sense of fully lucid dreaming (with part of awareness) and fully waking in the gross realm (with another part of awareness). When this sort of opening has occurred, we might say that gross and subtle realms are held open at all times. For those who have cultivated this capacity, there is no more passing away from the waking-state gross realm and into the dreaming state in the subtle realm. Because the subtle realm is always open, even as one's body falls asleep the process of lucid dreaming that has been unfolding already all day long, unceasingly, simply continues. The same is true as one begins to penetrate the causal realm as well. This would mean that during the waking state, one is simultaneously lucid dreaming, and simultaneously open into the formless causal realm. All three realms are held open all at once. From this perspective the linear process of moving through the cycle of states is transcended. As subtler realms begin to open even in the waking state, the practice of trans-dual vantage point development continues. All forms (whether arising in gross, subtle, or causal realms) are seen as nondual.

With this clearer understanding of how access to states/realms and vantage point practice can be combined, we can now turn to examine the role of our third aspect of spiritual development: structure-stages. Whether one opens realms as an end in itself, or is practicing the stabilization of deeper vantage points throughout all realms, the objects that arise in experience will be brought forth according to the developmental structure-stage of separate self. Another way of saying this is to understand the fact that realms determine the container of the experience, whereas one's structure-stage determines the content that is enacted within the experience.

As we progress on the spiritual path and increase our structure-stage, we are simultaneously increasing the content/objects that are available to fill up those realms and states of our experience. Even if one has developed access to gross, subtle, and causal realms, while holding a nondual/trans-dual vantage point he or she will only be able to see content that can be enacted from the highest level of structural development that he or she has earned. An individual at a traditional level of consciousness will only be able to enact traditional content (this means that all modern, postmodern, and Integral content will be unavailable to him/her). Higher structure-stages enact more reality. As a result, we can rightfully claim that reality enacted through higher stages of development (e.g., higher stages of spiritual intelligence) is more comprehensive.[242]

Taking all three aspects together, this would mean that a full level of realization today requires (1) a nondual/trans-dual vantage point that shines *through and as*, (2) an advanced Integral structure-stage, enacting all available content (that has emerged in the evolutionary process to date), and (3) full wakefulness throughout all states of experience. If each of these three factors are met, nothing arising in consciousness would be other than the suchness of the Absolute Self (due to the nondual/trans-dual vantage point), nothing would be out of view (existing at a higher structure-stage), and no dimensions of relative reality would be unexplored due to a lack of conscious access to gross, subtle, and causal states. A tall order indeed, but at the same time, it is an order that is destined to bring even more love, positivity, and power to the world the more it manifests in the years to come.

Integrating Our Shadow and Healing Our Wounds

Categorized by the three main aspects of spiritual development (vantage points, structure-stages, and states), the goals of Integral realization and embodiment listed above are all more associated with eros by their very nature. As such, each offers an important piece of the kosmic evolutionary thrust as it moves upward and onward. Accordingly, each might be said to be biased towards a more masculine typological orientation.[243] The full picture of an Integrally embodied realization would not be complete without an acknowledgment of agape or an embracing feminine orientation. (Whereas agape was discussed in chapter 7 in relation to conscious evolution through both complexity and identity, agape is examined here in relation to individual spiritual practice and shadow.)

Viewing practice through the lens of agape we find great value and importance in ensuring that development in all vectors is as healthy as possible. This includes integrating our shadow and healing our individual and collective wounds.

When speaking about his most recent and as yet still unpublished work, Wilber notes that shadow or potential pathologies can arise in vertical growth through structure-stages as well as through horizontal growth through state-stages.[244] At each fulcrum[245] of structural development, structure-stage pathologies tend to split off to create splintered sub-personalities (resulting in a kind of temporary regression when activated). Similarly, unhealthy vantage point development results in certain forms of what Wilber calls allergies or addictions at switch points[246]along state-stages. Just as sub-personalities can arise causing *temporary regression in one's structure*, state-stage pathologies can arise that create a *temporary loss of vantage point*. Because vantage point pathology (or what we can also call state-stage pathology) is a less familiar phenomenon than structure-stage pathology, an example will help to further illustrate what I'm pointing to. (I keep this section short and instead point the reader to Wilber's latest additions to the book *Transformations of Consciousness* – forthcoming.)

Sexuality is one area in our culture that tends to reveal quite a bit of vantage point pathology. Due to a general lack of presence around sexuality in our culture at large, some spiritual practitioners "lose" their vantage point in sexual situations. In an extreme situation, this might mean that even if one normally lives from a nondual vantage point, a sexual situation may arise that activates identity at the level of personality. In these situations rather than remaining anchored in a nondual vantage point, the obscuration of personality causes one to "lose" their level of realization. All of a sudden, the person who is normally awake to nondual reality is functioning from their egoic identity. Worse even still, because loss of vantage point can sometimes go unnoticed until after the fact the person may be under the conceptual delusion that he or she is still living from the deepest vantage point! (One of the prime characteristics of vantage point loss is a discontinuity of meditative presence – or what the Buddhist tradition calls *ignorance*.) Furthermore, as if the situation wasn't sticky enough, the person may then make excuses as to why their actions were justified because vantage point loss has gone unnoticed. The amount of hardship caused in spiritual communities because of this type of vantage point pathology is staggering. We can begin to see why it is necessary that each of us do the necessary work to address our pathologies and heal the wounds of our disintegrated self.[247]

Whether pathologies arise as a result of structure-stage shadow or state-stage shadow, an Integrally informed practitioner will be sure to include this more feminine dimension of practice into the fold every step of the way.

An Integral Frame for Spiritual Revolution: Wake Up, Grow Up, Clean Up, Show Up

The first two steps closer to an enlightened culture require a deeper consideration of both vantage points and structural development.[248] Wilber often uses the phrases "wake up" and "grow up" to point to each of these aspects respectively.[249] We have to "wake up" through deeper state-stages (vantage points) of spiritual realization as well as "grow up" through higher structure-stages through increasing our various levels of intelligence.[250]

In addition to "waking up" to deeper vantage points and "growing up" through higher structures, it is also vital that we integrate our individual and collective shadows. I like to add "clean up" to the string of phrases to point out the importance of addressing our broken and disowned parts of self.[251] This means that any integrally informed spiritual practice ought to engage in conscious practices that are designed to heal the state-stage and structure-stage pathologies that have accumulated over the course of a lifetime. In Integral parlance this parallels Wilber's call for an integral spiritual practice to focus on "states, stages, and shadow."

To the degree that we "wake up, grow up, and clean up" within ourselves, we set the individual conditions needed to enter into transpersonal levels of We-space. We-spaces can only flourish to the degree that each of us fully "show up" with commitment and determination to enact the future that we know is possible. To fully "show up" means that each of us must bring our experience, our autonomy, our gifts, and our wisdom to the inter-subjective field. We must own where we sit in the natural hierarchy within the inter-subjective space.[252] Each of us has a unique purpose and a unique obligation in the evolutionary process and it is our duty to bring everything we have to the table. "Wake up, grow up, clean up, show up."[253]

Updating Our World's Wisdom Traditions

All of our world's great wisdom lineages can benefit from including an Integral frame into their foundation. It is my aspiration that the three aspects of spiritual development and the imperative to "wake up, grow up, clean up, show up" can be embraced by religious traditions around the globe. (We can also add "open up" to this phrase to include the important dimension of states.) If this is accomplished, I truly believe it would serve as the perfect Integral frame for spiritual revolution. Our world's religious traditions would transition from being hindrances to evolution (to the degree they keep people contained to mythic/prerational levels of spiritual intelligence) to vehicles of transformation in the third millennium. And in this light, we will be one step closer to more fully enacting the Great Human Tradition.

Let's take a brief look at each piece of the frame. Encouraging religious traditions to acknowledge a dimension of "waking up" would liberate the mystical and esoteric teachings of the religions. This liberation would allow these once secret teachings to be taught openly alongside more exoteric expressions. If all religions embraced the call to "wake up," those traditions that already successfully track the whole ladder of vantage points could share their teachings with the rest of the world. In a similar vein, those traditions that have partial maps of these state-stages of identity could add to their own systems, complementing their own maps of human potential with the wisdom of other streams.

Acknowledging the fact that we all must "grow up" would give religious traditions the terminology necessary to embrace vertical dimensions of spiritual intelligence. This would mean that we could develop together an appropriate interpretation of each tradition at every level of spiritual intelligence; fully enacting what Wilber calls the "conveyor belt". In short, this means that there would be a traditional version, a modern version, a postmodern version, and an Integral version of each tradition. (See volume 2 in this series for a full account of how the conveyor belt shows up in four major traditions.) When religion is unbound from its association with traditional structures of consciousness and allowed to flourish at modern, postmodern, and Integral levels of development, all those who once abandoned religion because it lacked developmental legitimacy could authentically reengage with each other at a level of development appropriate to their stage. As ritual, prayer, and community are reinterpreted at higher stages of religious orientation, new forms of inter-subjective engagement become a realistic possibility.

To the degree that religions authentically embrace the importance of "cleaning up" shadow both individually and collectively we can increase the capacity for teachers and lineages to be clear and effective. The cleaner religious leaders are the easier it will be for them to transmit their realization (vantage point) and spiritual intelligence (structure-stage) to others. Similarly, the cleaner religious leaders are, the less likely they are to cause unnecessary pain to others as they act out shadow issues in their respective communities. On a collective scale, if communities and lineages consciously engage in shadow work, further "cleaning up" their broken aspects, the more they are likely to be honored and taken seriously on the global stage. Cleaner traditions will find much greater acceptance when sharing their lineage-specific gifts with others as part of the Great Human Tradition.

If religious traditions find ways to encourage individuals to "show up," religion will serve as a catalyst that calls individuals to continually live from and lean into their unique life mission. Historically religious communities have made strong efforts to encourage individuals to uphold specific character qualities and principles of faith. Many religious traditions have historically encouraged community and social engagement on a wide scale. The potential for communities of practitioners taking responsibility for their experience and "showing up" for communal engagement in configurations of trans-personal We-spaces is enlivening.

Finally, religious traditions have the capacity to "open up" multiple realms and states of reality. Single handedly, religions have been and to this day continue to be the gatekeepers of these realms. Today, death of the mythic worldview at the hands of modernity has also led to the fact that access to these realms has been cut off for the majority of individuals at modern stages and beyond. When access to realms and states are brought back online from higher stages of spiritual intelligence, we open the possibilities for inter-dimensional capacities beyond our wildest dreams.

If our world's great wisdom lineages are updated in this way, making commitments to value "waking up, growing up, cleaning up, showing up, and opening up," the future may very well be a place into which only the most fortunate of beings are born. With new dedication and devotion to bringing Integral intelligence into our world's great wisdom lineages, we have the potential to generate an unprecedented power for guiding the Earth in a positive direction. In this way, the pursuit and revelation of our Great Human Tradition is one of, if not the most noble endeavor we can explore together.

Integral Ethics

In an Integral age, when consciously cultivated We-engagements become the standard for interactions, the backdrop of an Integral ethic and the moral responsibility for right action that comes with it, gain significant importance. In addition to ideas like Wilber's notion of the "Basic Moral Intuition" (the greatest good for the greatest depth and greatest span), new applications of ethical insights can be uncovered in the Great Human Tradition. At its most basic level, an Integral ethic builds on the notions we've explored in this book.

How do we determine right action in a paradigm dedicated to integral ethics? As I see it, one example of right action might read something like the following: "In an Integral world, right action is any action that helps to catalyze the healthiest forms of awakening through vantage points and healthiest forms of growth through structure-stages for both individuals and collectives."

If we can agree that such a standard can serve as ethical backdrop for our actions, then the following moral checklist might be worth consulting before acting:

Awakening through Vantage Points (State-Stages of Identity)
1. Is this action coming from my deepest realization? What is my vantage point?
2. Is this action serving the awakening of the other person or person(s) with whom I'm engaging?

Growing through Structure-Stages (Honoring Evolution)
3. Does this action honor the past? Does this action serve to dignify all of those who have come before me and all the sacrifices that have been made to make this moment possible?
4. Knowing that in this moment I am laying kosmic grooves for the future, could this action serve as the foundation for all future action to be built upon?

Health
5. Could this action be coming from my own shadow or some pathology within myself? (If I am not sure then I should consult with those who know me and who I trust.)
6. Could this action serve to catalyze shadow or perpetuate pathology in the other person or in the community of which I am a part (local or global)?

When confronted with a moral dilemma, moving through the six-point checklist above can provide a series of useful data points. The list is in no way complete, but it does give the sense of what direction we might need to move in if ethics are to flourish as part of an integrally informed Great Human Tradition.

The Integral Rapture

The maps laid out by Brown and Wilber, along with the three aspects of spiritual development outlined in this book, provide the platform for what might rightly be called an "integral rapture." Rather than leaving behind all those unlucky souls (as might be the case in some form of traditional Christian rapture), the Integral rapture transforms all human activities into what I call "dual conveyor belts." These new dual-conveyor belts help to elicit higher vertical structures of development and deeper horizontal vantage point realization in all human beings. From transforming our religious traditions into vehicles of evolution, to using social networking sites, iphone apps, computer games and educational systems to stimulate growth, the coming Integral Age employs every medium conceivable as a vehicle for vertical and horizontal awakening. When these efforts are combined with technologies to help individuals access multiple realms and states, the light of an Integral rapture begins to shine its electric heart of love to every dark corner of the globe. Individual and collective shadows are highlighted and integrated. Unnoticed wounds are healed. In place of disintegration, the light of a collaboration of Integral minds, hearts, and hands will continue to construct an infinite number of new ladders leading into the kingdom of heaven. In the Integral Age, each breath, each step, each meal, each conversation becomes a portal to the divine reality here and now.

For those already here with us in the new world, keep rowing the great vehicle of Integral awakening and may no one or no thing be left behind. May the Great Human Tradition come to fulfill its destiny of planetary purpose here on Earth. And may we join in the Great Evolution of conscious co-creation with all of our brothers and sisters in the kosmos.

Chapter 8 - Integral Realization

Appendix 1
Historical and Contemporary Approaches to Spiritual Development

This appendix examines a broad swath of academic research related to spiritual development and religious experience. Providing this general outline serves two basic ends. First, a historical and contemporary survey of the field helps to position this book within a larger academic context. Although my work is based extensively upon the models of both Ken Wilber and Daniel P. Brown, it is important that I also offer a backdrop of other research so as to show where their models stand among their contemporaries. As a second, equally important end, the survey of methodological approaches I lay out here in the appendix provides a more expanded articulation of the basic content used in chapter 1 to show how Wilber's Four Quadrant Model can help to organize the field. The average scholar studying spiritual development does his or her best to coordinate vast amounts of information haphazardly, often giving preference to one particular methodology over another. With the Integral lens in place, instead of weighing one specific approach over another, all methodologies are given equal preference and integrated into a single comprehensive frame using Wilber's Integral Methodological Pluralism. All of this is vital to the successful emergence of the field of Integral Religious Studies.

Surveying Historical and Contemporary Approaches to Spiritual Development

A broad survey of all available information is a monumental

task. Attempts at surveying spiritual development in the Western world alone, such as Hood's *Handbook to Religious Experience*, dedicate over 600 pages to the topic. Whereas Hood was able to commit an entire book to surveying the research, my attempt at a general survey here is limited to a mere appendix. This is an obvious disadvantage. Nonetheless, some sort of broad brushstrokes are important so that we can assure some reference points for shared footing. I offer this appendix toward that end.

The examples I provide below are not an exhaustive account of all the available information but rather a representative depiction of the type of research and methodologies most often employed in the examination of religious experience and spiritual development.[254] The section that follows outlines four basic categories of methodological approach: (1) phenomenological and structural (UL), (2) neurological and psychopharmacological (UR), (3) cultural (LL) and, (4) sociological (LR). Each category represents one of the common Western academic methodologies used to examine spiritual development and religious experience.[255] Each category correlates to Wilber's Four Quadrants/ Quadrivia. After I've outlined each of the four categories, I expand my lens to look briefly at some of the insight garnered outside of Western academic institutions.

Phenomenological and Structural Approaches: The Interior of the Individual (UL)

Phenomenological Approaches

In the West, the concept and study of spiritual development as a whole, and spiritual experience in particular, is a relatively recent line of inquiry.[256] Although religion has always been an experiential matter, the idea of religious experience as an object of study is novel, developing only over the past two centuries.[257] The study of spiritual experience in the Western Academy was, at its inception, one of phenomenological investigation. In other words, despite the various ends to which it was employed, early researchers of spiritual phenomena began by examining the internal experiences of individuals.
Friedrich Schleiermacher

The concept and study of religious experience, as an end in itself, was first introduced in 1877, in a piece titled *On Religion* by Friedrich Schleiermacher.[258] Schleiermacher's work was a direct defense against a long line of modern thinkers whose disdain for religion was obvious. Voltaire, for example, claimed that religion was "the source of all imaginable follies, and disturbances...the parent of fanaticism and civil discord...the enemy of mankind."[259] Others from Decartes to Kant, fuelled by the critical reasoning instigated by the Enlightenment, systematically dismantled all religious belief based on metaphysical thought. To the intellectual modern thinker, religion was a dying legacy. It was in this light that Friedrich Schleiermacher saw it necessary to respond.

Motivated by "an interest in freeing religious doctrine and practice from dependence on metaphysical beliefs and ecclesiastical institutions,"[260] Schleiermacher developed an approach to save religion from the dismal fate proposed by modern thinkers. According to Schleiermacher's reasoning, if religion were based on experience and not mere metaphysical speculation, then it could, theoretically, survive the critical lens of modernity. That is to say, if emphasis was placed on the religious experience itself (e.g., affective feelings and noetic insight) instead of the belief in a particular doctrine, membership to a specific institution, or intellectual ruminations on ontological reality, then it could be freed from having to defend itself against spheres of knowledge that lay outside of its domain.

Schleiermacher focused on experience in order to fight against all forms of reductionism that tried to discount religion as a valuable source of insight. In doing so, Schleiermacher successfully demonstrated that religion was an "autonomous moment in human experience which ought not be reduced to be science, metaphysics, or morality."[261] Among other accomplishments, Schleiermacher's argument served to clearly differentiate the value spheres of human experience. By demonstrating that the value spheres of science, morality, and religion were not reducible to each other, Schleiermacher claimed that religion itself was immune from modern, scientific critiques. "Because religion is autonomous," claimed Schleiermacher, "all possible conflict between religion and science or morality is precluded. Any attempt to assimilate religion to nonreligious phenomena is an attempt to reduce it to something other than what it is."[262]

Schleiermacher's attempt to base religion on the experience itself and as a result, in its own autonomous sphere, was seminal to the field. Columbia professor Wayne Proudfoot calls Schleiermacher's work the "most influential statement and defense of the autonomy of religious experience."[263] Even though some theorists find fault in

Schleiermacher's thinking,[264] it cannot be denied that his arguments against modern, rational critiques of religion have instigated a stream of investigation and debate that continues to the present day.[265]

William James

In 1902, while a professor at Harvard, William James published *The Varieties of Religious Experience*, continuing Schleiermacher's demand for a persistent inquiry into the nature of religious phenomena. James' emphasis on individual experience (as it was felt from the inside) earned him titles like the "father of phenomenology" and the "father of the psychology of religion." In James' view, personal religious experience and mystical experience were deeply intertwined.[266] As such, James was one of the very first researchers to develop a common set of descriptions to distinguish mystical experiences from other more mundane forms of common religious experience. According to James, mystical experiences tend to be ineffable, noetic, transient, and passive. Many of these ideas are still used today in academic literature.

Walter Terence Stace

Following James' lead a half-century later, Walter Terence Stace continued to value the mystical as the pinnacle of all religious experience. Stace dedicated a large portion of his academic career at Princeton to developing a sound set of phenomenological categories to analyze and compare spiritual experience. In his two monumental works published in 1960, *Mysticism and Philosophy* and *The Teachings of the Mystics*, Stace argued that there were "common core"[267] elements, similar to what Wilber calls deep structures of mystical experience. According to Stace, these common core characteristics (e.g., a unitive quality, a noetic quality, transcendence of space and time, a deeply felt positive mood, paradox and ineffability) all hold true across diverse traditions despite the fact that each is likely to be interpreted variously according to ideological conditions.[268]

Ralph Hood

Fifteen years after Stace, Ralph Hood developed what he called the Mysticism Scale (M-scale), effectively operationalizing Stace's categories with an empirical foundation.[269] Macdonald and Friedman recognize Hood's mysticism scale as the most widely used academic psychometric to measure mystical experience.[270] Since its inception in 1975, Hood's scale has been utilized to establish an undeniable empirical record of mystical experience.

In addition to the fact that Hood's M-scale empirically supports Stace's original claims to a "common core," it also stands strong in the face of critics. In 2001, Hood's M-scale was implemented cross-culturally, in response to critiques that his model was culturally biased. Although his original work was conducted among mostly American Christians, Hood's more recent work included a study with a group of researchers in Iran working with Muslims.[271] The study showed that there are indeed phenomenological properties of mystical experience across cultures and that such experiences are subject to an interpretive factor. Hood's cross-cultural work further supported Stace's categories of mysticism and confirmed his claim that "identical experiences can be differentially interpreted."[272]

Structural Approaches

Complementing the research of phenomenological and mystical experiences described thus far, empirical data has also been collected to study spiritual development in other areas. For instance, some researchers over the past several decades have moved beyond simply studying the feelings and experiences of individuals from the inside to studying how spiritual development unfolds using research only obtainable from outside of the individual interior.

Ronald Goldman

In the 1930s, researchers following Jean Piaget's research into cognitive development began to look at how cognitive structures might be involved in religious and spiritual experience, specifically how these structures develop in complexity over time. One of the first studies was conducted by Ronald Goldman in 1964. In his research, Goldman concluded that Piaget's stages of preoperational, concrete operational, and formal operational could be accurately used to describe the process of religious thinking. In other words, according to Goldman, one's capacity to think about and therefore interpret religion developed overtime according to the psychological capacities of the individual.

Goldman used the following stages: intuitive (expressed in children up to 8 years old); concrete (expressed in children between 7 and 14 years old) and abstract religious thinking (expressed in children older than 13 years old) to mark the spiritual development of an individual as they progressed.[273] Because Goldman asserted that cognitive development tended to lead, he concluded that it was likely that not all adults reach abstract capacities in their religious thinking. Consequently, Goldman contended that "many young people and adults remain at the [basic] concrete level in their religious thinking."[274] Because religion is often limited to concrete levels of thinking, Goldman contended that if individuals did move beyond concrete levels of thinking it might result in either "the abandonment of religion or to an indifferent attitude toward it."[275] [276]

James Fowler

Continuing in the lineage of Goldman almost twenty years later, James Fowler's 1981 publication, *Stages of Faith*, took the field of spiritual development one step further. Instead of merely tracking an individual's level of spiritual intelligence as it unfolded in childhood and adolescence (as in previous studies), Fowler included the further reaches of adult development. Fowler contended that there were predictable stages of growth that human beings move through with regard to faith.[277] According to his research, these various stages of development lead to diversely different interpretations and expressions of religion. At early stages of faith development, individuals tend to take a more literal approach to religion (Fowler's mythic-literal/synthetic-conventional stages), only employing a limited range of perspectives. At later stages of faith development one learns to hold multiple perspectives simultaneously (Fowler's conjunctive/universalizing stages).[278]

Fowler's approach is not, however, without its detractors. The most common critiques come from those who contend that cognitive development is much more complex than both Fowler and Piaget's original model supposes. They argue that personal and cultural narratives, linguistics, social influences, and psychodynamic elements prevent Fowler's model from being as broadly applicable as he predicted.[279] Even while acknowledging these critiques, it is imperative that we do not throw the baby out with the proverbial bath water. That is, even if it is true that models of spiritual development that use cognitive development as the driving force need to be made more complex and sensitive to various postmodern considerations, it is erroneous to jettison the reality of faith development altogether. In addition, although his original research used mostly Christian subjects, subsequent research speculates that spiritual intelligence is clearly demonstrated across multiple traditions and in a multitude of cultural and social contexts.[280]

Neurological and Psychopharmacological Approaches: The Exterior of the Individual (UR)

Neurological Approaches

In 1984, James Ashbrook coined the term "neurotheology" in an article published in *Zygon: The Journal of Religion and Science*. His article, titled "Neurotheology: The Working Brain and the Work of Theology," sparked a robust field of inquiry into the nature of religious experience and the role of the human brain. Subsequently, biological and neurological approaches to religious experience and spiritual development have proliferated. As technology increases, we gain a greater capacity to measure changes in brain chemistry and the physiological correlates to spiritual experience. Interestingly, as we shall see below, neurological research increasingly demonstrates that there are permanent neurological changes to the brain when spiritual practice is enacted consistently over time.

Andrew Newberg

The research of Andrew Newberg and his team at the University of Pennsylvania's Center for Spirituality and the Mind is some of the very best in the emerging field of Neurotheology. In recent studies, Newberg and his team compared meditating brains of Franciscan nuns doing verbal meditation to earlier research results of Buddhist monks in visualization meditation. According to a SPECT scanner to measure cerebral blood flow, both cases showed decreased activity in the parietal lobes (the part of the brain that controls one's sense of self and spatial orientation).[281] Decreased activity in this region correlates to experiences wherein an individual feels a sense of unity with the surrounding environment. By showing the places of the brain directly affected by spiritual practice, Newberg's work offers some of the first examples of physiological evidence to confirm the claims that practitioners are indeed experiencing transcendence of their individual sense of self.

Despite the strict scientific and neurological lens he uses, Newberg is not a reductionist. He refuses to make materialistic claims about the source of causation. In other words, Newberg does not posit, as do some other scientists,[282] that spiritual experiences are merely results of decreased brain activity. Rather, being much more astute with his level of academic rigor, Newberg defends against positivist reductionism and leaves room for the possibility that the changes in the brain may be neurological correlates to real internal spiritual experience. In his book *How God Changes Your Brain*, Newberg maintains an agnostic view about the ontological reality that the experience points to, claiming that regardless of whether or not such experiences point to a "real" reality, the results and effects of practice are undeniable. Spiritual practice, according to Newberg, plays a positive role in a sense of well-being and one's capacity for social action.[283]

Among other conclusions, Newberg points out that "intense, long-term contemplation of God and other spiritual values appears to permanently change the structure of those parts of the brain that control our moods, give rise to our conscious notions of self, and shape our sensory perceptions of the world." Furthermore, he states that "contemplative practices strengthen a specific neurological circuit that generates peacefulness, social awareness, and compassion for others." Newberg's discoveries align perfectly with new insights regarding the brain's capacity for neuroplasticity. Although the brain was once thought to be an immutable structure with fixed pathways, the concept of neuroplasticity, also known as cortical remapping, points to new discoveries that experience has the capacity to literally rewire the brain.[284] Newberg concludes by stating that "spiritual practices also can be used to enhance cognition, communication, and creativity, and over time can even change our neurological perception of reality itself."[285]

Psychopharmacological Approaches

The speculation that particular spiritual experiences can be tracked with neurological correlates has also inspired other types of research. Rather than examine the neurological correlates of self-induced experiences, some researchers prefer to ask whether it is possible to induce spiritual experiences from the outside using various forms of psycho-pharmaceuticals. The results indicate that yes, it is indeed possible. When various psychedelics are used specifically to induce religious or spiritual experience, they are called *entheogens*.[286]

Timothy Leary and Richard Alpert

Some of the early psychopharmacological research conducted in the United States is infamous. Most well known is the work of Timothy Leary and Richard Alpert (Ram Dass). From 1960–1962 Leary and Alpert conducted a substantial amount of psychedelic research on human subjects at Harvard University. One of the aims of their research was to examine the capacity of psychedelics to induce religious experience. Before their studies were shut down by the university, Leary and Alpert were able to demonstrate promising results. In one research project, called the Marsh Chapel Experiment, 9 out of 10 students from Harvard Divinity School reported profound religious states as a result of taking psilocybin in a religious setting.[287]

Rick Strassman

Following a methodology similar to those employed in the early Harvard psychedelic studies, contemporary researcher Rick Strassman brings new insight to the fore. Strassman, a researcher in clinical psychopharmacology and a medical doctor specializing in psychiatry, conducted some of the first research on the effects of psychedelics on human subjects approved by the government in over twenty years. Strassman's research at the University of New Mexico's School of Medicine studied the effects of dimethyltryptamine (DMT).

Interestingly, many of the subjects reported that the results of taking DMT were spiritual in nature, despite the fact that the expectation for such experiences was not set before hand. Overtime, Strassman became so impressed with the capacity of DMT to induce profound religious and spiritual experiences that in his published research, he used the terms "God molecule" and "Spirit molecule" to describe it. As we saw in chapter 6, one of the findings that makes DMT research so relevant to spiritual development is that it is a naturally occurring chemical in the brain. According to Strassman's hypothesis, DMT is produced in the pineal gland and has a direct connection to events as extraordinary as near-death experiences and as common as dreaming.[288]

Cultural Approaches: The Interior of the Collective (LL)

Anthropological and cultural perspectives on spiritual development and experience represent our third category of methodological approach. Some of the first anthropological studies of the late nineteenth century focused specifically on the religious and spiritual experiences of the diverse cultures of the world.[289]

Cultural Study from the Outside

Most often, early scholars (mostly Western) made voyages

to remote tribes (mostly non-Western) to examine their beliefs and spiritual experiences. These early studies were often conducted from the outside, meaning the researcher remained an external observer. As a result of their fieldwork, scholars like E.B. Tylor and James Frazer came up with evolutionary theories to describe the cultures that they observed. Instead of positioning each individual along a developmental spectrum (which a developmental psychologist might do skillfully today), Tylor and Frazer instead, clumsily placed the religions themselves in a hierarchical order with Christianity on top and the more "savage" traditions below. Although early scholars like Frazer and Tylor are now criticized for their Western, Christian-centric biases and lack of cultural sensitivity, their pioneering efforts must be commended and recognized as some of the first attempts to study spiritual experiences from the outside across multiple contexts.

Contemporary surveys of spiritual and mystical experience from around the globe continue to offer perspectives from the vast majority of our world's traditions. Now, however, such studies are done with much more sensitivity. For example, Denise and John Carmody's book *Mysticism*, published through Oxford University Press in 1996, provides cross-cultural comparisons of mystical experiences from a large swath of traditions, including: Hindu, Buddhist, Chinese, Japanese, Christian, Jewish, Muslim, and oral. Instead of placing the various cultures on a hierarchy with Christian-centric Western values at the top (civilized) and all other cultures below (savage), today's scholars curb these colonialist tendencies and instead do their best to place the cultures on equal ground.

Cultural Study from the Inside

As cultural research continued, scholars gained even greater degrees of sensitivity to cultural differences. Some began to discover that what we call reality is in fact greatly conditioned by the shared values and beliefs of the particular collective that is defining it. In an attempt to refine research methods and to better understand multiple perspectives in many different contexts, some contemporary scholars decided that rather than using a single lens to view reality (e.g., a Western or Christian lens), reality itself must be understood on the same terms as those who are enacting it. As a result, scholars saw that it was necessary to study the shared values of a culture from the inside, as a participant in religious life, rather than simply observing the culture from the outside.

Michael Harner

Anthropologists like Michael Harner provide a sound example of this type of insider approach. In an attempt to understand the shamanistic tradition of Central and South America from the inside, Harner began to participate in their rituals directly. In doing so, Harner was able to legitimize and articulate the religious experience of native tribes from a first-person rather than third-person perspective.

Harner writes of the dramatic change in perspective that came from his participation in a shamanistic journey under the influence of yage (ayahuasca).[290] He writes of his experience:

> For several hours after drinking the brew, I found myself, although awake, in a world literally beyond my wildest dreams....transported into a trance where the supernatural seemed natural, I realized that anthropologists including myself, had profoundly under estimated the importance of the drug in affecting native ideology.[291]

Harner's participatory experience from within the world-space of the native tribe demonstrates how important a change in methodology from outside to inside can be. Although all anthropologists study the internal shared values of the collective, a change in perspective from that of an outside observer to that of an inside participant, radically influences the type of information and insight gained.

A Multi-Method Cultural Approach

It is vital to insert an important caveat before we proceed further with our survey. That is, not all scholars limit themselves to employing a single methodology. Some use multiple lenses to coordinate a more comprehensive view. In fact, as integrative impulses in consciousness emerge, more scholars will use a trans-disciplinary and mutli-perspectival approach.

Daniel P. Brown is a perfect example. Although Brown's work can be appropriately categorized as a study of the interior of the individual, outlining the fundamental stages of spiritual realization as they unfold phenomenologically, Brown's methodology also takes into consideration a broad cultural approach and therefore deserves mention in this section.

As we have seen, Brown's early research at the University of

Chicago compared the spiritual stages of meditative practice across multiple contexts of shared belief. Translating Buddhist and Hindu scriptures from their original language, Brown was able to track common paths within the traditions despite cross-cultural differences.[292]

At the time that Brown's work was published in *Transformations of Consciousness*, it was common for scholars to claim that although spiritual paths were diverse, all paths lead to the same end.[293] Brown's work demonstrates that quite the opposite is true. According to Brown's cross-cultural research, there is one common underlying path to spiritual realization (that can be tracked according to its deep structure), and many different ends. In other words, Brown's research demonstrates that not all forms of awakening are equal. His research stands in contrast to those striving for religious homogeneity. As we learned throughout this book, because a particular religious experience can never be extrapolated from its cultural matrices, religious experience will always be enacted within and then defined, at least in part, by the particular cultural and ideological setting in which it arises.

Sociological Approaches: The Exterior of the Collective (LR)

Our last category of methodological approach explores the work of those researchers who examine the role and function of religious experience and spiritual development using a broad social lens. In other words, these researchers study the external of the collective and how various social factors and systems influence spiritual experience.

Emile Durkheim and Max Weber

Rather than focusing on the phenomenological experience of an individual or the shared beliefs of a particular culture, early social theorists like Emile Durkheim and Max Weber tended to view religious experience through a social and systemic lens. Durkheim, for instance, concluded, that "even when religion seems to be entirely within the individual's conscience, it is still in society that it finds the living source from which it is nourished."[294] Along a similar line of thought and congruent with a sociological approach, Weber's early work looked at social economic systems and their relationship to religious experience. He concluded that the Christian tradition itself, and the Protestant experience in particular, was the reason that capitalism flourished in the West.[295] Both Durkheim and Weber demonstrate that religious experience, expressed more broadly, has been a significant part of Western sociological studies for centuries.

Daniel Batson and Larry Ventis
Similar to the way in which shared cultural values, language, and context influence the possibility and limits of religious experience, so too do social categories affect the quality and type of mystical experiences to which a particular individual will be susceptible.[296] According to Batson and Ventis, "what may seem to be a freely chosen and highly personal religious stance is in large measure a product of social influence....You are free to choose only the religious stance that your particular social background dictates."[297] Furthermore, they explain that "each of us is subject to subtle forms of social influence simply as a result of being born into a particular niche in society." Ultimately, Batson and Ventis confirm previously conducted sociological research[298] that suggests that by knowing simple data such as a person's sex, race, age, socio-economic status, educational level, town size, geographical region, family ethnic origin, parents' religion, political affiliation, and marital status, it is possible to make an accurate guess as to the type of religious experience an individual is likely to have. [299]

Research Outside of Academic Institutions

A substantial amount of research comes from sources outside of Western academic sources.

Academic Blind Spots
Academic approaches to spirituality do indeed bring a certain type of clarity to our analysis. However, as with any approach, the academic endeavor has a few rather startling blind spots. These blind spots are made even more obvious when academic assumptions are compared to the statements made by mystics within the world's great traditions themselves.
Teachings of some lineages directly contradict axiomatic assumptions that many Western researchers have taken for granted for over a century. For instance, William James makes the assertion that

"mystical states cannot be sustained for long" and that "except in rare instances, half an hour, or at most an hour or two, seems to be the limit beyond which they fade into light of common day."[300] James' statement is in direct contradiction to the scores of texts in Eastern literature dedicated to the idea that mystical states can indeed be stabilized as permanent acquisitions in awareness. (We addressed the subject of stabilizing identity in chapter 2 on state-stages.)

Similarly, as my own mentor Daniel P. Brown first pointed out to me, James' idea that mystical states are "ineffable" may be more the result of the West not having developed a technical language to describe them. This means that in certain circumstances experiences can indeed be articulated and that "ineffability" is not a native quality of the experience itself. Not only can mystical states be spoken about in communities that have developed the common language of "signifiers" and "signified" to describe them,[301] but as demonstrated by the Hindu sage Abhinavagupta (among countless others), descriptions of mystical realizations can be brought into clear written word, spoken discourse, theater, dance, poetry and lively aesthetic performance.[302]

The World's Spiritual Traditions

As we saw in our core chapters on the various vectors of spiritual development, the most robust and detailed spiritual maps of mystical phenomenon come not from within academia but from our world's great religious traditions themselves. Historically, spiritual heroes from every tradition have provided maps of extraordinary experience. A few exemplars here will help to land the point.

In the East, Buddhists such as Nagarjuna, Shantideva, and Longchempa, as well as Hindu sages like Abhinavagupta, Vasugupta, and Ksemeraja have mapped phenomenological spiritual realities that far surpass the original conceptualizations put forth in academia. Similarly, Western spiritual traditions also hold substantial keys. Mystics like St. Teresa of Avilia, St. John of the Cross, and Meister Eckhar stand as exemplars in the Christian Stream, while mystics like Ibn Arabi, Hafiz, and Rumi stand in the Islamic stream. In the Jewish stream we can draw on the work of mystics like Azriel of Gerona and Shimon bar Yocha. Each of the world's religious traditions points to critical elements that ought to be included in any comprehensive map of spiritual development. Rather than conducting an extensive survey here, I note these historical spiritual trailblazers as mere placeholders of the wisdom that we can continue to draw from our great traditions.

Non-religious and Non-academic Insight

Additional researchers outside of both traditional academic institutions and the confines of a particular religious affiliation also provide significant insight to an Integral approach to spiritual development. Pioneers like Mike Murphy and George Leonard founded their own institute called Esalen to conduct their research. Murphy's book, *The Future of the Body* is a definitive guide to what might be possible as the human species continues to evolve. Other contemporary leaders bring their own unique avenues of inquiry. For example, spiritual teacher Andrew Cohen and his organization EnlightenNext explore the edges of spiritual development in a post-postmodern context. Cohen and his students examine how cultural conditioning might be deconstructed to such a degree that a new culture of inter-subjective non-duality and conscious co-creation might be born. Other spiritual leaders like Adi Da Samraj have synthesized huge amounts of spiritual knowledge and made their own spiritual realizations available to the West. In an attempt to convey his teachings in a way that could properly reflect his experience, Adi Da developed much of his own language and writing style.

The list of contemporary contributors outside of both Western academia and specific religious institutions can continue to be expanded massively. Stanislav Grof (holotropic breathwork), Kenneth Ring (near-death experiences), Robert Monroe (out of body experiences/Monroe Institute), Ervin Laszlo (Club of Budapest), in addition to the now declassified research conducted by the United States Central Intelligence Agency,[303] should all be included in an Integral analysis. Similarly, additional insight can be gleaned from countless popular culture icons (some more controversial than others) that have explored the possibilities of consciousness through working with plant medicines and synthesized entheogens including: Terence McKenna, Aldous Huxley, Carlos Castanada, and John Lilly, among others.

The Four Quadrants Revisited

When we employ the tool of the Four Quadrants, instead of weighing one specific approach over another, all methodologies are given equal value and integrated into a single comprehensive frame. Examining religious experience in general and spiritual development in particular, we find that historical and contemporary researchers can be easily organized using an Integral framework.[304] The figure below (first offered in Chapter 1) shows how all of the academic researchers discussed above fit together in graphic form.

	interior	exterior	
	Upper Left		Upper Right
individual	Schleiermacher James Stace Hood Goldman Fowler	Newberg Leary Alpert Strassman	Major researcher organized using the Four Quadrants
collective	Frazer Tylor Carmody Harner	Durckheim Weber Batson Ventis	
	Lower Left		Lower Right

Why are the Four Quadrants useful?

In addition to a simple methodology for organizing research, the Four Quadrants help to secure at least two additional ends that are useful for this book and vital for the broader articulation of the Great Human Tradition: First, using the Four Quadrants ensures that any given research project is as comprehensive as possible. One can easily check to see where a particular approach might be limited and which methodologies are left out. Second, using the Four Quadrants helps to protect against gross and subtle forms of reductionism. Let's examine each of these benefits in turn along with their relevance to the thesis of this book.

Comprehensive Analysis

Using the Four Quadrants as a backdrop for our discussion on spiritual development will help to ensure that the perspectives included are as holistic and as comprehensive as possible. To fully appreciate the way we might uncover a deeper and more comprehensive analysis, we turn to two brief examples of how the research of several scholars might be supplemented using the Four Quadrants.

First, let's examine the historical researchers Stace and Schleiermacher (see Appendix 1). Both scholars focus their study on the interior of the individual (UL). They each study a particular type of phenomenology. Although both of their research approaches are perfectly sound in their own right (and in their own quadrant), both Stace and Schleiermacher leave out the individual's exterior (neurological correlates in the UR), along with social (LR) and cultural (LL) factors. In other words, their approaches miss three out of four quadrants.

Second, along a similar vein, scholars like William James hint at both the interior and exterior of the individual (UL and UR)[305] but still leave out the collective dimensions of culture (collective interior in the LL) and systemic influences (collective exterior in the LR). Using an Integral lens, we see that James successfully includes phenomenological and neurological approaches (satisfying requirements for inclusion of the UL and UR quadrants), but fails to include the LL and the LR quadrants in his analysis.[306] Although much of my study in this book focuses on the UL quadrant, I am careful to always consider the implications, influences, and correlates in all four quadrants.

Gross and Subtle Reductionism

In addition to helping to elucidate scholarly limitations and ensure more comprehensive analysis of a given subject, the Four Quadrants also help us to prevent what Wilber calls gross and subtle forms of reductionism. Wilber writes: "subtle reductionism reduces all Left-Hand interiors to the Lower-Right quadrant; that is, reduces all 'I's' and all 'we's' to systems of interwoven 'its' (systems theory is the classic example). Gross reductionism goes one step further and reduces all material systems to material atoms."[307] Let's first look at a brief example of gross reductionism to highlight the point. It is best once again to examine the examples in the context of the Great Human Tradition.

Some scholars insist that all spiritual experience is "nothing but" neurological synapses firing in the brain. Others claim that mystical experiences are caused by reduced oxygen or frontal lobe seizures. In both examples, researchers are quick to reduce all Upper Left phenomena to the biological quadrant in the Upper Right. Some researchers, like Matthew Alper, even state this explicitly. Alper argues that because some mystical experiences can be induced through psychopharmacology, they must necessarily be reducible to neurology and biology. Alper explains his position as follows:

> The fact that psychedelic drugs have a cross-cultural tendency to stimulate experiences we define as being either spiritual, religious, mystical or transcendental means we must possess some physiological mechanism whose function is to generate this particular type of conscious experience. If we didn't possess such a mechanism, there is no way that these drugs could possibly stimulate such experiences in us.[308]

In the above quote, we begin to see Alper's preference for biology (Upper Right) over internal experience (Upper Left). With a foundation for gross reductionism laid, Alper continues, "the fact that there exists a certain class of drugs—molecules—that can evoke a spiritual experience in us supports the notion that spiritual consciousness must be physiological in nature. In support of this, hundreds of ethnobotanical studies lend further substantiation to the neurophysiological origin of the mystical experience."[309] In these final two sentences, Alper concludes with a classic form of gross reductionism claiming that the very "origin" of mystical experience is in the brain.

Using Wilber's Four Quadrants we see that Alper's claim that spiritual experiences are *caused* by neurological correlates is a blatant form of reductionism.[310] He reduces everything to the UR Quadrant and denies the inherent validity of the UL Quadrant. Given the available information we have at our disposal, we cannot determine causation or "origin." To the contrary, all we can say is that there are direct correlations, or what Batson calls "observable tracks," in the brain that correspond to religious experience.[311] Said even more strongly, we might say that the brain is the exterior of the interior state.

This means that every given interior, subjective spiritual experience in the Upper Left co-arises with an exterior, objective correlate in the Upper Right. Avoiding the tendency for both scientism (the dominance of materialistic reductionism) and unwarranted metaphysical claims, we cannot determine either as causative.

Most social theorists are not as assertive as Alper and instead are careful not to make the same type of false conclusions. Thus many social theorists skillfully avoid gross reductionism. However, these same scholars are not immune to more subtle forms of reductionism. Just as we should be careful to avoid gross reductionism, reducing everything to biology in the Upper Right quadrant, it is equally important that we avoid assertions that spiritual experiences are merely social constructions or simply the products of collective factors and expectations (thus reducing spiritual development and experience to the Lower Left and Lower Right quadrants through a form of subtle reductionism). The approach taken in this book uses Wilber's Four Quadrant model to fully honor all four dimensions of reality.

Closing Remarks

All these examples remind us that this survey only begins to touch upon available information. Future scholars of Integral Religious Studies will have to extend beyond the limitations of my own Western academic bias to include much of the research happening at other universities and academic institutions around the globe. It is my hope that at a minimum, these examples begin to provide a background of the type of research already underway. Ultimately, Kalevi Tamminen, professor emeritus of religious education at the University of Helsinki, states the issue correctly when he writes:

Any model of religious experience alone is not enough to explain development; the various factors influencing experience should also be presented...for some time an urgent need for interdisciplinary collaboration has been felt among the researchers of this field. [312]

This book has been an attempt to elaborate the type of complex approach for which Tamminen calls. As such, it is vital that an Integral model of spiritual development not only touches upon all the various approaches, but that it also finds a way to organize and integrate them. As we've seen, the Integral approach provides just the type of framework we need for the Great Human Tradition to be fully recognized and for spirituality to have a lasting impression in all Four Quadrants during the twenty-first century and beyond.

Appendix 2
Mapping the Traditions Using the Three Core Vectors

The following chart offers a few orienting generalizations as to how some traditions might line up with reference to the categories of state-stage, structure-stage, and state access according to region and sect. Obviously, these regions and the traditions are not homogenous. There are clear exemplars in each tradition that are exceptions to the ideas suggested. So with that in mind please hold the chart lightly.

As you examine the chart please consider the "center of gravity" of what the tradition tends to teach on average. Ultimately, this sort of analysis will only be successful if we can develop sociographs of the various traditions, comparing their respective lines of development and areas of expertise. For now, it is my hope that the following initial outline is helpful for future projects considering the emergence of a universal spirituality and the role of Integral Religious Studies in honoring our Great Human Tradition.

Religion	State-Stage (Vantage Point)	Structure-Stage	State Access
Protestant Christianity in the United States	Gross	Mythic	Gross
Pentecostal/Evangelical Christianity in the United States	Gross	Mythic	Subtle
Eastern Orthodox Christianity	Nondual	Mythic	Causal
Buddhism in the United States	Nondual	Postmodern	Causal
Buddhism in South East Asia (Theravada)	Causal	Mythic	Causal
Buddhism in Tibet	Nondual	Mythic	Causal
Islam in the United States	Gross	Mythic	Gross
Islam in Middle East	Gross	Mythic	Gross
Islamic Sufism	Nondual	Mythic	Causal
Hinduism in the United States (e.g., Siddha Yoga)	Nondual	Postmodern	Causal
Hinduism in India	Nondual	Mythic	Causal
Judaism in the United States (non-orthodox)	Gross	Modern	Gross
Jewish Kabbalah	Nondual	Mythic	Causal
Shamanism in the United States (as practiced by non-natives)	Subtle	Postmodern	Subtle
Shamanism in the Amazon	Subtle	Magic	Subtle

Figure 26: Average state-stage, structure-stage, and state access as taught by various wisdom streams according to region

Appendix 2 - Mapping the Traditions Using the Three Core Vectors

Bibliography

Anandavardhana, Abhinavagupta, and Daniel Henry Holmes. Ingalls. *The Dhvanyaloka of Anandavardhana with the Locana of Abhinavagupta.* Cambridge, Mass.: Harvard University Press, 1990.

Alper, Matthew. *The "God" Part of the Brain : A Scientific Interpretation of Human Spirituality and God.* Rogue Press, 1996.

Argyle, Michael. and Benjamin Beit-Hallahmi. *The Social Psychology of Religion.* London ; Boston: Routledge & K. Paul, 1975.

Batson, C. Daniel, Patricia Schoenrade et al. *Religion and the Individual : A Social-Psychological Perspective.* New York: Oxford University Press, 1993.

Brown, Daniel P. *Pointing Out the Great Way : The Stages of Meditation in the Mah¯amudr¯a Tradition.* Boston: Wisdom Publications, 2006.

Bucke, Richard Maurice. *Cosmic Consciousness : A Study in the Evolution of the Human Mind.* Dover ed. ed., Mineola, N.Y.: Dover Publications, Inc., 2009.

Burckhardt, Titus. *Introduction to Sufi Doctrine.* [2008 ed.]. ed., Vol. Library of perennial philosophy. Spiritual classics series. Bloomington, Ind.: World Wisdom, 2008.

Clayton, Philip, and Zachary R. Simpson. *The Oxford Handbook of Religion and Science.* Vol. Oxford handbooks Oxford ; New York: Oxford University Press, 2006.

Cohen, Andrew. *Being and Becoming: Exploring the Teachings of Evolutionary Enlightenment.* 2010.

Combs, Allan. *Consciousness Explained Better : Towards an Integral Understanding of the   Multifaceted Nature of Consciousness.* 1st ed. ed., St. Paul, Minn.: Paragon House, 2009.

Dyczkowski, Mark S. G. *The Doctrine of Vibration : An Analysis of the Doctrines and Practices of Kashmir Shaivism.* Vol. SUNY series in the Shaiva traditions of Kashmir. Albany: State University of New York Press, 1987.

Emmons, Robert A. *The Psychology of Ultimate Concerns: Motivation and Spirituality in Personality.* New York: Guilford Press, 1999.

Fowler, James W. *Stages of Faith : The Psychology of Human Development and the Quest for Meaning.* San Francisco: Harper & Row, 1981.

Goleman, Daniel. *The Meditative Mind: The Varieties of Meditative Experience.* 1st ed. ed., Los Angeles, New York: J.P. Tarcher, Inc. Distributed by St. Martin's Press, 1988.

Grof, Stanislav. *The Cosmic Game : Explorations of the Frontiers of Human Consciousness.* Vol. SUNY series in transpersonal and humanistic psychology Albany: State University of   New   York Press, 1998.

Hood, Ralph W. *Handbook of Religious Experience.* Birmingham, Ala.: Religious Education Press, 1995.

Hubbard, Barbara Marx. *Conscious Evolution : Awakening the Power of Our Social Potential.* Novato, Calif.: New World Library, 1998.

James, William. *The Varieties of Religious Experience: A Study in Human Nature.* New York: Longmans, Green, and co., 1902.

Katz, Steven T. *Mysticism and Philosophical Analysis.* New York: Oxford University Press, 1978.

Michon, Jean-Louis, and Roger Gaetani. *Sufism: Love & Wisdom.* Vol. The perennial philosophy series Bloomington, Ind.: World Wisdom, 2006.

Proudfoot, Wayne. *Religious Experience.* Berkeley: University of California Press, 1985.

Bibliography

Schultes, Richard Evans & Robert F. Raffauf. *Vine of the Soul: Medicine Men, Their Plants and Rituals in the Colombian Amazonia*. Oracle, AZ: Synergetic, 1992.

Stace, W. T. *The Teachings of the Mystics: Selections from the Great Mystics and Mystical Writings of the World*. [New York]: New American Library, 1960.

Stewart, John. *Evolution's Arrow : The Direction of Evolution and the Future of Humanity*. Rivett, A.C.T.: Chapman Press, 2000.

Tart, Charles T. *States of Consciousness*. 1st ed. ed., New York: E. P. Dutton,   1975.

Tillich, Paul. *Dynamics of Faith*. New York: Harper, 1956.

Underhill, Evelyn. *Mysticism : A Study in the Nature and Development of Spiritual Consciousness*. Mineola, N.Y.: Dover Publications, 2002.

Visser, Frank. *Ken Wilber: Thought as Passion*. Vol. SUNY series in transpersonal and humanistic psychology Albany, NY: State University of New York Press, 2003.

Voltaire. *The Philosophical Dictionary for the Pocket*. London: S. Bladon, 1765.

Walsh, Roger N. *The World of Shamanism: New Views of an Ancient Tradition*. 1st ed. ed., Woodbury, Minn.: Llewellyn Publications, 2007.

Wilber, Ken., Jack. Engler, and Daniel P. Brown. *Transformations of Consciousness: Conventional and Contemplative Perspectives on Development*. Boston, New York: New Science Library Distributed in the U.S. by Random House, 1986.

Wilber, Ken. *The Spectrum of Consciousness*. Wheaton, Ill.: Theosophical Pub. House, 1977.

――――. *Collected Works of Ken Wilber: Sex, Ecology, Spirituality : The Spirit of Evolution*. 2nd, rev. ed. ed., Boston: Shambhala, 2000.

――――. *Integral Spirituality: A Startling New Role for Religion in the Modern and Postmodern World*. 1st ed. ed., Boston: Integral Books, 2006.

――――. *Integral Psychology: Consciousness, Spirit, Psychology, Therapy*.

Boston: Shambhala, 2000.

———. *A Sociable God: Toward a New Understanding of Religion.* Boston: Shambhala, 2005.

Zohar, Danah, and I. N. Marshall. *Sq: Spiritual Intelligence, the Ultimate Intelligence.* London: Bloomsbury, 2000.

Endnotes

1 The conveyor belt, in its simplest articulation, is a theory proposing that each level of psychological developmental complexity interprets/enacts religion and/or spiritual differently. If we follow Wilber's basic metric of five stages of development (ranging from magic to mythic to rational to pluralistic to Integral), we'll see that the theory suggests that every new level of psychological complexity has a corresponding religious interpretation. There is a magic version, a mythic version, a rational version, a pluralistic version, and an Integral version of each tradition. A fully articulated and established "conveyor belt" would outline each stage of development within each religious tradition. Ultimately, if each of those outlines were made explicit it would allow our world's religions to be stewards of psychological transformation and growth around the globe, rather than the prerational obstacles that they now most often pose.

2 I explain faith development in this chapter in more detail in two different places: 1) when I survey the existing work in the field, and mention Fowler's work and 2) in my definition of spirituality as a specific line of intelligence.

3 Cindy Wigglesworth's term "spiritual intelligence" is more closely aligned with my broader term "spiritual development." In my opinion, Wigglesworth's Spiritual Intelligence Assessment is not a measure of a single specific line of development (vis-a-vis Fowler) but perhaps the only test extant to measure an individual's spiritual development in its entirety.

4 Similar conclusions are made by other scholars as well. For example, Margaret Poloma uses the terms religious experience and mysticism interchangeably: "Religious experience and mysticism are essentially the same phenomenon, differing only in degree. As such, these two terms can be used interchangeably." See Hood, 1995, p 166.

5 Alfred Korzybski's first coined the phrase in a 1931 paper. "A Non-Aristotelian System and Its Necessity for Rigor in Mathematics and Physics," a paper presented before the American Mathematical Society at

the New Orleans, Louisiana, meeting of the American Association for the Advancement of Science, December 28, 1931. Reprinted in *Science and Sanity*, 1933, p. 747–61.

6   Wilber, *The Collected Works of Ken Wilber: Sex, Ecology, Spirituality*, 2000, p 127

7   A full version of the model shows increasing levels of complexity and development. Evolution in all Four Quadrants is shown in the graph below (adopted from Wilber's *Sex, Ecology, Spirituality*, 2000)

8   Wilber, *The Collected Works of Ken Wilber: Sex, Ecology, Spirituality*, 2000, p 127

9   More properly stated this refers to "quadrivia" and not the Four Quadrants.

10   It is important to recognize that few researchers fit into the Four Quadrants perfectly. Many researchers employ minor degrees of cross-methodologies. However for the purposes of this Integrative model, I organize research of religious development and spiritual experience according to the more dominant methodology employed by the particular researcher. Furthermore, the examples are meant to be representative of the type of research methodology used to examine spiritual development.

11   Rather than viewing figure 2 as if each scholar is somehow "in" a particular quadrant, it is better to understand that scholars are associated with quadrants due to the fact that they give methodological preference to either the interior or exterior of the individual or the collective. That is to say, each researcher uses a methodology that is biased towards one of the Four Quadrants.

12   Wilber, 2006, p 149

13   On a positive note, some scholars (i.e., Newberg) are already moving into an integral perspective and do their best to account for social, cultural, and phenomenological experiences without reducing causation to any single quadrant. Scholars such as Newberg who fully acknowledge their methodological limitations within a much larger framework are harbingers of the type of research that we can expect in an Integral Age.

14   Wilber's Eight Zones: For an even more detailed and more balanced analysis, the Four Quadrants can be expanded into Eight Zones. Just as any event can be viewed from an individual or collective perspective and from an interior or exterior orientation, each quadrant also has an inside or outside. Each inside and outside perspective revealed can be labeled as a particular zone, as shown in figure A below.

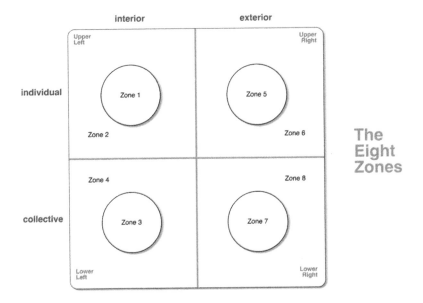

Figure A: Wilber's Eight Zones (adapted from *Integral Spirituality*)

Zone 1 is the inside of the Upper Left Quadrant, whereas zone 2 is the outside of the Upper Left Quadrant. Zone 3 is the inside of the Lower Left Quadrant and zone 4 is the outside of the Lower Left Quadrant, etc. Historically all of the mystics of religious traditions use the same methodology. That is, they examine the interior of their own individual experience; they are examining their own Upper Left Quadrant. Furthermore, they are examining their own interior from the inside and reporting their subjective experience. This means that mystics, the world over, tend to take a zone 1 approach.

A zone 1 approach (i.e., viewing the inside of the Upper Left) is quite different from a zone 2 approach where a researcher examines the outside of the Upper Left. As Wilber points out in *Integral Spirituality*, in contrast to the approach taken by mystics, researchers like James Fowler examine stages of spiritual unfolding from the outside of the Upper Left. Figure B below shows the distinction between zone 1 and zone 2 approaches.

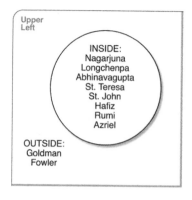

Figure B: Inside and outside of the Upper Left Quadrant

We quickly see how when the Eight Zones are added to Wilber's Four Quadrant Model we are able to get a more clearly organized sense of the complexity described in chapter 1 and appendix 1.

Over the course of this book, I touch on each of these eight perspectives. Although I include some of the neurological correlates (Upper Right Quadrant), and will account for the fact that spiritual development is necessarily influenced by cultural and social influences (Lower Left and Lower Right), the majority of my exploration centers on the interior of an individual (Upper Left Quadrant) and examines the complex interaction of zones 1 and 2.

15 As Wilber correctly points out, although Fowler studies the interior developments of the individual as stages of spiritual intelligence, his approach is quite different from the methodologies of Nargarjuna or Abhinavagupta (two sages who study mystical states directly in their own experience). Whereas Fowler studies the individual interior from the outside (zone 2), Abhinavagupta and Nargarjuna study the individual interior from the inside (zone 1).

In a similar vein, it is clear that we can make parallel distinctions when examining other scholars of religious experience and spiritual development in the Lower Left Quadrant. For instance, E.B. Tylor examined cultures from the perspective of zone 4, the outside of the interior collective. Whereas Michael Harner entered into the culture and practiced ceremonies from the inside of the collective interior space (zone 3). Figure C below shows this distinction in the Lower Left Quadrant.

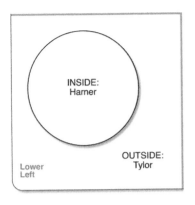

Figure C: Inside and outside of the Lower Left Quadrant

(zone 3 and zone 4)

16 See Wilber, 2006, p 90. All summaries of the Wilber-Combs Matrix are adapted from Wilber's *Integral Spirituality*.

17 In volume 2 of this series, *Evolution's Ally*, I use the terms mythic, magic, rational, and pluralistic to describe each stage of individual psychological development as they show up within multiple religious traditions; whereas I reserved the terms traditional (premodern), modern, postmodern, Integral to refer to major paradigm shifts in collective consciousness. Although in volume 2 the distinction helped to maintain a sense of clarity between collective and individual transformation, in this volume, I use the two sets of terms interchangeably.

18 See Wilber's *The Spectrum of Consciousness*, 1977.

19 See the PhD work of Jeffery Martin: *Ego Development Stage Does Not Predict Persistent Non-Symbolic Experience* completed at the California Institute of Integral Studies in 2010.

20 See Jeffery Martin's dissertation. Using empirical research to compare the reports of individuals in both Hood's Mysticism Scale (consistency and type of state experiences) to Cook-Greuter's Ego Development Scale (structure-stage development), Martin shows that the structure-stages do not predict any sort of correlation with state development.

21 Wilber states: "Putting zone-#1 and zone-#2 research together gives us the W-C lattice [i.e. Wilber-Combs Matrix]." (Wilber, 2006, p 93)

22 Wilber, 2006, p 90

23 As Wilber points out: "That bold sentence was for us early researchers the breakthrough and real turning point. It allowed us to see how individuals

at even some of the lower stages of development—such as magic or mythic—could still have profound religious, spiritual, and meditative state experiences. Gross/psychic, subtle, causal, and nondual were no longer stages stacked on top of the Western conventional stages, but were states (including altered states and peak experiences) that can and did occur alongside any of those stages." (Wilber, 2006. p 91)

24 In the original spectrum of consciousness as shown in figure 4, this type of state access would not be possible but was rather held open to only those at the highest stages of development.

25 Wilber writes: "A person will interpret that state according to the stage they are at." (Wilber, 2006, p 90)

26 Wilber makes a similar note, highlighting the fact that interpretation will always occur "according to the entire AQAL matrix" operative at that time. (Wilber, 2006, p 94). This means that interpretation will be conditioned according to levels, lines, states, types, and all Four Quadrants. See appendix 1 for details on Wilber's Four Quadrants.

27 As discussed in chapter 8, an even more complete model would also include shadow.

28 However, at a certain point of structural development beyond Integral, a nondual vantage point becomes a pre-requisite for further growth.

29 Private conversation, Jan 22, 2012, in Denver, Colorado.

30 In chapter 5, we explored how all three of these elements come together to form the Spiritual Development Cube.

31 For further details on the terms "deep structure" and "surface feature" see Wilber's *Integral Psychology* and *A Sociable God*. In his original usage the term, a "deep structure" refers to the cross-cultural commonalities of a particular psychological or spiritual phenomenon. His use of the term "surface feature" refers to the various ways that those deep structures show up in experience according to the unavoidable influence of the Four Quadrants (including dimensions of self, biology, culture, and social system among others).

32 Once the deep structure of the single, underlying path to spiritual realization is distilled, each stage can be reverse-engineered and adapted to fit both religious and secular circumstances alike. This means that the basic outlines offered in this chapter can just as easily be adapted into a psychological context as they can into a tradition specific spiritual context. Furthermore, within the realm of spirituality, the deep structures outlined in this basic model also allow it the flexibility to be adapted into both theistic (e.g., Christian, Jewish, Islamic, Hindu) and nontheistic (e.g., Buddhist) models of growth with equal ease.

33 Brown's work traced the similarities and differences using three

authoritative texts: Patanjali's Yoga Sutras (Hinduism), Buddhaghosa's Visuddhimagga (Theravada Buddhism), and *Bkra' Shis rnam rgyal*'s main commentary on the Mahamudra, *Nges don. . . zla zer* (Mahayana). See Wilber, Ken., Jack. Engler, and Daniel P. Brown. *Transformations of Consciousness: Conventional and Contemplative Perspectives on Development.* 1st ed. ed., Boston New York: New Science Library Distributed in the U.S. by Random House, 1986. p 222. Brown's more recent work is also relevant to tradition specific contexts. See Brown, Daniel P. *Pointing Out the Great Way: The Stages of Meditation in the Mahamudra Tradition.* Boston: Wisdom Publications, 2006.

34 Many other Western researchers have inquired into the stages of the meditative path and various types of mystical experience. Historically, I look to early scholars like Bucke (*Cosmic Consciousness*), James (*Varieties of Religious Experience*), and Evelyn Underhill (*Mysticism*). More recently, we turn to the work of Daniel Goleman (*The Meditative Mind*), Charles Tart (*States of Consciousness*), as well as the work of Stan Grof (*Cosmic Game*) and Allen Combs (*Consciousness Explained Better*), all of whom have generated substantial data and insight. A next generation of researchers, including scholars like Jeffery Martin, have also begun to look towards a more comprehensive three-vector model. Following the lead of Wilber, Combs, and others, Jeffery suggests that there may be a third dimension of spiritual growth related to identity. (See his dissertation titled *Examining Claims of Self Reported Persistent Non-symbolic Experiences in Adults Using the M Scale and WUSCT.*) In short, although I allow all of the aforementioned researchers to both explicitly and implicitly influence the models offered in this text, none of them offer a more comprehensive understanding of identity transformation than Daniel P. Brown.

35 In a similar way that a scientific discovery in Germany is applicable to a study in Japan, the distinction between the "event perspective" and "mind perspective" holds cross-cultural significance despite the fact that it was originally discovered by the Tibetans. For this reason, it is included here in our more generalized outline of vantage points.

36 Note that both aspects of awareness can be inside the individual interior (UL) so that "objective" here does not require an exterior (UR). This will be explored further with regard to zone 1a and zone 1b.

37 Brown, 2006, p 286.

38 Brown, personal interview, August 9, 2011.

39 Looking through the lens of Integral theory, both the mind perspective and event perspective provide further distinctions within what Wilber would refer to as zone 1 of the Upper Left Quadrant. Using these new aspects we can further delineate zone 1 to show zone 1a pertaining to the mind perspective and zone 1b signifying the event perspective.[66] Both the mind perspective and the event perspectives arise in the inside of the individual interior and can be noted as aspects of phenomenological experience.

40 Whereas Brown's work as presented in *Transformations of Consciousness* traces eighteen stages of the meditation path including six stages of preliminary practice, six stages of concentration (with support and without support), and six stages of insight practice (ordinary and extraordinary), in this chapter I focus most of my attention on those higher stages of the path revolving around insight meditation wherein the practitioner begins to gain a deeper sense of identity and the various ways that awareness constructs reality moment to moment.

41 See Brown in Transformations of Consciousness, p 223.

42 See Brown's University of Chicago dissertation Mahamudra Meditation Stages and Contemporary Cognitive Psychology: A Study in Comparative Psychological Hermeneutics, Chicago, Il 1981. p 689.

43 At this early level of practice, awareness is sometimes also confused with being the physical body.

44 In each of these vantage point shifts, zone 1a (subject) is transformed into zone 1b (object). This means that Robert Kegan's insights around structure-stages can also be applied to vantage point development. To paraphrase: the *seeming* subject of one stage becomes the *seeming* object of the subject of the next stage. I use the word *seeming* because eventually even the subject object duality is seen through.

45 A deep thank you to my friend and teacher Bruce Lyon for pointing out the importance of including the masculine aspect of "penetration" alongside the feminine dimension of "inclusion."

46 For example, ego development is a function that unfolds within the confines of a shallower set of vantage points (often thought and personality). That is, although ego development is many things, it is mainly a function of gross and subtle identity. Even though ego development also proceeds through a process of increasing embrace, it is a process of developing complexity and not a process of transcending the construction of identity. I might only have a vantage point of what Brown would call "awareness" or what Wilber would call "subtle identity" but might still have a very high level of ego development reaching structures of autonomous, integrative, etc.

47 We explore this idea at the end of the chapter and then again in chapter 8.

48 From a certain perspective, spiritual realization can be viewed as a function of the speed of awareness. One way to consider it is to think about each level of obscuration as vibrating at a different rate. If awareness is vibrating at a slower rate than the particular vantage point than it is obscured by it. If awareness is faster than a particular level than that vantage point can be seen through as transparent.

49 It seems that if this is true, then we must begin to explore the pragmatic value of certain beliefs to determine which perspectives and expectations are more useful than others. I suspect that Integral practitioners of the future will judge meditative paths not only on the degree to which they can induce spiritual realization to a vantage point of awakened awareness but also by the degree to which the initial "setting up" results in a type of awakening that leads to the creation of a better planet, culture, and individual.

50 Brown, Transformations of Consciousness, 1986 p 266.

51 Brown, Transformations of Consciousness, 1986 p 267.

52 Because each account below is fairly brief, those readers interested in more in-depth accounts are encouraged to consult the material in the bibliography. Furthermore, a more exhaustive and nuanced account from the traditions is in the making. I am currently in the process of gathering teams of scholars to produce religion-specific volumes that cover each of the vectors of growth presented in this book. These tradition specific volumes will compose future books in this series. Scholars interested in contributing to future volumes can contact me directly.

53 Furthermore, because the Tantric Hindu example was not originally examined by Brown it helps to provide further evidence that his deep structures do indeed have cross-cultural relevance.

54 A reference point precisely because the model employed here transcends and includes other versions of spiritual realization. A tradition that pushes only to subtle or causal identity is not incorrect but rather not as full as one that pushes all the way to a witness or nondual identity state-stage. In a complementary fashion, the traditions that do point all the way to a full nondual awakening usually have mapped the lower state-stages to at least some extent.

55 The examples below are meant to be descriptive. In each example below, I'll point out where corresponding vantage points are relevant. Rather than an exhaustive description, the examples below are meant to be descriptive. Ultimately, it will be clear that in each tradition it is the final collapse of the subject and object that allows for the full recognition of an identity non-separate from whole of reality.

56 Brown, 2006, p 366.

57 Brown, 2006, p 366.

58 The term "awareness-itself" is used here idiosyncratically and not necessarily to refer to the specific level of awareness beyond personality in particular.

59 Brown, 2006, p 366.

60 Brown, 2006, p 441.

61 Brown, 2006, p 442.

62 Dyczkowski, Mark S. G. *The Doctrine of Vibration: An Analysis of the Doctrines and Practices of Kashmir Shaivism.* Vol. SUNY series in the Shaiva traditions of Kashmir Albany: State University of New York Press, 1987. p 139.

63 Dyczkowski, 1987, p 142.

64 Dyczkowski, 1987, p 153.

65 Dyczkowski, 1987, p 141; also see his footnote.

66 Dyczkowski, 1987, p 140.

67 In addition to the difference in language (i.e., theistic vs. nontheistic), Brown also makes an important point that the fundamental experience of reality is different depending on whether one is a Buddhist or Hindu. Whereas the Buddhists see all events as a moment to moment discontinuity, Hindus tend to experience reality as a continuous stream. See Brown, *Transformations of Consciousness*, 1986 p 225.

68 Burckhardt, Titus. *Introduction to Sufi Doctrine.* [2008 ed.]. ed., Vol. Library of perennial philosophy. Spiritual classics series. Bloomington, Ind.: World Wisdom, 2008. p 69.

69 Michon, Jean-Louis., and Roger Gaetani. *Sufism: Love & Wisdom.* Vol. The perennial philosophy series Bloomington, Ind.: World Wisdom, 2006. p 96.

70 Burckhardt, 2008, p 69.

71 Burckhardt, 2008, p 69.

72 Burckhardt, 2008, p 65–66.

73 He goes on to describe the two vantage points (divine and human) with even greater clarity using the phrase "point of view": "This is the Unique Prototype (*al-Unmudhaj al-farid*) or 'Clear Prototype' spoken of in the Qur'an and already mentioned above. It should also be recalled that from the divine 'point of view' creation is integrated in this prototype in which we are reflected all the Divine Qualities or 'relationships' (*nisab*) without their being either confused or separated; it is only from the point of view of the creature that the universe appears as multiple. Now the great mediators, whose spirit is identified with the Divine Spirit, are by this fact related to this synthesis of the universe, the great Prototype, which is the unique and direct 'object' of the Divine Act." (Burckhardt, 2008, p 65–66)

74 Burckhardt, 2008, p 66.

75 This is not to say that the Sufi tradition lacks stage models of realization. They do indeed offer several models. However, these models often conflate zone 1a (mind perspective) and zone 1b (event perspective). As a result, they

resemble other Christian mystical accounts in that many only truly offer one shift in identity but several stages of sequential changes in the field of experience.

76 A second problem with regard to the denial of shallower identities is worth noting in brief. As we explored in chapter 7 in relation to conscious evolution, there is a *responsibility* of all those with deeper levels of awakening to embrace and nurture all shallower identities. This process of acknowledging and embracing shallower identities allows one to meet others at their particular level of realization with compassion. (Another way of wording it is to say that there is an inseparability of wisdom and compassion. Each vantage point can be viewed as a deepening of the mind as well as a deepening of the heart. Each deeper vantage point allows one to act from a "place" of more care and deeper love.) If shallower identities are denied, there is no capacity to reach into relative reality in order to serve. Practitioners consciously participating in the Great Human Tradition protect against this sort of disaster and are sure to bring these critical dimensions of health and well being to the process of spiritual realization.

77 See Zohar, *Spiritual Intelligence: The Ultimate Intelligence*, 2001.

78 Emmons, *The Psychology of Ultimate Concern*, 1999, p 176.

79 When we return to Wigglesworth's definition of spiritual intelligence in chapter 9, you will find that her definition is much more closely aligned with what I call spiritual development. In other words, Wigglesworth's definition requires much more than structural growth. It also requires vantage point development and state access. In general, Wigglesworth's model of spiritual intelligence is broader and more holistic than the narrow version used in this chapter.

80 See volume 2 of this series *Evolution's Ally*.

81 All of this is discussed in detail in volume 2.

82 In that initial endeavor, because the efforts were all made within a religion specific context, I use the term "religious orientation" interchangeably with the term "spiritual intelligence." In both cases (religion-specific and faith-neutral uses), spiritual intelligence always relates to issues of ultimate concern and, as a result, it plays a determining factor in how an individual interprets and orients toward reality.

83 See Wilber's work in *Integral Spirituality*, 2006.

84 Gardner, 1983.

85 Fowler, 1981.

86 As a side note about spiritual intelligence, Michael Schwartz has purposed that because spiritual intelligence (faith development) relates to ultimate concern, its influence is so strong that when it is activated that it may

have the power to drag other lines up or down depending on its developmental relationship to the other areas of growth (personal conversation). Important to note here that if this is true, spiritual intelligence will not be able to pull things higher than the highest stage they have developed thus far. It may however be able to cause regression.

87 See Fowler's groundbreaking work in *Stages of Faith*, 1981.

88 The term "conveyor belt" refers to the fact that each stage of psychological development will interpret religion differently according to their developmental capacity. See Wilber, 2006.

89 See Wilber, 2006.

90 This correlates to culture in the LL, socio-economic shifts in the LR, and increase in subtle mass-energy in the UR. At the end of the chapter we tracked how the move into modern, postmodern, and Integral levels of consciousness have been stunted due to an overall abandonment of spirituality as a result of the modern enlightenment values. I call this the pathology of Modern Endarkenment.

91 Interpretation is always an all-quadrant affair. As I have shown in my other work, religious interpretation will also be influenced by the regional cultural values as well as the various factors in the right-hand quadrants.

92 Wilber, 2006, p 194.

93 See Wilber, 2006.

94 The traditional level of development described here combines the magic and mythic stages of development as outlined in volume 2.

95 It is important to remember that there are healthy and unhealthy versions of each stage. Moreover, each stage is valid and deserves its place on the spiral. This distinction helps us understand that traditional isn't "bad." Even though it is indeed ethnocentric. Those at this stage are not necessarily terrorists. Terrorism stems only from an unhealthy version of traditional consciousness.

96 Spong, John Shelby. *A New Christianity for a New World: Why Traditional Faith Is Dying and How a New Faith Is Being Born*, San Francisco: Harper San Francisco, 2001. p 2.

97 Although, this is changing as more individuals in the West are brought up in a secular environment wherein such orientations might represent conforming levels of consciousness and not necessarily self-reflective ones. If raised in an agnostic household or a strictly secular culture, then an expression of agnosticism or atheism can still be trapped at a traditional level of development. One might only be an atheist because his or her parents are atheists.

Endnotes

98   As paradigmatic examples see Dawkins' *The God Delusion* and Harris' *End of Faith*.

99   See Wilber, 2006.

100   Ramakrishna. *Sayings of Sri Ramakrishna; the Most Exhaustive Collection of Them, Their Number Being 1120*, 10th ed., Madras: Sri Ramakrishna Math, 1965.

101   In both cases, Hafiz and Rumi often speak of the pluralistic nature of God. It is important to notice that both Rumi and Hafiz also express a nondual vantage point of total union with the Divine. This vantage point (state-stage identity) is not to be confused with the level of development of spiritual intelligence (structure-stage at postmodern).

102   Wilber notes some of the pathologies that can occur at this level of development in *Transformations of Consciousness*. See Wilber, Englar, and Brown, 1986. Wilber's writing in 1986 is still in the context of stacking states on top of structures (a claim which he has now corrected showing that states are a different vector than structures), however his points about pathology are still relevant.

103   When this level of spiritual intelligence is hijacked by lower levels of development it can be used as an excuse for fundamentalism and acts of terror. "You don't have a right to judge my actions. It's my religious right..." etc. This is, as Sean Hargens calls it, premodern content in a postmodern context. [Personal conversation.] Other examples include the ways that a teacher or spiritual leader might use postmodern arguments to justify breaking ethical codes around sexuality with students.

104   Often this means that leaders with an Integral level of spiritual intelligence spend much of their time drawing adequate maps that help show the possibilities for vertical growth in each tradition.

105   The following account takes a specifically Western perspective at first, only to eventually show that Western trends and pathologies have begun to infect much of the rest of the globe.

106   The term Dark Age is derived from the Latin saeculum obscurum. See Dwyer, John C., *Church History: Twenty Centuries of Catholic Christianity*, (1998) p. 155. Baronius, Caesar. Annales Ecclesiastici, Vol. X. Roma, 1602, p. 647.

107   Of course there were exceptions. Multiple versions of rational spirituality have persisted and evolved over time. I cover many of these in volume 2 of this series. However, on a whole, spirituality was stunted at mythic stages.

108   To make matters even worse still, as other countries around the globe modernize, and in certain cases Westernize, the pathology of a stunted

line of spiritual intelligence is infectious and is making its way to all corners of the globe.

109   Wilber, 2006, p 183.

110   Wilber, 2006 p 183.

111   The shift from more mythic/traditional worldviews led to major improvements in civilization. For instance, a mythic to rational transition in culture led to a corresponding shift from agricultural modes of techno-economic production in the Lower Right to more industrial forms. Although it is certainly not without its downfalls, this transition has led more people out of poverty and malnourishment than ever before. This shifts also plays a role in ending slavery.

Alongside the many benefits it brought, modern consciousness also instigated new modes of destruction and war. As self-reflective and representational modes of thinking increased in capacity, there emerged a massive disassociation between mind and body, mirrored almost identically in an increasing divide between humanity's small scale but sustainable exploitation of the earth to the current unsustainable levels we see today. These splits between mind/body and humanity/earth continue today. It is not unrealistic to suggest that such splits can be directly correlated to contributing factors in both the obesity epidemic (mind/body divide) as well as the massive environmental degradation currently underway (humanity/earth divide).

112   Wilber, 2006, p 193.

113   Wilber accounts for both modern and postmodern critiques of religion and spirituality in *Integral Spirituality*, 2006, p 45.

114   Again, this is not a blanket statement true for all individuals alive today. There are some individuals who have already rescued their spiritual intelligence from lower stages of development to allow it to mature through modern, postmodern and Integral levels.

115   As we shall explore, a fuller depiction of the lens of knowing is made up of all Four of Wilber's Quadrants and not just the stage of individual structural development in the Upper Left.

116   This vital distinction between changes in the subjective aspect of awareness and changes in the objective aspect of awareness is well-established within the Tibetan and Hindu Tantric traditions. The important point was most recently elaborated and clarified to me by Daniel P. Brown. (Brown himself learned the distinction from one of his own teachers Denma Locho). As we saw earlier, Brown refers to this distinction as the difference between the event perspective and mind perspective.

117   The differences suggested in this chapter between states/objects/realms on one hand and vantage points on the other will be implicitly

transmitted by the very nature of introducing and clearly defining this third vector. In the next chapter, I spoke more explicitly about how all three areas of spiritual development relate to each other. It is there, in chapter 5, that I develop a full case for why an Integral model of spiritual development ought to distinguish clearly between all three vectors. And why the three vectors cannot be conflated with the each other.

118 Brown, 1981.

119 Although it is true that these extraordinary states are associated with a particular realm, several of these states can be induced while in the waking state. That means that the correlating realm that holds the experience can be entered into from the waking state even while the dominant container of experience is the gross realm. This same idea comes up again later in relation to my discussion on wake-induced lucid dreams (WILDs).

120 At a certain point in the process of spiritual realization, all distinctions between interior and exterior collapse. The same is true for objective and subjective aspects of awareness.

121 See Wilber, *1-2-3 of God*, Sounds True (Audio), 2006.

122 This is an articulation first offered by Wilber. [personal conversation.]

123 See Ferrer, Jorge N., and Jacob H. Sherman. *The Participatory Turn: Spirituality, Mysticism, Religious Studies*. Albany, NY: State University of New York Press, 2008.

124 This refers to all quadrants, levels, lines, states, and types.

125 See Wilber, *Excerpt B —The Many Ways We Touch*. <http://wilber.shambhala.com/html/books/kosmos/excerptB/>; we'll explore this more in the next chapter. For now Wilber sets the tone for us in part 3 of excerpt B. He writes: "We must forgive each other our arising, for our existence always torments others. The golden rule in the midst of this mutual misery has always been, not to do no harm, but as little as possible; and not to love one another, but as much as you can. Therefore, let a calculus of torment as well as one of compassion guide the maps with which we navigate samsara."

126 Although we'll be using the category less often, states can also refer to emotional changes in the affective quality of experience, including states of flow, ecstasy, depression, compassion, delight, wonder. As with all types of states, whether ordinary, extraordinary, or emotional, each can be experienced regardless of one's vantage point. In other words, changing states do not effect one's state-stage identity. As we explore in the next chapter, one can have any state from any vantage point.

127 See Tart, Charles T. *Altered States of Consciousness*. San Francisco: Harper, 1990 and Tart, Charles T. *States of Consciousness*. New York: E. P. Dutton, 1975.

128   This is similar to Wilber's notion that each state/mind of consciousness has a body (gross, subtle, and causal).

129   Most major changes in the field of experience are in some ways related to the three realms of normal human existence: gross, subtle, and causal. Each of these three realms can be thought of as an energetic container— almost like a vibrational world or dimension in and of itself. For instance, major states like waking, dreaming, and deep sleep are all encompassing. As such, they are associated with the gross, subtle, and causal realm, respectively. Minor states like emotional and mental fluctuations can arise within different realms and even within different major states (e.g., I can be filled with bliss in the waking state/gross realms or in the dream state/subtle realm).

130   See Tart, Stace, James, Hood, just to name a few.

131   Brown, 2006, p 423.

132   Grof, Stanislav. *Psychology of the Future: Lessons From Modern Consciousness Research.* Vol. SUNY series in transpersonal and humanistic psychology Albany, N.Y.: State University of New York Press, 2000. p 2.

133   Grof, 2000. p 2.

134   Grof, 2000, p 3.

135   Grof, 2000, p 3.

136   Wilber, 2007, p 93.

137   Wilber, 2007, p 93. In the next sentence, Wilber then goes on to speak of nondual mysticism which is "to experience a oneness with all phenomena arising in gross, subtle, and causal states." In the model I present in this book, I consider "nondual mysticism" a vantage point because it can only be experienced from a first-person perspective. The other states listed here (nature, deity, formless) are all variation on gross, subtle, and causal, respectively. Relationships in the causal are more challenging to detirmine as a result of their formless nature.

138   Wilber, 2007, p 76.

139   In all the examples above, James and Stace along with other contemporary researchers (i.e., Brown, Wilber, etc.) are pointing to the event perspective (zone 1b) or that which is "known." They are not focusing on the mind perspective (zone 1a) the "knower" as described in our discussion of vantage points in chapter 2.

140   Most of the theories addressing the universal commonality of states have been strongly critiqued by postmodern scholarship. Claims to universals appear to violate the foundational understanding that cultural and linguistic matrices play a role in co-creating experience. Further, postmodern scholars worry (correctly) that if we say similar experiences exists in all traditions that we

could potentially slide down the slippery slope to then claim that all traditions are essentially the same. Monolithic approaches that essentialize traditions erroneously homogenize differences. Such approaches, most often associated with the modern paradigm of academic inquiry, tend to leave little room for the particularities and almost always fail to see the cultural and linguistically created reality in which each of us is embedded. The postmodern corrective to essentialization is important and is one that the Great Human Tradition ought to embrace as far as it goes.

With that said, however, because an Integral approach points to common deep structures that are true across traditions, postmodern scholars are often overwhelmed by their own knee-jerk reactions against all universal claims. Because the Integral scholar points to underlying commonalities, the postmodern scholar mistakenly assumes he or she must be making the modern error (ultimately falling victim to the "myth of the given"). In actually, the Integral scholar has included the postmodern critique but has also transcended it to a new level of organization and complexity.

Ultimately, the Integral endeavor to point out cross-cultural deep structures strikes the heart of postmodern scholars concern about grand narratives and universals. What the postmodern position fails to see (as both Habermas and Wilber have pointed out), is that their own claim that "there are no grand narratives" is itself a grand narrative and is therefore a category error in that it renders its own foundational claim untrue by the very nature of asserting it. I'll address these specific issues again in the next chapter in relation to Integral participatory co-creation.

141   It is helpful to briefly reintroduce the Four Quadrants and Eight Zones of Wilber's Integral Theory. Summarizing the discussion above in this way will offer an orienting frame for the conversation. The first point, and the one that often causes the most confusion, is that the objective side of experience (i.e., all the experiences that I can know and see) arise in both the exterior and interior of an individual holon. Wilber's Integral lens is helpful here. Let's start with the Upper Right Quadrant.

As outlined in chapter 1, the Upper Right Hand quadrant refers to the exterior of the individual. Most commonly, when referring to this quadrant, we speak of the brain, the physical body, or behavior. In addition to these commonly referred to items, Wilber also discusses the Upper Right Quadrant in relation to what he calls "artifacts." Artifacts might be simple external objects like a chair, a desk, a rock, or a book. All of these objects, from the physical body to a book, are exterior to the individual. They are exterior objects.

Simple enough so far. However, there is second category of objects. This second category of objects includes those particular events that arise in the objective field of awareness interior to the individual. We can call these interior objects. Here in the footnotes we took an in-depth look at zone 1, (the inside of the interior individual). As we tracked vantage points of awareness to greater and greater degrees of depth and identity we noted that each of those state-stages was highlighted along a spectrum following the subjective aspect of awareness. In an earlier footnote, I briefly referred to this as zone 1a.

An understanding of interior objects allows us to further articulate zone 1. Rather than focus on the subjective side of awareness, one can also look at the objective side of awareness. I call this Zone 1b. This means that although both vantage points and internal objects arise in zone 1, vantage points refer to what arises in zone 1a (the subjective aspect of awareness) whereas interior objects refer to what is arising in zone 1b (the objective aspect of awareness). Brown calls this the difference between the "mind perspective" (zone 1a) and the "event perspective" (zone 1b). Figure D below illustrates the difference between the two categories of objects using Wilber's Four Quadrant model:

Figure D: Exterior objects and interior objects and states

Before we get too far ahead of ourselves, let's look at more complex and practical examples of exterior objects using multiple dimensions. Once we've laid those tracks we can move onto the interior objects in the same way.

Exterior Events

One of the easiest ways to begin to dissect the concept of an external object is to use something like the breath. The breath arises as part of the exterior of the individual, in the Upper Right quadrant. When one focuses attention on the breath one notices all the fluctuations of the gross level of breath. Simple enough, so far.

But the breath, as an exterior object, co-arises in multiple dimensions simultaneously. The breath exists not only on the gross level of reality, that is the molecules, and atoms of nitrogen, oxygen and carbon dioxide that you inhale and exhale but also on the subtle and causal levels of existence. An external object like the breath is made up of gross, subtle, and causal energies. As spiritual cultivation increases so too does an individual's access to these multiple levels of reality, including the energy signatures that correlate. This means that as I cultivate this vector of spiritual development my access to see, feel, and sense objects beyond their gross form, into subtle and causal form also increases. Again, all of this arises in the Upper Right. For a fuller account of this sort of outline see Wilber's Excerpt G toward a comprehensive theory of subtle energies.

Interior Events

Interior objects and changes to the interior field of awareness.

Coming back to the example of meditation. As progress on the path develops, the objects of meditation move from external objects like the breath to internal objects of the mind. Considering that, we now proceed to further study zone 1. Earlier in the footnotes, zone 1 was further divided into a subjective and objective aspect of awareness. This is what Brown calls the "event perspective vs. mind perspective." The mind perspective tracks state-stages of identity—that is, how subjectivity shifts as it moves to a deeper and deeper vantage point (zone 1a). In this section, we track zone 1b the objective side of interior awareness.

In addition to the external objects described above, there are other types of objects. For example a shift in the field of experience is something that can be seen phenomenologically. A change in emotional states can be seen or felt. The same is true for states that involve luminosity or light. Perhaps intense patterns of fractalized geometry, or sounds. All of these phenomena arise in zone 1, in the interior of the individual. How do we know that something like light isn't UR or shared energy in LR? (Are these UR or UL?). The answer would depend upon whether or not the events are intersubjectively verifiable.

If you and I shared a subtle-realm experience in meditation or a dream, then it would indeed be fair to say that such events were in UR or LR.

142   Wilber, 2011 [personal conversation].

143   This last sentence is a technical point but worth further elaboration: The nondual vantage point itself is beyond state experiences involving subject and object. However, because a stabilized nondual vantage point transcends and includes all shallower levels of awareness, and because the shallower levels of awareness don't disappear, state experiences of identity, union, and communion (among others) can and do still arise in participatory creation by the apparent subject-object duality at any shallower level of awareness.

144   Note: It is important that we do not confuse a temporary experience of identity with a particular object on one hand with the types of subjective identity shifts in vantage point explored in chapter 2. To avoid this confusion, I will for the rest of the book be more strict about my use of the term vantage point to represent the degree of transcendence of the separate-self.

Another easy way to think of this is to note that each shifting subjective vantage point has a corresponding object. At any given vantage point there can be a temporary experience of identity with any object (i.e., arising as the object). This is true until the final vantage point wherein subject and object collapse. A nondual vantage point is, therefore, one in which all levels of awareness, all states, and all objects in all realms arise as a single identity—the self-aware Great Gesture of reality. This is what the Tibetan traditions call Mahamudra.

145   For example, St. John of the Cross writes, "When God grants this supernatural favor to the soul, so great a union is caused that all the things of both God and the soul become one in participant transformation, and the soul appears to be God more than a soul. Indeed, it is God by participation. Yet truly, its being (even though transformed) is naturally as distinct from God as it was before, just as the window, although illumined by the ray, has been distinct from the ray's. (*The Ascent to Mount Carmel*, 1979, p 117–118 in K Kavanaugh & O. Rodriguez, (Trans.), *The Collected Works of St. John of the Cross*. Original work published in 1585.)

146   Here, I shall speak most specifically about extraordinary and holotropic states that fall more broadly into the category of major states. This is in contrast to conscious access to minor states like positive emotional well being, or empathy, etc.

147   An interesting conference took place recently called Technologies of the Sacred, sponsored by the International Transpersonal Association. It explored the various technologies that exist in cultures around the world that can help catalyze access to states and realms.

148   Sometimes states and realms (i.e., the objective side of experience)

can unfold in a sequential order from gross to subtle to causal. It is important to differentiate these particular types of experience (wherein one tracks the changes in the objective field) – like those described in chapter 4 -- from the types of changes in subjective source of awareness outlined in chapter 2.

149   Wangyal, Tenzin, and Mark Dahlby. *The Tibetan Yogas of Dream and Sleep.* 1st. ed. ed., Ithaca, NY: Snow Lion Publications, 1998.

150   LaBerge, Lucid Dreaming, 2004/2009. p 27.

151   Wangyal, Tenzin., and Mark. Dahlby. *The Tibetan Yogas of Dream and Sleep.* 1st. ed. ed., Ithaca, NY: Snow Lion Publications, 1998.

152   Lucid dreaming, for example, can be induced from both the waking state and from within the dream state itself.

153   LaBerge, 2004/2009. p 3

154   LaBerge, 2004/2009. p 4.

155   Stephen LaBerge. *Lucid Dreaming.* New York: Ballantine. 1985.; See chapter 9: "Dreaming, Illusion and Reality." <http://www.lucidity.com/LD9DIR.html>

Stephen LaBerge, *Lucid Dreaming* New York: Ballantine. 1985.; See chapter 9: "Dreaming, Illusion and Reality." <http://www.lucidity.com/LD9DIR.html>

In yet another example, LaBerge writes: "There are suggestions that mutual dreaming abilities have been cultivated to a high level by a number of Sufi mystics. Aside from various stories of Sufi masters being able to appear in the dreams of anyone they chose, there is the report of a group of dervishes who explored the world of dreams on the island of Rhodes in the 16th Century." Stephen LaBerge, *Lucid Dreaming* New York: Ballantine. 1985.; See chapter 9: Dreaming, Illusion and Reality. <http://www.lucidity.com/LD9DIR.html>

156   Some chemical compounds like MDMA open profound subtle state shifts into feelings of empathy, love, intimacy, and interconnectedness but do not necessary facilitate a transition of reality into subtle and causal realms.

157   See also, Schultes, Richard Evans & Robert F. Raffauf. *Vine of the Soul: Medicine Men, Their Plants and Rituals in the Colombian Amazonia.* Oracle, AZ: Synergetic, 1992.

158   Typically the caapi vine is mixed with leaves of shrubs from the Psychotria genus.

159   For details see the case of *Gonzales v. O Centro Espirita Beneficente Uniao do Vegetal* heard by the U.S. Supreme Court on November 1, 2005. The decision, released February 21, 2006, allows the UDV to use the tea in its ceremonies pursuant to the Religious Freedom Restoration Act. See also, the decision made by U.S. District Court Judge Panner who ruled in favor of

the Santo Daime, acknowledging its protection from prosecution under the Religious Freedom Restoration Act.

160   One major difference between Strassman's studies and the traditional use of Ayahuasca is the duration of the   medicine's effect. Traditionally, ayahuasca ceremonies, with the combinations of caapi vine and DMT containing leaves, provide a DMT experience of several hours. Strassman's studies on the other hand only last 5–15 minutes.

161   Strassman, 2001. p 143.

162   Strassman, 2001, p 68–70.

163   Strassman, 2001. p 185.

164   Strassman, 2001. p 185–6

165   Strassman, p 186.

166   Wasson, *Life* magazine, May 13, 1957. Wasson's article from *Life* magazine is republished on Google Books: <http://books.google.com/books?id=Jj8EAAAAMBAJ&lpg=PA100&dq=wasson%20life%20magazine&pg=PA100#v=onepage&q&f=false>.

167   **Pahnke WN.** *LSD and religious experience.* In: DeBold RC, Leaf RC (eds) LSD Man & Society. Wesleyan University Press,Middletown, CT. 1967. p 67.

168   Entheogen is a term that literally means to "generate the god within."

169   R. R. Griffiths & W. A. Richards & U. McCann & R. Jesse. "Psilocybin can occasion mystical-type experiences having substantial and sustained personal meaning and spiritual significance." *Psychopharmacology* (2006) 187:268–83.

170   R. R. Griffiths & W. A. Richards & U. McCann & R. Jesse. "Psilocybin can occasion mystical-type experiences having substantial and sustained personal meaning and spiritual significance." Psychopharmacology (2006) 187: p 281–2

171   R. R. Griffiths & W. A. Richards & U. McCann & R. Jesse. "Psilocybin can occasion mystical-type experiences having substantial and sustained personal meaning and spiritual significance." *Psychopharmacology* (2006) 187:281.

172   Ideally, in an Integral embrace, all three aspects of spiritual development ought to be honored and emphasized— spiritual intelligence (structure-stages) and spiritual cultivation (states) deal with relative reality, and spiritual realization (state-stages/vantage points) deals with ultimate reality. Because ultimate reality and relative reality are not two, it is vital that we include the full experience of relative reality, from moment to moment. If

we fail to do so, we risk merging with the nonmanifest aspect of reality, while bypassing the entire relative dimensions of being.

173   In addition to the major collective repercussions outlined above specifically in relation to accessing multiple states and realms of reality, it is useful to explore some of the concrete benefits that can come from such cultivation. The original term used to describe alternative states of consciousness was "non-ordinary." Other scholars like Charles Tart used the term "altered states of consciousness." However the term "non-ordinary states of consciousness" tended to be far too broad and the term "altered states of consciousness" could be taken to mean that these states are in some way less important or less real than ordinary waking consciousness. Even worse, in some circumstances, these states which can be profoundly important and positive are incorrectly categorized as psychotic (Grof, *Psychology of the Future*). In this light, I agree with Grof that it is important to specify a particular category of non-ordinary states that he calls holotropic. As we saw earlier in the chapter, holotropic states are specifically those states that provide substantial benefit to the person who experiences them. That benefit might bring anything from healing (both psychological and physical) to heuristic insight (See Grof, *Psychology of the Future*, chapter 1, "Healing and Heuristic Value of Non-ordinary States of Consciousness," p 1–19). In reference to nearly four decades of research into these types of states, Grof writes that careful attention ought to be given to the "healing, transformative, and evolutionary potential of these experiences" (Grof, *Psychology of the Future*, p 1). The vector of spiritual cultivation is almost always in reference to access to those states that lead to this end.

174   In much of our shared postmodern culture for example, there is a romantic view of native and indigenous tribes. Due to a lack of discrimination between prerational and trans-rational thought some of the logical and critical perspective is lost.

175   Grof makes a similar argument and I follow his expertise closely in my analysis. See his work in *The Future of Psychology* (2000). He writes, "All the human groups of the preindustrial era were in agreement that the material world, which we perceive and in which we operate in our everyday life, is not the only reality. Their worldview included the existence of hidden dimensions of reality inhabited by various deities, demons...." p 206.

176   Imagine for example what it would mean if eventually access to opening these realms was stabilized to such a degree that communion with multi-dimensional beings and multiple realms of existence becomes the norm. This should not be from a prerational space but from a trans-rational space of Integral post-metaphysics. What if we threw out angels (subtle realm inhabitants) with the bath water of prerational thought? Without positing the ontological existence and reality of such beings an Integral scholar would want to be open to these questions without automatically having a knee-jerk

response of rational reaction and closed mindedness. I suspect that if collective medicine ceremonies with ayahausca are engaged in together with individuals strongly at a rational level of development, we may discover realities similar to those seen by Galileo in his telescope. Ayahausca (exogenic catalysts) and particular forms of meditation and prayer (endogenic catalysts) may very well be today's new (oldest) telescopes.

177   See Wilber, 2007.

178   A Christian at a modern level of spiritual intelligence, living from a stabilized causal vantage point, has a vision of Jesus (subtle communion) during prayer:

Figure E: A modern level of spiritual intelligence, a causal vantage point,

and a state experience of subtle communion

179   See Wilber, 2007.

180   An interesting speculation revolves around the participatory

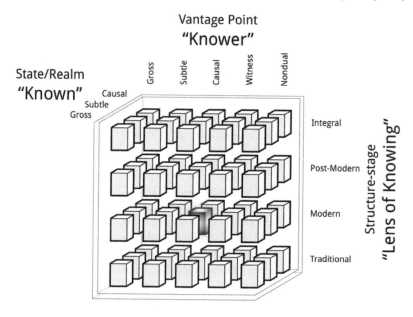

enactment of objects according to one's vantage point. For instance, I suspect that in waking state, a person will enact objects in the gross realm to the degree to which the vantage point has been realized. This means that while waking in the gross realm with a subtle vantage point, one will have access to gross and subtle objects while in ordinary consciousness. (When a vantage point has not been stabilized access to subtle objects will only arise in temporary experiences.) Looking at it in the reverse direction, I speculate that if one has developed to a causal vantage point and has an extraordinary experience of a subtle object in the subtle realm, the causal vantage point stays anchored in the causal even as the shallower, subtle identity enacts the experience in participatory creation. We'll examine these types of experience in the main text toward the middle of the chapter as it relates to a trans-dual vantage point.

181   Eventually a stabilized nondual vantage point does often lead to increased access to realms.

182   As all of the great spiritual teachers have pointed out historically: Spiritual realization simply has to be recognized as that which is always-already the case. An awakened and fully nondual vantage point is present right now, regardless of the changing state or any of the events in the field of experience. All that is needed is to recognize the source of awareness that rests deeper than the confusion with thought, personality, time/space, and individual consciousness. If awareness is quick enough to recognize itself in this very moment as the entire sphere of awareness, before falling down the involutionary staircase of identity confusion, then right now, right here is spiritual realization.

183   Although this is true for states and realms, certain types of access to energy may be an exception. For instance, if I have access to subtle energy in the objective field of awareness and am in the waking state, I will also have access to gross energy that makes up the object itself. This means that gross energy and subtle energy coexist. Another way of saying it is that subtle energy is more fundamental than gross energy and therefore when gross energy is present it necessarily arises out of subtle energy. (Same is true for the fact that subtle energy arises out of causal energy.) This type of distinction regarding energy can be contrasted with access gained to a particular realm (e.g., subtle) wherein immediate access to other realms is not available while the subtle realm is the dominant container.

184   Needless to say this is not a hard and fast rule. At advanced levels of practice one can hold open all realms at all times and may very well open all states at all times. However, more often than not, states arise independently from one another.

185   Again, changing states (chapter 4) and vantage points (chapter 2) are not mutually exclusive because they refer to different aspects of awareness.

186   Things do get a little tricky here. It is still uncertain whether an experience of a deeper realm requires a vantage point of equal depth to enact it. For example, if I usually have a gross vantage point and I have an experience of subtle communion with some sort of subtle light or deity, it is still unclear if this also means that I am simultaneously having a dip to a subtle vantage point in order to enact the subtle entity. My initial thought is

subtle vantage points are not necessary to enact subtle experiences, through I am open to dialogue and learning otherwise. Vantage points are defined by an insight into the subjective nature of the mind and how it constructs reality. My logic is as follows: Vantage points, by definition, mean that one has moved beyond confusion with (i.e., exclusive identification) that which it has transcended. A subtle experience of a deity, although arising in subtle state does not imply that I have also gone beyond my exclusive identification with thought.

187   Wilber, Engler, Brown 1986, p 224–5

188   It's still speculative, but I suspect that there are two more categories of state experience. The first is called complete union. In complete union gross, subtle, and causal are all experience in a great union. The second is complete communion, in which gross, subtle, and causal are all experienced at once in a great communion. Complete union might be something like Underhill's "unification" whereas complete communion might be more like Bucke's "cosmic consciousness." If this is true, it would mean that each perspective (first, second, and third) can be taken to the fullest extent. A first-person realization enacted to the full extent is nondual vantage point (or complete identity), second-person taken to the full extent is complete union, third-person taken all the way is complete communion. This would provide the deep structural pattern for a comparative mysticism that truly takes both perspectives and enactment into consideration. An integral expression of a tradition would want to at the very least acknowledge and at best incorporate all three. (The hesitancy I have here is around the fact that a nondual vantage point isn't exactly a first-person perspective but is rather beyond all perspectives.)

189   Underhill, p 423.

190   Vasudev, 2004.

191   Again, these rules about biasing perspectives aren't hard and fast and this is the beauty of the Integral perspective. It is flexible to accommodate the various nuances in the traditions. For instance, Meister Eckhardt, who clearly comes from a perspective that biases the objective side of experience in second-person God is well-known for explaining what certainly sounds more like a vantage point shift than a state of unification at his final culmination. He writes "The eye that I see God with is the very same eye with which god sees me." Even in cases where the final stages of realization might change from explaining states as objective changes to speaking from a subjective change in vantage point, it is safe to say that the majority of practitioners in the tradition will resonate with one perspective over the other due to philosophical biasing. In a second example from Eckhardt we see that even when the objective field (zone 1b) was emphasized during early stages using a second- or third-person perspective, final stages of realization may suddenly switch to a first-person

recognition of the Divine. Meister Eckhardt offers us another classic example of this trend: "To gauge the soul we must gauge it with God, for the Ground of God and the Ground of Soul are one and the same..... The knower and the known are one. Simple people imagine that they should see God, as if He stood there and they here. This is not so. God and I, we are one in knowledge." (Huxley, *Perennial Philosophy*, 1970 p 11-12).

192   Let me make a few initial caveats here as we move into the second half of this chapter to show how the Spiritual Development Cube might help to address some common scholarly concerns. Thus far, I have tried to illuminate several categories of spiritual development that might hold true across various cultural and religious contexts. This means that shifting vantage points through state-stages, increasing levels of spiritual intelligence through structure-stages, and vision into particular realms and states are all deep structures that tend to unfold among a diversity of people despite the fact that their cultural, historical, and social circumstances are often quite different.

Some scholars today worry about claims that assert these kinds of universal underlying structures. (See Ferrer's work in *Revisioning Transpersonal Theory* as a paradigmatic example.) My intention in introducing the topic here is twofold: First, I seek to create some initial awareness of postmodern critique for all those readers who might not already be familiar with the issues. Second, it is my hope that by openly acknowledging the problems that can arise with universal claims, that the more savvy postmodern critics will at least take a breath of relief that this is not just another reiteration of the "modernity project". I am confident that those who do decide to take my proposal all the way through to the end will find that I honor postmodern concerns while simultaneously attempting to go beyond them using a more constructive integral perspective.

In short, postmodern critics often accuse earlier scholars of essentializing religious traditions. This means that many modern scholars overlooked differences in single traditions and spoke about them as if they were all the same, across cultures and in different contexts. This means, for example, that they spoke of Christianity as if it were the same in all corners of the globe no matter who was practicing it. We now know that this is an inaccurate perception. Christianity is quite different depending on the culture, time period, and the identity of the person practicing it. Let it be clear then, that although I do explain deep structures of commonalities within and across spiritual traditions this does not mean that I am essentializing them. I am well aware of the differences within traditions and systems. However what I have found even more useful here in this project is to speak of the deep structures that are common. In addition to acknowledging deep structures, I use them to develop one of the most sophisticated methodologies available to show how the enacted differences between spiritual experiences can be deeply profound. Building on postmodern methodologies employed to show differences in spiritual events (e.g., Ferrer's participatory enactment), I include the fact that spiritual events are also co-created according to the individual's developmental level and stage of vantage point realization and within certain categories of experience (gross, subtle, causal).

A second common concern stemming from postmodern critiques is that most claims to universal structures fall victim to what Wilfrid Sellars called the "myth of the given." Major arguments against universals using the myth of the given as spearhead usually follow three steps:

First, they assert in order to claim that there exist any sort of universal structures in the universe, one has to accept the premise that there is an objective reality "out there" somewhere in space in a kind of atemporal reality. As such, it is this apparent universal reality that is then uncovered or discovered by different people in different contexts. This view of a monological reality, the critics point out, was the fatal error of modernity.

The critics bring up a relevant second point: All sound postmodern critical analysis (beginning in its earliest forms in the work of Kant, lasting through Derrida, and continuing into the present day) shows that reality is context dependent and that the idea of a monological "view from nowhere" is non-existent. Therefore, modern claims to universals are erroneous.

In place of universals, postmodern critics of modernity argue that reality is always relative to things like context, culture, and the identity of the perceiver. The assumption is made, then that because *some* claims to universals fell victim to the myth of the given, then all such claims must also be in error.

However, crude and oversimplified the above outline might be, most postmodern critiques against universals (including those critiques aimed at most development schemes) follow a similar train of logic like the one proposed. In some cases today, postmodern critics cling to relativistic arguments as a way to scaffold their own logic so as to not fall back to a modern level of scholarship. Others simply play self-serving egoic power games and try to deconstruct past theories and narratives in order to make scholarly names for themselves. In both cases, critics hold the critique of modernity so tight that they don't leave room for the possibility that perhaps both modernists and postmodernist each hold some piece of the overall puzzle. Rather than getting stuck in an "either/or" dilemma between universal (modern) and participatory enactment (postmodern) agendas, those few scholars who have bravely pushed beyond the postmodern paradigm into some sort of post-postmodern or integral context, understand that the solution to the dilemma of "universals" lies in the use of "both/and" thinking. That means that yes of course reality is in part participatory, co-created, and both culturally and context specific. Yes, of course this is something to include in any good form of critical scholarship today. Simultaneously, using both/and logic, this also means that yes of course there are deep structural patterns to the universe that are also true across all cultures and traditions regardless of the linguistic or cultural paradigm enacting that knowledge. Just as the human body has the same number of bones no matter where the person is from, and just as the laws of physics and mathematics hold true as deep truths. (As we shall see later in the chapter, these universal structures are not pre-given in some sort of way that rests outside of time, but are rather evolutionary emergents that have *unfolded in time* to create what Wilber calls kosmic grooves and kosmic habits.)

193   Brown's conclusions in *Transformations of Consciousness* (p 266–7) are twofold: (1) There is one common underlying meditative path that is universal across multiple traditions and (2) because of biasing perspectives the goals of each path will be experienced differently. As Brown often says: "Not all enlightenments are the same!" When Ferrer draws on Brown's work in *Revisioning Transpersonal Theory* (p 147) he includes the second half of Brown's analysis to say that different experiences mean different spiritual outcomes (or as Ferrer calls it "an ocean with many shores") but almost entirely excludes the first half of Brown's conclusion: there is one universal, underlying spiritual path that shares the same deep structures across traditions. Precisely because there is one underlying path that they all share, we can pass judgments about which path leads to deeper realizations. This first half of Brown's discovery regarding deep structures is the very piece of the puzzle I resurrect when I critique Ferrer's approach below to show how an Integral approach can include both deep structures as evolutionary emergents (kosmic habits) and the fact that outcomes will be enacted through participation.

194   See Katz, S. (1978). *Mysticism and Philosophical Analysis*. New York: Oxford University Press; Katz, S. (1992). *Mysticism and Language*. New York: Oxford University Press.; Ferrer, Jorge. (2000) *Revisioning Transpersonal Theory*. Albany, New York: SUNY Press; and Ferrer, Jorge (2008) *Participatory Turn*. Albany, New York: SUNY Press.

195   Brown, Dissertation, p 85.

196   Brown, Dissertation, p 85.

197   Brown, Dissertation, p 85.

198   Katz, 1978. p 26.

199   Brown, Dissertation, p 86. For further details see also: Anthony F.C. Wallace, "Cultural Determinants of Response to Hallucinatory Experience," Archives of *General Psychiatry* 1 (1959): 58–9.

200   Brown, 1986, transformations of consciousness.

201   Wilber helps us to see how we can make judgments—since judgments are unavoidable—with as much compassion as possible. Wilber explains what he calls the "calculus of torment" as follows: "Here is the basic problem. If

I am going to act on the principle that 'Everybody is right,' then, as we have seen, sooner or later I run into the fact that everybody cannot be totally right or equally right. Some views are 'more right' than others. And as soon as we say that somebody is 'more right' than somebody else, we generate pain or uncomfort on the part of those judged less right, as well as on the part of those who even dare to make such unkind judgments.... But my point is that those judgments are categorically impossible to avoid. I know not a single person who is innocent of such judgments (and the reason that nobody is innocent is that some views are indeed 'more right' than others, and we all *already know* that some views are more right than others, which is exactly why we all have those kinds of judgments in the first place). The question, needless to say, then becomes: 'Fine, some views are more right than others. So which views are more right, wise guy?'.... And there begins the calculus of torment for all parties involved. As we have seen, I believe that the principle of unfoldment can help us with that difficult question. The reason that I believe so is that, on balance, it is the solution that causes the least pain." (See Wilber, excerpt B, part 3)

202   In making his critique of universals, Ferrer himself is self-contradictory in that he asserts a universal claim. In a sidebar to his book *Boomeritus* Wilber critiques Ferrer's work in the voice of Joan Hazelton. As the voice of Hazelton, Wilber writes:

In other words, these authors [Ferrer and the reviewer of his book *Revisioning Transpersonal Theory*] do not actually believe that there is a plurality of ultimates; they do not really believe that there are many waves on this shore. Rather, they believe that participatory pluralism is the one, true, and only correct way to view spirituality. They do not believe that pluralism is true for those who believe it, and absolutism is equally true for those who believe it. They believe instead that pluralism is the only essentially correct stance, period. Thus, their view is the one and only way that it actually is for all people everywhere, whether those people know it or not, like it or not. The postmodern approach that denies strong universals (and instead postulates a plurality of equally valid ultimate truths) does so only by creating a *meta-language* and a series of strong *meta-claims*, and these meta-claims themselves are NOT culture-dependent, contextual, interpretive, and pluralistic, but are instead held to be absolutely and universally true for all people, in all cultures, at all times.... For example, the typical postmodern pluralist maintains that there are few if any context-transcending truths that are universally and cross-culturally valid. Rather, all truth is actually intersubjectively constructed; it is not a series of facts but a series of interpretations; all truths are situated in cultural backgrounds that mold or even create the form of the truth at any given time; truth is therefore not a matter of objectively representing facts correctly (or a matter of representing a single, pregiven world), but is rather a matter of intersubjective mesh within a particular cultural hermeneutic and social practice; and that, finally, notions of truth that claim to be universal are therefore imposing their own particular values on everybody else, which results in oppressing and repressing the pluralistic richness of the Divine.... But, you see, *all of those claims* are asserted to be true for all people, at all times, in all cultures. Those assertions are a series of literally dozens of truth-claims (such as the contextuality of all knowledge, the interpretive component of all knowledge, the intersubjectivity of all knowledge, etc.) that are claimed to be universally and absolutely true and binding on all people. These claims are not merely true for those who believe them. These claims are not merely interpretations that hold only for those who embrace them. These claims themselves have not an ounce of pluralism in them. They are instead an incredibly extensive, sophisticated, cognitively generated meta-theory about truth and knowledge that is claimed to be absolutely binding on all people, with no exceptions, whether those people believe it or not, like it or not. (See Wilber, sidebar F: Participatory Samsara)

203   Ferrer, Revisioning Transpersonal Theory, p 133.

204   Ferrer, Revisioning Transpersonal Theory, p 162.

205   A deeper understanding of Wilber's book *Up from Eden* recognizes that he tracks the ways in which both structures and access to states/vantage points have evolved overtime. He calls structures "average mode" and calls the leading breakthrough into new states and vantage points the "advanced tip."

206   We mustn't confuse the container of the experience (gross, subtle, or causal) which is universal, with the events that are enacted in those containers. In addition, it is helpful to point out the distinction between the realm and the event. The realms—gross, subtle, and causal—are invariant (the same is true for the major states of consciousness waking, dreaming, and deep sleep), however the events that arise in each of those realms are participatorily enacted according to the entire AQAL matrix.

207   Wilber, sidebar F.

208   Wilber, sidebar F.

209   It should be clear that we are not ranking the traditions against each other as a whole. This would be an error made by modern level of consciousness. Instead we are judging and ranking specific contexts according to specific content. This type of ranking uses a post-postmodern nuance that understands kosmic address and relativity of every interaction. (In volume 2 of the series we look at comparing individuals within a single tradition. In doing so we don't compare the views of the individual as a whole but more specifically we compared the particular line of development I call spiritual intelligence. The same criteria applies when comparing religious or mystical

traditions. First, we have to ask which element of spiritual development are we comparing (capacity for vantage point development, capacity to enter into realms and states, capacity for ease of vertical translation through lenses of spiritual intelligence). See appendix 2.

Wilber says it in another way that also helps to relieve concern about making judgments: "Human beings (or any sentient beings) are not what is being judged or ranked here, but simply the views that they may or may not adopt." See Wilber, excerpt B, part 3.

210   Wilber, sidebar F.

211   Although first used in John Welwood's work in a general way, the specific use of the terms "grow up" through structure-stages and "wake up" through state-stages was coined by Wilber (personal conversation).

212   Segilman's research in the tradition of positive psychology shows that a meaningful and engaged life are vital means to greater degrees of happiness. See Seligman, Martin, et al. "Positive Psychology Progress: Empirical Validation of Intervention," *American Psychologist*, July–August 2005. p 413.

213   As a point of conceptual orientation, the shifts in context and worldview explained above can be roughly correlated to changes in one's structure-stage of development. In the case of this book, changes in structure-stage relate to a shift in one's ultimate concern according to the basic levels of spiritual intelligence.

214   As Wilber points out in *Integral Spirituality*, the criticisms that modernity leveled at spirituality are only the beginning. Even worse are the criticisms outlined by postmodernity which decimates even the modern paradigm by pointing out the erroneous assumption in the fact that modern paradigms failed to take into consideration the perspective of the observer and instead posited one universal reality (i.e., "myth of the given"). See Wilber, 2006, p 283.

215   Once updated, our world's religious and spiritual traditions will likely instigate a contextual change on the collective scale that moves us first from an ethnocentric to a worldcentric context (wherein universal human rights and responsibilities become the foundation), and then from a worldcentric to kosmo-centric contextual paradigm (where in universal and evolutionary rights and responsibilities become priority). A new kosmo-centric context will offer a faith neutral/scientifically satisfying planetary purpose to help guide the evolutionary process. Just as mythic religious traditions and a mythic level of spiritual intelligence helped family tribes align across bloodlines under a common religious ideology, our common universe story of evolution, and an Integral level of spiritual intelligence, can help to align human beings across various religious traditions. With power of spiritual intelligence released to

250

help redefine ultimate concern and meaning, it seems we might be poised, perhaps for the very first time, to realize a vision of one humanity, one story, one planet, all aligned and cooperating in an evolutionary direction.

216   In *Pointing out the Great Way*, Brown lists the three special states as luminosity, bliss, and non-conceptual stillness.

217   This distinction between the "evolution of complexity" and the "evolution of identity", relates to Wilber's distinction between structure-stages and state-stages. In a 2d-matrix, the y-axis can be used to represent the evolution of complexity, and the x-axis the evolution of identity (state-stages).

218   This same basic logic of evolution, relating it to higher levels of complexity and greater levels of self-organization, can be extended even more broadly. When we look at the evolution of the brain, for instance, we know that the brain's emergence was marked by successive stages. The brain evolved from a reptilian brain stem, to include first a limbic system and then the simple and complex neocortex cortex (UR). Each of the new forms of complexity moved beyond but included the emergent properties that came before it. For instance, the brain of a complex life-form with a complex neocortex (e.g., human) also includes the limbic system and brain stem. The opposite is the not the case. That is, the brain of an organism that has developed a limbic system (e.g., horse) will not necessarily include a complex neocortex. In each of these cases, the less complex forms of life preceded the more complex forms in their emergence. Mammals with a limbic system emerged prior to humans with a complex neocortex. The emergence of reptiles, with only a cerebellum and brain stem, preceded both.

219   See Wilber, *Sex, Ecology, Spirituality*, p 22 for a discussion on holarchy.

220   Although it may seem obvious, the ideas that evolution is directional and progressive is not without its opponents.

221   Cultural complexity requires a little more nuance. Because cultures are the result of the shared values of a group of individuals, they too move through a series of developmental unfoldings according to the center of gravity of the individuals who compose it. Over time, as the average mode of consciousness (UL) of individuals has increased, we can simultaneously track an increasing and correlating increase in cultural complexity. Historically, we know that the magic worldview emerged prior to the mythic worldview; we know that the mythic worldview emerged prior to the rational worldview; and we know that the rational worldview emerged prior to the full emergence of postmodern and Integral stages of cultural development (see figure 24). (Lower Left cultural stages beyond the modern stage [postmodern and Integral] are represented by the term centauric in figure 24.) At some point in the future, today's Integral consciousness will represent the average cultural mode of consciousness only to be transcended and included by broader and more complex levels of understanding.

Because cultures are composed of individuals, the agreed upon mode of discourse will always be determined by the particular group engaged at a specific point in time. This means that even when the average mode of consciousness is modern or postmodern (as it is in the West today) a specific subculture's center of gravity within that larger culture might range along the whole spectrum from magic to mythic to rational to pluralistic to Integral and beyond, depending on the specific level of consciousness (UL) of those involved.

222   Depending on how much metaphysical allowance we give ourselves (and only a bare minimum is required) we might speculate that vantage points are preexisting and laid down as ontological pre-givens as involution unfolds in each moment, the stages of awakening or spiritual realization of identity through vantage points is therefore available at every stage of development. The evolution of identity is always available and ever present. It is not emergent. The evolution of complexity or the evolution of structures are not pre-given and are emergent in each and every moment. This type of evolution occurs at every stage of development according to the preset grooves laid out by previous travelers for most people. However, for the leading edge of evolution these structures are created as we go: conscious co-creation of reality in each moment.

Now, it is also worth speculating that the highest structures of development only begin to be accessible if the individual has shifted identity (either with temporary access or with permanent abiding) to a nondual vantage point. This means that at a certain point (sometimes called third-tier), creation of the universe as the universe is occurring instantaneously. Or, using theological terms, we might say that God creates his creation, while being both incarnated in the creation and as the entire creation itself.

223   Because the process of vantage point development is a process of transcending and including, the dual nature of multiplicity that results from gross, subtle, causal, and witnessing identities never goes away; and because gross, subtle, and causal identities are in time, they follow the patterns of the evolution of complexity. This realization of awakening + evolution of form is what we will call Integral Evolutionary Enlightenment in chapter 8.

224   This distinction is analogous to Wilber's distinction between states and structures.

225   As we shall see below, many forms of collective identity and intelligence have persisted in the past. This type of "We" that I am speaking about is something that can only emerge after a self-authoring, modern consciousness is in place. Traditional consciousness, for instance, was communal without a strong sense of agency. In traditional consciousness there is a tendency for conforming. (See Cook-Greuter's work on the stages of ego development). Traditional consciousness also contained a lack of reflection

about the way that culture and linguistics construct reality. These realizations are novel to postmodern consciousness. As such a truly self-reflective "We" cannot emerge until after a postmodern stage of development.

226   I first introduced the "Unique We" in an article I wrote for the *Journal of Integral Theory and Practice*, "Rejuvenating Religion for an Integral Age: The Emergence of the Unique Self and the Unique We," published in 2011 through SUNY press. I draw extensively from that article in this section.

227   I thank Clint Fuhs here for suggesting the name "kosmic," and for helping me to flesh this out.

228   The term "Supermind" refers to the highest structure-stage available at a given point in time. Supermind requires that one also have a state-stage center of gravity at nondual identity. As Wilber puts it, "Supermind includes Big mind, but Big Mind doesn't necessarily include Supermind"

229   Creating culture consciously requires at least some degree of transcendence of both the individual ego and the cultural ego as foundation. Most spiritual practice today stems from traditional structures and lacks even an understanding of cultural matrices. As a result most spiritual practice available in the market place today only examines individual ego. Today, postmodern forms of spiritual practice are emerging in which collective ego and collective shadow is being addressed directly (see the work of Thomas Hubl and Andrew Cohen as two examples).

230   Cohen, Andrew, and Ken Wilber. (2007). "A living experiment in conscious evolution" [transcript]. *What is Enlightenment?*, *35*, January–March. Retrieved January 10, 2011, from www.enlightennext.org/magazine/j35/ guru-pandit.asp.

231   The phrase often used here is that one must move beyond "exclusive identification with the ego." Wilber notes this in *Eye of Spirit* (2001) when he states, "And in order to discover being, one must surrender exclusive identification with the ego..." (p. 368). In *One Taste* (2000), Wilber acknowledges the earlier work of Hubert Benoit, first citing Benoit's claim that "it is not the identification with the ego that is the problem, but the exclusive nature of the identification" (p. 297). In a similar way, Gafni uses the term "evolution beyond exclusive identification with the ego." I suspect the emphasis here is to distinguish himself from others like Cohen who often use the phrase "evolution beyond ego." Cohen's teachings can be taken to mean, incorrectly I believe, that no individuality exists beyond ego. Although Gafni's point of clarification is certainly useful, it is my experience that in each of their teachings, both Cohen and Gafni include some degree of separate self (Cohen in the degree to which he emphasizes the individual's position of natural hierarchy in the higher "We" and Gafni in emphasizing the "unique self").

232   Cohen, Andrew, and D.G.M. Genpo. (2009). "Spirit is Higher."

EnlightenNext, *45*, September–November. Retrieved January 9, 2011, from www.enlighten-next.org/magazine/j45/genpo-merzel-roshi.asp.

233   I speculate as well that this "we" intelligence is a new line of development.

234   Surrender to the collective can fall victim to a pre/trans fallacy: pre-individuative surrender and post-individuative surrender. Mythic surrender is full communion at the expense of autonomy. Integral surrender to the Unique We is full communion by way of choice using the fully autonomous consciousness of the individual. Mythic surrender continues unconsciously while Integral surrender will only continue for as long as the agent wills it. In both cases, whether or not the individual has moved through the fulcrum of modern individuated consciousness determines the difference.

235   Whereas Cohen refers to this collective emergence with terms like *intersubjective nonduality* and *Authentic Self*, others like Buddhist leader and activist Thich Nhat Hanh use more traditional language to explain it: "The next Buddha," Hanh explains, "may not take the form of an individual. In the 21st century the Sangha may be the body of the Buddha." I suspect that in time poly-centric Integral consciousness will produce a diversity of "We" holons that will check and balance the evolutionary process.

236   See Tenzin Wangyal, *Yoga of Dream and Sleep.*

237   Wangyal, *Yoga of Dream and Sleep,* p 17.

238   Again the main point here is that vantage point training (subjective shifts) and realm access (objective shifts) do not necessarily equal the other.

239   Wangyal, *Yoga of Dream and Sleep*, p 205.

240   As my colleagues Zak Stein and Clint Fuhs are quick to point out, more comprehensive does not necessarily mean more accurate.

241   This of course, all depends upon how we define the term "masculine." In this case, I use masculine to refer to the evolutionary movement forward (eros). And I use the term "feminine" to refer to the reaching backward (healing, integration, etc.) of agape. We each have both masculine and feminine drives within our being. A healthy integral practitioner is in touch with both of these drives.

242   Wilber, Personal Conversation, 2010.

243   A "fulcrum", according to Wilber, is the transition point between one structure-stage and the next.

244   A "switch point," according to Wilber, is the transition point between one state-stage and the next.

245   One piece worth highlighting here is that access to realms and states plays a critical role in the "cleaning up" process. Whether we take

a psychological stance and say that subtle realms provide a backdrop for projection of our unconscious or if we take it a step further into a trans-rational space to state that subtle realms provide a glimpse into individual and collective fabrics of reality, both circumstances provide the opportunity for massive healing and integration.

246   In the fullest expression of such a culture, conscious access to states and realms of reality would also be key.

247   John Welwood used the terms "wake up" and "grow up" in his book *Toward a Psychology of Awakening* (p xviii and p 231).

248   Given the model outlined in this book we now also understand how important it is that we allow our waking up and growing up to unfold as we continue to "open up" access to multiple states and realms of experience.

249   Wilber often uses the phrase "states, stages, and shadow". I build on his phrases wake up and grow up here to offer the new term "clean up" in reference to shadow. "Cleaning up" Shadow and healing the broken aspects of ourselves is even more complex as we begin to realize that shadow is both individual and collective.

250   In an article published in the Integral Journal of theory and Practice, titled "On Spiritual Teachers and Teachings" (2011), Zak Stein reminds us that "natural hierarchy" (particularly as it arises in the teacher and student relationship) is always content and context specific.

251   One of the keys to the inter-subjective sphere is the way that learning takes place. In a new culture we pass information and learn from each other at hyper-speeds. Rather than learning from generation to generation, when true community emerges we learn from the experience of those who are our elders even if the difference is only a few years. With this, a new network of growth and development emerges. Fully "showing up" allows us to learn from those more developed than us, to engage new levels of intimacy and evolutionary love with those at our same level of development, and to take responsibility for everything that we have learned in our relationships with those less developed than we are. In addition, shadow also plays a critical role in inter-subjective space. Because shadow is the definition of something that is in our blind spot, its effect on us is minimal (save a few egoic contractions). Where shadow really begins to matter is in our interactions with others. The cleaner we are as a vehicle, the easier it is to transmit our realization (vantage point) and vertical growth (structure-stage) to others.

252   The following analysis is a measure of some of the key areas that an Integral approach to spiritual development will be sure to include. My attempt points toward what I call the Great Human Tradition. Some researchers in the area of religious development are quick to dismiss the idea of a single grand theory that unifies existing theories. Tamminen and Nurmi (Hood, 1995),

for example, conclude "there is no 'United Grand Theory' of religion or religious development" despite attempts by scholars like K. H. Reich to create one. Although I agree with them that "different theories have very different points of departure" and that "more longitudinal data" is needed, I also know that integral methodological pluralism (IMP) places scholarship on a path that begins to reconcile some of these major methodological differences to show how each can be positioned to complement the other rather than contradict.

253   Although researchers do tend to use multiple lenses for their studies, it is usually the case that a researcher will disproportionately favor one particular methodology over others. In the survey in appendix 1, I organize scholars according to the methodology they tend to preference. In the section on cultural approaches, I list Daniel P. Brown as an example of a multi-methodological researcher.

254   Proudfoot, Wayne. Religious Experience. Berkeley: University of California Press, 1985. p xii.

255   Proudfoot, 1985. p xi–xii.

256   Schleiermacher, Fredrich Daniel Ernst (1958) On Religion: Speeches to its Cultured Despisers, Trans, J. Oman. New York: Harper Row.

257   Voltaire, Philosophical Dictionary, 1764.

258   Proudfoot, 1985. p xi–xiii.

259   Proudfoot, 1985. p xiii.

260   Proudfoot, 1985. p xiv.

261   Proudfoot, 1985. p xiii.

262   Although a theologian like Barth employs a similar strategy and claims that religion is an autonomous sphere and therefore not susceptible to scientific critiques, he also accuses Schleiermacher of "heteronomy and idolatry because Schleiermacher describes religious experience in terms borrowed from philosophical anthropology rather than the language of Christian Doctrine." See Proudfoot, 1985. p 236.

263   Schleiermacher's argument is still used today by some contemporary social theorists. See Berger, 1979.

264   James, 1902. p 379.

265   The theme of a "common core" has been greatly expanded upon by Ralph Hood. For example, see Hood's "The Common Core Thesis in the Study of Mysticism" in McNamara's edited volume *The Psychology of Religious Experience*, Volume 1. Later scholars like Steven Katz argued against the "common core" theory claiming that we can never truly get to an experience void of conceptual interpretation. He writes "The experience itself as well as the form in which it is reported is shaped by concepts which the mystic brings

to, and which shape, his experience." See Katz, *Mysticism and Philosophical Analysis*. New York: Oxford University Press. p 26.

266   Stace, W. T. *Mysticism and philosophy*. Philadelphia, 1960.

267   Martin, 2010. (Dissertation Manuscript)

268   MacDonald, D. A., & H.L. Friedman (2002). "Assessment of humanistic, transpersonal, and spiritual constructs: State of the science". *Journal of Humanistic Psychology*, 42, 102.

269   Hood, Ralph, et al, "Dimensions of the Mysticism Scale: Confirming the Three-Factor Structure in the United States and Iran," *Journal for the Scientific Study of Religion*, Vol. 40, No. 4 (Dec., 2001), Blackwell Publishing. p 691–705.

270   Hood, 2001.

271   Tamminen, Kalevi and Kari E. Nurmi, "Developmental Theories and Religious Experience" in Hood, *Handbook of Religious Experience*, p 277.

272   Tamminen, Kalevi and Kari E. Nurmi, "Developmental Theories and Religious Experience" in Hood, *Handbook of Religious Experience*, p 277.

273   Tamminen, Kalevi and Kari E. Nurmi, "Developmental Theories and Religious Experience" in Hood, *Handbook of Religious Experience*, p 277–8.

274   Following Goldman's work, John Peatling conducted a similar study in 1973 using the categories of very concrete, concrete, abstract, and very abstract religious thinking. Four years after his main study, Peatling was of the strong conviction that "religious thinking continues to develop during adult years." (Tamminen, Kalevi and Kari E. Nurmi, "Developmental Theories and Religious Experience" in Hood, *Handbook of Religious Experience*, p 278) Peatling's claim and prediction that religious thinking continues into adulthood, was later continued by James Fowler.

275   Fowler defined faith following the lead of theologian Paul Tillich (Dynamics of Faith, 1956), using the phrase "ultimate concern."

276   See Fowler, Stages of Faith, 1981.

277   See the work of Streib, Day, Rizzuto, McDargh, as presented at the Symposium on Faith Development Theory and the Modern Paradigm. Further work is published here: *The International Journal for the Psychology of Religion*, 11(3), 2001.

278   See DiPerna, *Evolution's Ally*.

279   Newberg, A. B., D'Aquili, E. G., & Rause, V. (2001). *Why God Won't Wo Away : Brain Science and the Biology of Belief*. New York: Ballantine Books.

280   See Alper, M. (1998). *The "God" Part of the Brain : a Scientific Interpretation of Human Spirituality and God*. [Boulder, Colo.]: Rogue Press.

281   Newberg, A. B., & Waldman, M. R. (2009). *How God Changes Your Brain : Breakthrough Findings from a Leading Neuroscientist*. New York: Ballantine Books.

282   Books like Doidge's *The Brain That Changes Itself* give a good overview of the latest research and examples of neuroplasticity. See Doidge, Norman (2007). *The Brain That Changes Itself: Stories of Personal Triumph from the Frontiers of Brain Science*. New York: Viking.

283   Newberg, *How God Changes Your Brain*, 2010. p 7

284   Entheogen is a term preferred to many in place of the more common term psychedelic due to its lack of cultural baggage.

285   The Marsh Chapel Experiment also known as the Good Friday Experiment was run by Walter N. Pahnke under the direction of Leary and the Harvard psilocybin project.

286   Strassman, DMT: *The Spirit Molecule*, 2001.

287   For examples see: Frazer, J. G. (1894). *The Golden Bough: A Study in Comparative Religion*. New York and London: Macmillan and co.; Tylor, E. B. (1958). *Primitive Culture*. New York: Harper.; and more recent work: Geertz, C. (1973). *The Interpretation of Cultures: Selected Essays*. New York: Basic Books.

288   It is significant to note that the psychoactive ingredient in ayahuasca is DMT, the same entheogen studied by Strassman.

289   Harner, *Hallucinogens and Shamanism*, 1973.

290   Also supported by Stace and Hoods research.

291   Wilber, Ken, Jack Engler, and Daniel P. Brown. *Transformations of Consciousness: Conventional and Contemplative Perspectives on Development*. Boston New York: New Science Library Distributed in the U.S. by Random House, 1986.

292   Durkheim, *On Morality and Society*, 1973. p 198.

293   Weber, Max. *The Protestant Ethic and "The Spirit of Capitalism,"* 2002, trans. by Peter Baehr and Gordon C. Wells.

294   Batson, *Religious Experience*,1982. p 29.

295   Batson, *Religious Experience*,1982. p 27.

296   Argyle and Beit-Hallahmi demonstrate that social influence is so strong that it is even possible to predict the range of spiritual access an individual might have when provided with only basic sociological data. See Argyle and Beti-Hallahmi, *The Social Psychology of Religion*, 1975.

297   The examples provided above in the four methodological categories described thus far are only the tip of the iceberg when it comes to sound

academic research into the nature of spiritual development. Research at the University of Arizona Center for Consciousness Studies, the Center for Spirituality and the Mind, California Institute of Integral Studies, Maharashi University of Management, and JFK University, among others, are providing consistent research on spiritual development. As this book proceeds, I draw on other academic researchers as necessary, but maintain the main focus of my work on the insights of Wilber and Brown.

298   James, 1902, p 381.

299   The terms "signifiers" and "signified" originally come from the philosophical work of Ferdinand Saussure. Since then the study of "signs" has grown into an entire field of philosophical and linguistic discourse called semiotics.

300   See the Ingalls, *The Dhvanyaloka of Anandavardhana with the Locana of Abhinavagupta*, 1990.

301   See Puthoff's article on CIA's involvement in Remote Viewing research at Stanford; Puthoff, H.E., "CIA-Initiated Remote Viewing Program at Stanford Research Institute," *Journal of Scientific Exploration*, Vol. 10, No. 1, p 63–76, 1996.

302   It is important to recognize that few researchers fit into the Four Quadrants perfectly. Many researchers employ minor degrees of cross-methodologies. However for the purposes of this Integrative model, I organize research of religious development and spiritual experience according to the more dominant methodology employed by the particular researcher. Furthermore, the examples are meant to be representative of the type of research methodology used to examine spiritual development.

303   For example, although research in 1902 pales in comparison to the type of research we have access to today, nevertheless, William James titles his first lecture, "Religion and Neurology." (James, 1902, p 1–25)

304   Instead of simply dismissing a researcher for his or her partiality, the Four Quadrants allow us to see where a particular researcher may contribute the most value and where he or she is still partial. For instance, Stace and Schleiermacher bring great insight when it comes to the Upper Left Quadrant, but use of the Integral lens informs us that they are each partial in that their research fails to take into account the influence of cultural and socioeconomic factors on religious experience. The Integral scholar would know to integrate the work of Stace and Schleiermacher for what it does best (UL), but would turn to other scholars like Batson and Ventis (LR), Harner (LL), and Newberg (UR) to fill in their methodological blind spots.

Although the Integral approach encourages researchers to be as comprehensive as possible, it does not require that scholars include all the information available from all quadrants. The Integral approach does, however, require that all researchers become what Wilber calls, "integrally informed."[17] That is to say, each scholar ought to know which approach he or she is taking, how it fits in with other available approaches, and what its potential limitations are given its specialized focus.

305   Wilber, *Integral Psychology*, 2000, p 71

306   Alper, *God Part of the Brain*, 1996, p 131

307   Alper, 1996, p 131

308   Alper is not alone in this sort of positivistic reductionism. Other theorists like Eugene d'Aquilli and Charles Laughlin used similar but more complex arguments to explain that "all religious phenomenon arose from neuropsychology." See D'Aquili, *The Mystical Mind*, p 4. (After pointing out their tendency to find causation in neuropsychology, the author defends early research by claiming that it was "much more complex than simple reductionism.")

309   "The person's description of the experience of nonverbal cues and changes in belief and behavior are all tracks or symptoms that serve as observable criteria. They provide clues both to the existence and to the character of the experience. The scientist can use these tracks as publicly verifiable observations, making it possible to test explanatory theories concerning the nature and function of an individual's religious experience. (Batson, C. Daniel, Patricia. Schoenrade et al. *Religion and the Individual: A Social-Psychological Perspective*. New York: Oxford University Press, 1993. p 18)

310   Tamminen, Kalevi and Kari E. Nurmi, "Developmental Theories and Religious Experience" in Hood, *Handbook of Religious Experience*, p 274.

311

Also available from Dustin DiPerna:

Books

Streams of Wisdom (Integral Religion and Spirituality Volume 1)
Evolution's Ally (Integral Religion and Spirituality Volume 2)
Earth is Eden (Integral Religion and Spirituality Volume 3)
The Coming Waves: Evolution, Transformation, and Action in an Integral Age

iPhone App

Enhance: Meditation for Modern Life

Audio

The Great Human Tradition (Available on iTunes and on Amazon)

CPSIA information can be obtained at www.ICGtesting.com
Printed in the USA
BVOW10*1314020115

381723BV00001B/1/P